SPIDERS IN THE HOUSE
AND
WORKERS IN THE FIELD

SPIDERS
IN THE HOUSE
AND
WORKERS
IN THE FIELD

ERNESTO GALARZA

UNIVERSITY OF NOTRE DAME PRESS

NOTRE DAME   LONDON

Copyright © 1970 by

UNIVERSITY OF NOTRE DAME PRESS
Notre Dame, Indiana 46556

Library of Congress Catalog Card Number: 77-105730
Manufactured in the United States of America by
NAPCO Graphic Arts, Inc., Milwaukee, Wisconsin

To the men and women of Local 218,
National Farm Workers Union—A. F. of L.

This study was produced through the U.S.-Mexico Border Studies Project at the University of Notre Dame, under the direction of Julian Samora, sponsored by a grant from the Ford Foundation. The opinions expressed in the report do not necessarily represent the views of the Foundation.

CONTENTS

PART FOUR

ACKNOWLEDGEMENTS

I could not have continued a documentary search that lasted nearly twenty years without the assistance of many persons. They are almost as numerous as the scattered pieces of the story they helped me bring together. Not naming them all does not diminish my debt to each one. With special appreciation I want to thank Dwight E. Mitchell for meticulous checking of the Congressional Record Index; Robert Cooney, who tracked down hopeless leads and forgave me for setting him on them; Harry Hollins, whose long acquaintance with Kern County labor organizations I have exploited; Lewis Deschler, Parliamentarian of the House of Representatives, for technical points on its rules and precedents; Francis Gates whose cues and comments helped me over some arid spots; Harry W. Flannery, the source of details on the production of *Poverty in the Valley of Plenty;* Russell C. Derrickson, former administrative officer of the Committee on Education and Labor of the House, who allowed me to harass his staff with repeated requests for information; Robert W. Gilbert, for permission to examine his files; Ralph R. Roberts, onetime Clerk of the House, and his assistants, for their diligent examination of records inaccessible to me; Rep. Don Edwards and his staff, whose courtesy I am sure I strained; Frank Henshaw, an expert in public records whom I repeatedly called on for help with bibliographical snags; his many fellow librarians, especially at Stanford University, the University of California and the Library of Congress, who were not fazed by my importuning even after they knew that I was looking for something that wasn't there, and never had been; James Murray, without whose legal skill and devotion to my task this work would not have been possible; Dr. Julian Samora, the enabler, in a very real sense, of the publication of the manuscript he befriended; and Mae, my wife, who endured "Spiders" in her house with patience and understanding.

Flawless workmanship would have been the best evidence of my gratitude for all this. Where it is good, the credit is ours. Where it falters and perhaps falls I must answer alone. There would have been many more lapses but for the hard work of the editor, Mrs. Theresa L. Silio.

FOREWORD

California is a state of stories—the Missions, the Gold Rush, the Chinese, Bonanza Farming, Disneyland, Hollywood, The Faith Healers (nowadays replaced by the Touch Therapists), the Dust Bowl Migration and many others—intimately interlaced, dramatic, ongoing in consequence and interest, constantly being retold (as they should be) and updated.

Of these stories none is more dramatic, socially relevant or humanly absorbing than the century-old story of farm labor. It has great qualities: conflict, tension, pathos, humor, far-ranging implications and ironies galore. A never-ending saga, it will go on until mechanization has eliminated the last farm laborer and all the orchards and vineyards have been ripped out to make way for jerry-built subdivisions.

No one knows this story better than Ernesto Galarza, for he has lived it, and not merely in California but in Louisiana, Hawaii, Puerto Rico and Latin America. He has lived it as a day laborer, harvest hand, cannery worker, and labor organizer. It is also in his "blood," so to speak, for he is of Spanish-speaking background and was born in Tepic, Mexico. He is also a scholar, with degrees from Occidental College, Stanford and Columbia.

In *Merchants of Labor: The Mexican Bracero Story* (1964) he wrote a fine account of the "managed migration" of Mexican farm labor to California in the period from 1942 to 1960. In his latest work he relates still another "installment" in the ongoing farm labor story in California—the decade-long effort of the National Agricultural Workers Union to organize farm labor and the spider-like intrigues which frustrated it.

In a sense, it is the pre-Chavez, pre-Delano phase of the story with which this work deals. Apart from its inherent interest and social and historical importance, it has special theoretical significance as a study of how institutionalized power—as represented in the courts and committees of the Congress—can be used on occasion to block the legitimate aspirations of impoverished farm workers to achieve self-organization. The story of this gallant effort is told here for the first time and, because of Galarza's personal involvement, told with a wealth of detail and close observation.

There is a legend on the State Capitol in Sacramento which reads: "Bring Me Men To Match My Mountains." In its latter-day history California has not always produced men to match its mountains or its foothills, or even its hillocks for that matter. Too many of its "outstanding public figures" nowadays are pigmy types. But it still has some men and women in active life who measure up to the high standards of public service that, in times past, provided a long list of remarkable leaders and spokesmen and, in the best sense of a much-abused term, practical agitators. Ernesto Galarza belongs to this vanishing breed. He is a man of courage, integrity, scholarship and compassion, an idealist who remains quite unapologetic about his special brand of social idealism, which today is all too rare.

                                                            Carey McWilliams

New York
March 27, 1969

PREFACE

In 1968 the University of Notre Dame, under a grant from the Ford Foundation, embarked upon a research project to investigate the problems of the United States–Mexico Border and to provide some analysis of Mexican-American history.

The project has come to be known as the U.S.–Mexico Border Studies. At a time when the "invisible" minorities have suddenly appeared, this project hopes to contribute to knowledge about the second largest minority group in the United States namely the Mexican-Americans, the majority of whom live in Texas, California, New Mexico, Arizona and Colorado. This is the primary objective of the project.

In order to understand the present status of Mexican-Americans in the United States it is imperative that we investigate the conditions on the U.S.-Mexico Border. Since the turn of the century Mexico has supplied, legally or illegally, a large portion of the labor force, mostly unskilled, which has contributed to the development of the Southwest. The fluctuations of the U.S. economy are clearly reflected in the movements of people across the border. Much of this labor force has first found a place, however precarious, in agricultural endeavors before moving into the urban environment. Many continue working as farm laborers although living in the city. Whether they have come as legal immigrants, as *"braceros,"* as "commuters," as "Wetbacks" or as "visitors," they have left an imprint in the society. Thus what happens on the border has repercussions in Detroit, Chicago, Denver, San Antonio and certainly Delano.

Professor Ernesto Galarza (Research Associate, Department of Sociology and Anthropology, University of Notre Dame), makes a major contribution through this book, to our understanding of the plight of the farm worker as well as to our knowledge of Mexican-Americans, as they have moved in, and out, and through the farm labor movement in California.

In this scholarly and well-documented report we can begin to see with greater insight the powerful forces at work which have affected and continue to affect the lives of struggling agricultural workers, be they citizens, legal aliens or illegal aliens. We see also the obstacles which they must necessarily face and overcome as they seek a place with justice in the society.

This report, together with Galarza's earlier *Merchants of Labor,* also provides the background for an understanding of the present situation in California agriculture.

Julian Samora
University of Notre Dame

INTRODUCTION

At nine o'clock of the morning of 7 May 1950, a lone union•
picket was at her post in front of the main gates of the DiGiorgio
Farms near Arvin, California. She sat on a weathered lug box
turned on its side, the kind that can hold fifty pounds of grapes.
Her heavy work shoes, thick socks and a board laid in front of the
box fended her feet from the cold damp ground. Her pepper-and-
salt topcoat reached well below the knees. Below the hem of the
coat the cuffs of her Levis showed. Her clenched fists stuffed in the
pockets of the topcoat made two small bulges resting on her lap.
The shirt, buttoned close, was three sizes too big for her thin,
corded neck. The knitted wool cap was pulled down over her ears
and down in back, snug. The picket sign, a white cardboard as
wide as her shoulders and a yard long, hung from a loop of string
around her neck. The sign read:

DiGIORGIO WORKERS

ON STRIKE

FOR A LIVING WAGE

Local 218 A.F. of L.

The face of the lone picket could have been that of a Grant
Wood painting of American Gothic. The lower jaw was angular
and slightly square, set tightly against the upper. Her lips, pursed
by the cold, were a suture of tiny wrinkles. The skin was tight and
smooth only over the two small knobs of her cheekbones and the
ridge of the nose. The rest of her face was the furrowed countenance of a working woman of fifty years, a palimpsest on which
poverty had written and erased and written again the diary of the
southern sharecropper.

The lone picket was looking through metal-rimmed glasses on a
familiar scene. At that time of the morning the sun was still probing through the breaks in the overcast above the eleven thousand

acres of the DiGiorgio Farms. The gray, pastel light that filtered through was mirrored in the roadside puddles framed in umber mud. Opposite the main entrance to the Farms, a block-long packing shed faced the county road, parallel to the railroad tracks. The branches of the leafless trees, stained dark by showers, spread like cracks against the smooth, grey horizon over the ranch buildings. Beyond them fanned the naked vineyards, recently pruned. The empty stake-bed trucks rattled and grunted down the county road toward the gates after delivering the field crews to their appointed tasks. They wheeled into the corporation yard, a hundred feet away from the lone picket, the drivers as unmindful of her as she was of them.

In the back seat of a travel-beaten jalopy parked near the picket on the shoulder of the county road, a young man dozed. Next to him was the picket's black umbrella, in case it rained. He had brought the lone picket, and would take her back to Arvin at the end of her stint for the day. Another car was parked directly opposite across the road and headed in the same direction. It was a patrol car. One of Sheriff Johnny Loustalot's deputies relaxed behind the wheel, bored above and beyond the call of duty.

The weather, on the following morning of 8 May 1950 at nine o'clock, had not changed enough to speak of. The landscape was the same still life of dark-brown telephone poles, smooth puddles, and the slanted wooden crosses on which the vines rested. Somewhere above the grey ceiling a rising wind was pushing the fog. Where it broke, the sun spotlighted erratically bits and pieces of the scene—the road sign that identified the corporation buildings as the town of DiGiorgio, the metal lace of the cyclone fence along the packing shed, the windshield of an incoming truck.

Weather aside, the scene was different in some details. The lone picket was gone from her place next to the telephone pole. So was the black jalopy. The deputy and his car had vanished. Where the lug-box seat of the lone picket had rested there was a rectangular frame of gumbo.

These were the signs on the morning of the eighth that the DiGiorgio strike had come to an end. It had lasted, wasting away, thirty-one months and twenty-four days.

The departure of the picket from the gates of the DiGiorgio Farms, as a simple token of defeat, seemed trivial. It was in fact an episode between the significant events of four years preceding that foggy morning and of those that were to follow during the next twenty years. This account begins with the high point in that quarter-century struggle, fought first on the picket line and then in the courts.

This point was the appearance in the Appendix of the *Congressional Record* dated Thursday 9 March 1950 of an Extension of Remarks by the Hon. Thomas H. Werdel, whose congressional district included Kern County and the DiGiorgio Farms located near the town of Arvin. The Extension was published on March 10, and in the following days set in motion a rumble of publicity in the newspapers of the nation.

The Werdel Extension of Remarks proved to be a political bolt of lightning.

The charge behind the bolt had been gathering since November 1949, when a subcommittee of the House Committee on Education and Labor had held two-day hearings on the strike in Bakersfield, fifteen miles away from the DiGiorgio Farms. Four congressmen had attended the hearings. The top echelons of corporation farming were there—the zamindars of the Imperial Valley, the cotton kings of the San Joaquin basin, the lettuce manufacturers of Salinas and the fruit managers and their surrogates from as far north as Yuba City. In the hearing room, and taking their turn at the witness table, were the officers of the National Farm Labor Union, the leaders of the strike and a few rank-and-file members of Local 218. On the evening of the first day of the hearings two sound motion pictures were shown. One was *The DiGiorgio Story,* produced by the Corporation; the other, *Poverty in the Valley of Plenty,* by the Hollywood Film Council (A.F. of L.) on behalf of the Union.

Nearly four months after the subcommittee met in Bakersfield, its report had not been published. Werdel's Extension of March 9 seemed, on the surface, to end the delay. It purported to be the official report of the subcommittee, and appeared over the names of Richard M. Nixon, Thruston B. Morton and Tom Steed. In some forty-four hundred words it lashed the Farm Labor union with words seldom printed in the name of Congress. It indicted the union film on multiple counts of defamation.

Three days before the hearings the DiGiorgio Fruit Corporation

filed a suit for libel against the NFLU and the producers of the
Union motion picture. The Corporation sued in the Superior Court
of Los Angeles County, praying for $2 million in damages.

Behind the scenes, the strike collapsed rapidly. Early in May
settlement was reached between the Corporation and the defendants. The Corporation was paid one dollar. The producers of the
Union film agreed to recall the prints and destroy them. The
NFLU agreed also to end the strike.

With the breaking of the strike, Local 218 shrank to a small
guard of seasoned union men and women. Many left California.
Others found work elsewhere in the state. Carrying the lessons
of Arvin with them, they formed the core of NFLU locals in
the major farming areas. In the next ten years they maintained a
watch over agribusiness, as the complex of corporation farming
called itself.

Agribusiness had, by the mid-1950s, become a remarkably efficient system of production and a loose but effective power federation of employers to protect all of the vital factors of that system.
The DiGiorgio Fruit Corporation was never far from the center of
that power. Against it, the thin line of farm labor locals set up a
resistance the length and breadth of California. They struck in the
tomato, the peach, the melon, the cotton and the potato harvests.
In a decade of lost engagements of this type, the Union forced the
great ranches to the picket lines. The results were always the same
—small wage gains for the harvesters, the adamant refusal of
growers to recognize the Union, and a growing accumulation of
facts on how the agribusiness system, as production and as power,
operated on all levels.

In 1959, its time and money and stamina having run out,
the National Farm Labor Union, now the National Agricultural
Workers Union, died with its boots on. It had been broken by
attrition from its enemies while its friends in the high circles of
organized labor, watching in disappointment mingled with relief,
made other plans.

Out of these plans came the Agricultural Workers Organizing
Committee, created in the Spring of 1959. Someone on the staff
of the AWOC borrowed a surviving print of *Poverty in the Valley
of Plenty*. It was shown in various parts of the Central Valley, in
ignorance of the ban of 1950. Word of the showings promptly

reached the officers of DiGiorgio. Within ten days, the Corporation filed a suit for defamation demanding $2 million in damages. Heard at Stockton in the Superior Court of San Joaquin County, a judge found the film libellous, and the AFL-CIO and other defendants were ordered to pay $150,000 as damages. On appeal, the judgment was sustained with damages reduced to $60,000. In the pleadings and the trial of this lawsuit, the Nixon-Morton-Steed report, in the familiar print of Werdel's Extension of Remarks, figured prominently. Natural lightning, it is said, never strikes the same place twice; political lightning can, and did.

The Stockton trial and the appeal were a financial and judicial success for DiGiorgio. But they raised certain issues of law that remained unresolved. Counsel for the Corporation skirted them, and none was pursued by the judges who sat on the case.

The trail of Werdel's Extension of the Nixon-Morton-Steed report picked up again, but now took a different direction. The twist was unexpected, the effect of carelessness and haste. In announcing to the public the filing of the suit following the showings of *Poverty in the Valley of Plenty* in 1960, DiGiorgio issued a press release charging innocent parties with responsibility for the scandalous exhibitions by the AWOC. In this the Corporation and its advisers had tripped over poor research and lax investigation; a libel suit against DiGiorgio was filed in the Superior Court of the County of San Francisco with a prayer for damages of $2 million.

The issue raised in the San Francisco trial was no longer the offending film, but the circumstances that had surrounded the appearance of Werdel's Extension. A cloud no bigger than a lawyer's brief was beginning to cast shadows on those circumstances. The result was something of a stalemate. But a reporter for a chain of labor newspapers who had been following the subject for some years published an account of it. This article was republished in the *Valley Labor Citizen* of Fresno. It was a blunt piece which, among other things, said that the Nixon-Morton-Steed print was a "phony" congressional report.

The re-publication in Fresno was promptly noticed by DiGiorgio. It became the basis for the next suit for defamation—a complaint for libel against the Central Labor Council of Fresno, the original author of the piece and others. Moral and political issues were beginning to twine themselves into the lengthening chain of lawsuits, and the Corporation moved to the attack again, with the declared aim of silencing its critics once and for all.

In the Fresno trial, as well as in the pleadings and legal maneuvers that preceded it, the cloud no bigger than a lawyer's brief darkened. It had, nevertheless, a silver lining. DiGiorgio's attorneys won the contest. The jury awarded damages in the amount of $30,000. Defendants appealed and were upheld by the appellate court sitting in the same city. The case was sent back for retrial, and there the matter of *DiGiorgio v. Valley Labor Citizen et al.* rested for the time being.

In the meantime DiGiorgio had filed three additional suits in libel against other labor newspapers that had carried the piece about the "phony" report. In the superior courts of Monterey, San Francisco and Shasta counties identical complains were filed, demanding $1.4 million in damages. But with the adverse decision of the appellate court in the Fresno case the three suits were dismissed on motion of DiGiorgio's attorneys.

Like all human stories, this one frays before it is over, leaving loose ends where the evidence, for one reason or another, stops. The evidence, nevertheless, goes far enough to provide an extended footnote to the history of farm labor in California. The nine lawsuits upon which the account turns, considered with the hindsight of twenty years, were variations on a theme in the form of a simple question: How did the reputation of one of America's great corporations become entangled with a printed paper without a date and without an author?

The appearance of the Werdel Extension in the Appendix was at first glance inconsequential. It was, by itself, a mere drop of verbiage with no more prospects of fertilizing the congressional mind than the dropping of a pigeon on the dome of the capitol. There were, in fact, hidden potencies in so small a thing. It became a powerful weapon of publicity. In the succeeding lawsuits it served to punish alleged libelers and repair the supposed damage to reputations. As a crucial piece of evidence, used adroitly by DiGiorgio's attorneys, it was exposed time and again to close cross-examination. In the process it cracked, revealing step by step the circumstantial connections between events as far apart in time and place as the picketing at the DiGiorgio gates and a publication in Washington, D.C. It was a case in point of the precept for the

inquiring mind laid down by Justice Oliver Wendel Holmes: "To
see as far as one may and to feel the great forces that are behind
every detail . . ."

The litigation of which so much is made in the pages that follow
should be taken as it is offered—as the frame on which the connections between unseen forces are hung. An incident was peeled,
and there appeared an episode, within which there was wrapped
an event, the event in turn unfolding a process that was a part of
the social history of the Republic. The process reached a climax
which turned the tide against the migrant farm workers of California and in favor of the corporate power they were resisting.

The simple facts that strike the eye about this protracted affair
would themselves suggest deeper, underlying meanings. Professor
Max Radin, respected teacher of law at the University of California, wrote that "cases of litigation that last more than a generation
. . . are practically impossible today." Yet here was one that
already was close in duration to the famous courtroom feuds of
the eighteenth and nineteenth centuries to which he referred.
Around the nine complaints for defamation were collected nearly
thirty depositions and files fattened by innumerable subpoenas,
pleadings, demurers, affidavits, declarations, briefs, interrogatories,
remittiturs, motions and transcripts.

Papers, in fact, compete with human beings for the leading roles
throughout this narrative. There is a reprint of the Werdel Extension, making its way into the currency of legal evidence with a
borrowed credit card; a mimeographed twin of the reprint that
came no one knew whence and vanished no one knew whither; a
thick printed volume of a congressional hearing that is absent
without leave from a trial. These paper characters are shadowed
by ghost documents that in all probability never existed except for
a fleeting moment on the witness stand to support an alibi or accredit an evasion—a congressman's letter that had been burned;
an important brief that was never filed; a report that was never
submitted; a transcript that was destroyed in Washington, reap-
peared in San Francisco, and disappeared again in Fresno; holographic signatures in invisible ink that appeared in Roman type
when brought to court; a reprint that was offered to the court
undated and untitled so that it might testify to the truth.

Not all the players have this eerie air about them. There are other players, also made of paper, whose credentials stand the test of genuineness and who speak their lines plainly under oath.

Upstaged by paper and printer's ink, the human beings in the story look more like supporting players than stars: five presiding judges, six justices of appeal, more than a score of attorneys, seven congressmen and a parade of witnesses and deponents. Listening and looking on were twenty-four jurors. In scarcely twelve or fifteen hours of service in the jury box, they were sworn to get safely through the labyrinth and bring back a true verdict on the credibility of dead men, unwritten writings, congressional non-proceedings and absent politicians, all meshed in events that stretched back nearly two decades.

Better than they knew, the jurors were themselves dealing with economic interests and political powers that were moving in the depths of their society. These forces were exploited by agribusiness to break the threat of competing organization from a hostile quarter, that of farm labor. The processes of the House of Representatives were used to that end. That is how the reputation of a great American corporation became entangled with the questioned authenticity of a printed paper without a date and without an author.

The success of agribusiness in this respect could be measured by the results. A rare motion picture documentary was condemned to destruction. Politicians not yet famous were given a footing on the backs of other men for a practice climb to fame. It produced a piece of multipurpose propaganda that could be circulated discreetly among government officials, or announced to the world in press releases. It shielded the piece from criticism by giving it a double armor of privilege, congressional and judicial.

It is a tribute to the repugnance with which the American mind regards privilege that these works could not be produced in the open. In part the congressional processes lent themselves to the concealment. As the late Congressman Clem Miller wrote, "most of the action now takes place rather quietly and methodically behind closed doors and in private conversation." Other than the facts that will unfold, perhaps more than Congressman Miller's words should be cited to justify the overtones of such a title as *Spiders in the House*.

Professor Bailey in his book, *Congress at Work*, observed a committee during an investigation and drew from it "an edifying picture of the cunning spider carefully weaving a web to trap an unwary fly." He was referring to the techniques of a staff member. And why not? Caillois, the Frenchman, once asserted, that "les hommes et les insèctes font partie de la même nature." And Crompton, a close and sympathetic student of spiders, thought that detective writers might do worse than study them as models. Spider silk, he said, is the strongest stuff that exists; but, in its own way, so is a myth. However different their worlds, Arachnis and a congressional technician, as parts of the same nature, salute each other in this book because they are, indeed, "parts of the same Nature."

PART ONE

I

THE ENCOUNTER

Joseph and His Kinsmen. / Joseph DiGiorgio, the founder and architect of the DiGiorgio Fruit Corporation, arrived in New York in 1888 and went to work as an apprentice fruit jobber. He was born and reared on a farm in Cefalu, Corsica, where, as he was fond of recalling after he had become a multimillionaire, "I worked for $8.00 a month." By the time he was twenty-one he rose, with the help of relatives, to the directorship of a bank. He scaled the ladder of the fruit business by leaps and was soon well on the way to the top. While climbing he organized fruit auctions in the largest cities of the Atlantic seaboard. In the banana trade he was battered in a collision with the United Fruit Company, but in consolation he said, "I have my honor." He also had a wide and detailed knowledge of produce merchandising which he put to use with the aggressive bounce of an American tycoon "making it" fast and handsomely.

On the rebound from his failure in the tropical fruit trade he landed in California. He bought the Earle Fruit Company, looked more closely at the brokerage profits and decided to become a producer on his own account. By 1926 he had acquired large acreages near Arvin and Delano, on which there flourished his experiments with grapes and plums, with deep-well drilling, and with gang labor closely supervised and abundantly supplied. His gamble against sagebrush paid off, parlaying investments of $90 an acre into developed orchards and vineyards that he would not sell for $3,000 an acre in 1946.

When he died in 1951, Giuseppe DiGiorgio was the almost legendary Mr. Joseph, the classic example of the entrepreneur

13

who is free to enter and take, and does. Rugged he was, with the
rootstock of a Corsican and a peasant; he fitted as a peer among
his peers—Ford, Wier, Girdler, Sewell Avery.

Like them, DiGiorgio expertly used the prime instrument of
success in America, the corporation. He chartered his, the DiGiorgio Fruit Corporation, in Delaware on 10 December 1920. The
articles declared it the business of the Corporation "to plant, cultivate and grow and buy, sell, import, export and generally deal
. . . in the products and growths of the earth."[1] Twenty-six years
later his eminence and success were credited by *Fortune* magazine
to "his early perception that the small grower and the city jobber
who supplies the small retailer both require a free, open and
honest market."[2] The man who had at one time dispatched twenty-
nine vessels carrying bananas over the seven seas now had un-
counted ships, airplanes, trucks and freight trains supplying the
world with the grapes, peaches, plums, pears, nectarines, apples
and other choice products of the California earth.

And Mr. Joseph could claim to his credit not only the mounting
cash balances that his contemporary, Amadeo Giannini, husbanded
for him in the Bank of America, but also the ecological miracle
which he never tired of admiring. In the 1920s the Delano and
Arvin countryside was anything but a produce farmer's paradise.
Much of it was a wasteland of saline flats and Russian thistle with
an annual rainfall, in the favorable years, of five to six inches. In
the summer the tumbleweeds of jimson and sandblasted sage
rolled over the windswept ground like giant grass balls kicked
around by unseen players in a lunatic soccer game. These parched
flats were the areas of the dust storms that darkened the sun over
Bakersfield. In full sight of them, Joseph DiGiorgio bent down,
fingered the soil, asked questions, and calculated the promise of
that desolate land.

He bought it in large tracts, altogether some sixteen thousand
acres. But the land was only half of it. Without water it would
remain useless. He discarded the traditional windmills and drilled
hundreds of feet into the earth to tap the water table with powerful electric pumps. The blistered wilderness bloomed.

The showpiece of so much enterprise was the DiGiorgio
Farms, eleven thousand acres of grapes, fruit orchards and vegetables within a nineteen-mile perimeter, and valued in the late

1940s at $24 million. The packing shed was one of the largest and most efficient in California. In the winery, set well back from the main road, the Farm's own grapes were crushed. The administrative buildings and the living quarters, painted white, huddled in the center of the vast spread of the vineyards. Along the irregular boundaries a windbreak of tamarisks framed the property. On a clear midsummer day the Farms were visible from the top of the Grapevine grade, a buttress of the Tehachapis twenty miles to the south. Against the desert the tamarisk fringes, the full-blossomed vines, the irrigation ditches gleaming like streaks of quicksilver, the pearl-grey trim of the buildings formed a scene for superlatives. Gordon Pates, reporting it in the *San Francisco Chronicle,* coined one: "DiGiorgio is to farming what Tiffany's is to jewelry." Sierra Vista Ranch, twenty-five miles north near Delano, was less spectacular, but equally prosperous. The five-thousand-acre ranch was a self-contained community with its own volunteer fire department, restaurant, recreational facilities, dormitories, and police force.

DiGiorgio Farms and Sierra Vista were only a part of the far-flung holdings of the Corporation. In California proper these operations stretched from Borrego Valley, near the Mexican border, to Marysville, six hundred miles to the north, with way stations of farms, orchards, packing sheds and brokerage facilities between. In Florida the Corporation operated several thousand acres of citrus lands.

From these components of production the business moved, by railway and truck, ten million boxes of fruit and five hundred thousand packages of vegetables. That was in the late 1940s. DiGiorgio Farms alone could harvest, process and ship 70 carloads of asparagus, 350 of potatoes, 400 of plums and 1,200 of grapes. The Corporation was the second largest producer of wine in the United States.

The destination of this enormous flow of produce was the chain of auctions controlled and operated by DiGiorgio in Baltimore, Pittsburgh, Cincinnati, Chicago and New York. The Corporation sold its own products through these auctions. It also handled on a commission basis the fruits and vegetables of other growers. The auctions were the hub of the nation's produce business.

In the eight years immediately preceding the DiGiorgio Farms strike, the Corporation's total revenue rose from $5,717,000 to

$18,154,000. Ninety percent of this revenue was from farm sales.

It was a closely held family corporation, for Joseph DiGiorgio had no children. His nephews—Joseph S., Joseph A., Philip and Robert DiGiorgio—were trained to become the administrators and heirs apparent of the aging tycoon. The elder Joseph and his family owned more than 59 per cent of the common stock of DiGiorgio Fruit and a controlling portion of the cumulative preferred. Of the four young nephews it was Robert who was headed for the top. As a Yale and Fordham man, he was quickly accepted into the élite circles of California clubdom. He moved, along with DiGiorgio's diversified investments, into the boards of directors of the Bank of America, the Union Oil Company and other enterprises collateral to agribusiness. For the duration of the strike Robert was public relations director for the corporation and in charge of employment and personnel matters.

By reason of their strategically distributed farms throughout California, their brokerage connections with a host of small growers and their vital concern for the steady flow of produce to the eastern markets, the DiGiorgios worked closely with the organizations that watch-dogged the labor market. Principal among these organizations in the 1940s and '50s was the Associated Farmers, which Mr. Joseph helped to launch and to which the Corporation contributed directly or through its county affiliates.[3] In a letter addressed to the Santa Fe Railway, the Tidewater Oil Company, the Food and Machinery Corporation and other fellow farmers, he solicited contributions. The purpose was "to combat the attempts of radical elements to stir up trouble between the farmer and his employees."[4] This was in the days of rural vigilantes, pick-handle persuasion, hired goons, and tear gas confrontations, and before angry business men had acquired the restrained image of agribusiness men.

That image began to take form in the years preceding the investigation by the LaFollette Senate committee on violations of the civil rights of farm workers. February 2, 1937, was declared Joseph DiGiorgio Day by the Kern County Board of Supervisors. Homage was paid on this occasion by Mayor Rossi of San Francisco, Governor Merriam and the presiding officers of many important commercial, transport, finance and public utility corporations: "a great organizer," "a mind of scientific exactitude," a man who "believes in a single dominant trade organization. . . ."

These tributes were somewhat tarnished in November 1942 when Joseph DiGiorgio, his corporation and certain associates in the produce trade were indicted by a federal grand jury "for wrongful and unlawful combination to fix, control, peg and stabilize prices . . . by controlling and restricting the channels and methods of distribution."[5] Some of the polish was restored, however, by Senator Sheridan Downey, whose book, *They Would Rule the Valley*, appeared in 1947. It carried no publisher's imprint. One of its chapters was entitled a "Portrait of an Excess-Land Owner," in praise of the Corporation and its founder.

Now in his sunset years, the farm boy from Cefalu was the prototype and symbol of success and prestige. Physically he was a small man. His natty attire gave him the prosperous, compact look of what he was, the little giant of Montgomery Street, the financial center of San Francisco in which his headquarters were located. The broad forehead, gently swept back, the slightly beaked nose, a countenance creased with the scars of merciless business battles, were the features of a will streamlined and weathered for success. A bust of Mr. Joseph that adorned the reception hall of his headquarters memorialized him in bronze with a clipped mustache, the puckered lips of one who has just nipped a not-quite-ripe plum, and the gimlet stare of a man who knows he will not be stared back at.

Mr. Joseph gave to charity and good works in Arvin; schools and churches received gifts of land and money, and the community center in the town was a gift of the Corporation. In the small, grass-covered courtyard a replica of the bust had been mounted upon a hewn-stone pedestal. The stern stuff of the man came through better in this setting, more like the Kublai Khan of Kern County, as *Fortune* magazine had dubbed him, a grim philanthropist glaring at the desert he was determined to hold at bay.

There was something else that Mr. Joseph was bent on keeping in leash. That was his labor force. Between 500 and 600 year-round workers lived in the bunkhouses and cottages of the Farms, whose premises were well policed. On the job he was a barking martinet to everyone, including his nephews. He wanted "no strike on my property."[6] His reasons were straightforward and elemental: "Fruit is nothing but water, labor, more labor and freight." The meticulous, time-table organization of water and freight were vital to the profits of the business. So was the submissiveness of its labor. "Trees, vines and plants" ran the Corporation's rationale, "are growing, living things . . . a work stoppage at the harvest season could only mean that a grower could lose his entire investment in his crop that year."[7] With teamsters, cannery workers and longshoremen DiGiorgio bargained collectively. With his farm hands, he would not. His nephew Robert carried on this simple philosophy well into the 1960s. In lieu of a contract, DiGiorgio Farms provided two swimming pools for the help, a baseball diamond and a soccer field and, in special kitchens, "soul" food for ethnic tastes.

These thoughtful amenities served less and less to quiet the stirring discontent of the DiGiorgio field and shed employees as the 1940s went by. Persistent talk of grievances and of organization spread through Arvin, Lamont, Weedpatch, Government Camp, Rockpile and other neighboring communities where hundreds of DiGiorgio's employees lived. These were the farm labor settlements that marked the

Migrant Trail's End. / The caravans of trucks weighted down with people and household goods and the jalopies that had streamed along U.S. Highway 66 from the southern dust bowl in the 1930s and '40s halted in the barren surroundings of the DiGiorgio Farms. They had crossed the plains, climbed the desert 4,000 feet to Tehachapi and rattled their way to the southern end of the San Joaquin Valley. Against the mountains to the south and west the stringy, battered convoys slowed down, eddied and settled into pools of thousands of men, women and children from Oklahoma, Arkansas and Texas. They camped on the weedpatches and the rockpiles of Kern County, many moving on north where the horizon looked flat and negotiable and where work might be available. Between 1930 and 1940 it was estimated that over a million of these refugees entered California. They made the Valley their home base.[8]

On their long trek they seemed, as a religious people, to be seeking the fulfillment of Samuel's prophecy: "I will appoint a place for my people Israel, and will plant them, that they may dwell in a place of their own, and move no more, neither shall the children of the wicked afflict them any more as beforetime." It was a hope wrapped in a prophetic promise, a flight, seemingly, from the fate of other tribes before. In Joseph's time "the Egyptians sold every man his field, because the famine prevailed over them: so the land became Pharaoh's." In Oklahoma the sharecroppers sold every man his tools, because the dust had prevailed against them; and the land became the bank's or the furnisher's. Tenants, croppers and laborers were tractored out and bulldozed relentlessly to the other side of the continent.

In Kern County sand lots were available for $25 down and $10 a month in the open spaces of the desert between the cultivated lands. On these lots refugee families built their towns. The outskirts of Arvin and Lamont became settlements of trucks and trailers hoisted on bricks or jacks; stained plywood shacks roofed with patches of tarred paper and canvas; army issue tents with conical tops and sixteen-foot-square dirt floors. Squatters gathered building scraps from the dumps and improvised lean-tos against their trucks or cars, ready to move out on short notice. Beyond these, they stretched a fringe of even more precarious footholds—a camp in the shelter of a railway bridge, burlap curtains strung between the pastel pillars of tall eucalyptus trees, or stops in trailer "parks" for fifty cents a day.

The people waited for farm jobs between the last of the cotton bolling and the first of the pruning. In the interval they kept probing into this new land looking for work. A few got more or less steady jobs as "arragators," as they said. Others labored in the nearby oilfields. They learned to pack fruit in the sheds. They were signed on as tractor drivers. As they "rested their things" and made themselves "to home," a quiet expectancy was in their talk. In the cool of the summer evenings their conversation was about the work and the wages at "Die-george," as they called the Farms. From out of the dark came the staccato raps of the diesel rigs. carrying DiGiorgio's produce to Los Angeles, San Francisco and the East. They sped through the Okie towns like mad cicadas, leaving in their wake a slight stink of burnt fuel. To the men and women sitting on their porches something else was also bad—the working conditions at "Die-george."

In the fall of 1947 nearly half of the population of Arvin had arrived after 1940 from the dust bowl states.[9] The flavor, the style of life were unmistakable. Small children in the streets of the town asked: "Is they kinfolk to we'uns, grandmaw?" Men shook hands with fingers like iron clamps. To Sunday "meetins" the men came in fresh-washed overalls, the fabric worn to grey patches and streaks; the women, in the skirts and blouses they picked over at the Saturday auction.

Cultural kinship had crossed the plains intact. These migrants were surely not those Senator Downey had written about: "displaced persons, who arrived with scant money, few skills, little education and no sense of identity with the community."[10] The Senator had never been on the street in Arvin to hear the small boy ask a question of his grandmother. Nor is it likely that he ever heard the remark of a passing "arragator": "Hell, he ain't no bettern'n what I am." These were the people who formed

Local 218, A.F. of L. / Bob Whatley, a wiry little man missing his right arm, had talked persistently and quietly about a farm worker's organization. His empty shirt sleeve tucked into his belt, he trudged from camp to camp and house to house, the typical Jimmy Higgins who has been the point man of every labor union. When Whatley talked, the words barely reached beyond the brim of his straw hat. Jimmy Price, a foreman in the DiGiorgio shed, heard him. So did Jim Mitchell, the plump "arragator" who repeated the message thumpingly and aggressively on street corners and porches. They signed up the Herrons, the Adays, Copelands, Lawhorns, Shadowens and the Ramseys. Luis Chavez and his wife, who lived in a tent on the edge of Arvin with their four children, joined. Chavez, brown as burnt toast, had migrated from Texas. He "talked union" in Spanish in the fields. His wife made friends with the brown women, keeping the union grapevine busy wherever they met to exchange talk.

DiGiorgio hired no blacks, but across the county, on Cottonwood Road and in Carversville, they were gathering in shanty towns of their own. White and brown union men from Arvin visited them, signing up the first members. The Corporation provided separate camps and mess halls for the Filipinos, Mexicans and Anglos. The reason, Gordon Pates reported, was that management bowed to ethnic prejudices to avoid trouble. The DiGiorgio labor force was a mix of Oklahomans and Arkansans and Texans "who do not take more kindly to Mexicans than to Negroes."[11] The

Union gathered them all into a common effort across color lines.

What the segregated workers at DiGiorgio had not seen through the spectrum of skin colors they began to understand in the integrated union meetings. Former tenant farmers, sharecroppers and *peones,* they were all wage laborers now. Whether paid for by piece rates or by the hour, a unit of man-work was neither black, brown nor white. The price offered for the unit by the employer, moreover, was based upon the lowest wages the blacks and whites and browns bid against one another. Among the bidders, to make matters worse, were Mexican *braceros* brought by DiGiorgio under contract for a season—a contract that had been negotiated in Washington or Mexico City by diplomats and their employer advisors. Looking more closely at the wage system that prevailed, it became clear to the union men that the yardstick for *bracero* wages in turn was the *Wetback,* the smuggled Mexican who gratefully accepted work on any terms. DiGiorgio Farms had 130 *braceros* on its payroll the day the strike began, 1 October 1947. The U.S. Border Patrol regularly raided the Farms and hauled away crews of illegals for deportation.

Such were the basic conditions that kept the wage structure soft and the yearly earnings low. To these there were added even worse irritants. There was open sewage for some of the dwellings on the Farms. Men and women who travelled to the main gates for the shape-up complained of being sent home without call-in pay. Packers worked in extreme temperatures in the shed. Men were fired by foremen on the spot without appeal. Neither DiGiorgio nor any other farm employer provided unemployment insurance. Above all there was no way in which these common complaints could be discussed and negotiated with management.

To bring matters to a head, Bob Whatley wrote to H. L. Mitchell, president of the National Farm Workers Union. Mitchell had organized and led the Southern Tenant Farmers Union in the early 1930s. He led the first strike of tenants in 1935 working out of his dry-cleaning shop in Tyronza, Arkansas. In the next ten years the STFU set pickets marching in the cotton fields, organized Locals of white and black landworkers, and gradually developed a technique of publicity that brought the agrarian terror in the deep south to the attention of the country. Mitchell sent Henry Hasiwar

and Ernesto Galarza to Arvin. With Whatley and Price they began
the organization of Local 218, chartered by the successor to the
STFU, the National Farm Labor Union.

By September 1947 the Local had 858 signed and paid members who worked for DiGiorgio.[12] The Corporation's payroll at
that time comprised 1,345 employees. The members of Local 218
agreed to a set of demands: a wage increase of ten cents an hour,
seniority rights, a grievance procedure, and recognition of the
union as the collective bargaining agent for the workers. A letter
to Joseph DiGiorgio dated 22 September 1947 requested a meeting to discuss these matters. He was advised that a majority of
the DiGiorgio employees had designated the Kern County Farm
Labor Union, Local 218, as their representative.

Mr. Joseph DiGiorgio did not reply. Robert, the industrial relations director, refused to consider an election. The union's offer to
produce the signed authorizations was rejected.

The particulars set forth in the Union's letter were viewed by
the DiGiorgio's in the larger framework of the status quo. The
migrants from the dust bowl, Professor Goldschmidt had observed,
came from a rural society that "does not include organization
along special interest lines."[13] They brought to California no social
experience with the machinery of democratic processes for making
civic decisions. He found no history of meetings held before the
Union local was formed in Arvin in which the good and welfare of
the community were openly and freely debated.

To the DiGiorgios it was clear that this favorable state of affairs
was being threatened. The membership meetings of the Union and
the smaller home discussions began to provide the community with
the machinery of democratic experience whose absence Professor
Goldschmidt had noted. Through such experience new leadership
was being trained. It may be assumed that neither Mr. Joseph nor
Robert misread these portents. Their practical experience in making money in a closed system had revealed to them the alarming
dangers of the Hegelian statement: "The one essential canon to
make liberty deep and real is to give every business belonging to
the general interests of the state a separate organization whenever
they are essentially distinct." To prevent or at least delay such
organization was a basic policy of the DiGiorgios.

It was not likely that the new Union would be content with the provision of iced water in the fields on hot summer afternoons, or with sanitary drains, or by wages rising a dime per hour. The National Farm Labor Union propagandists were already holding meetings in Delano, Wasco, Pixley, Earlimart, Farmersville and Fresno. A chain of union locals extending north into the Central Valley was in the making. Mitchell was promoting a legal attack on the Taft-Hartley Act. The Union was registering voters and manifesting a preference for liberal congressmen. Something new was being added to the social landscape of Kern County. On an acre plot donated by Mrs. Bertha Rankin, a small cotton farmer who almost single-handed resisted the powers of agribusiness about her, the members of local 218 built a Union hall. Such was the background of

The Strike. / It began with a meeting of several hundred Union members at the Grange Hall in Weedpatch on 30 September 1947. They were told of Mr. Joseph's silence and the unavailing efforts to bring the Corporation's officials to a meeting. The vote was in favor of beginning the strike the following day.

A mass picket line of men and women formed at the gates of the DiGiorgio Farms on the morning of October 1. A Union head count on the county road showed that the majority of the shed and field hands, irrigators and tractor drivers was out. The statistics given by the Corporation were contradictory; they showed, when they were released years later, only a handful of absentees. But in its first weeks, despite reports of normal operations, the strike was real. The work stoppage was short but impressive. And the tactics and strategies it was to bring forth were those of determined men on both sides, propelled by deep passions and vital interests.

Strike headquarters were set up in an old trailer parked in the back yard of a Union member's home. The Union immediately set about to force the removal of the 130 Mexican *braceros*, who had laid down their tools on the first day of the strike. Three days later they were persuaded to return to work by Sheriff Loustalot and an official of the Department of Agriculture.[14] The *braceros* cushioned the effect of the walkout during six critical weeks while the company regrouped its labor force. But there were provisions in the *bracero* agreement against their employment during a labor dispute. The Union insisted on enforcement. On November 17 the *braceros* were removed over the bitter protests of management.

Later in November union pickets were placed in front of the Farm Labor Office in Bakersfield. It was referring workers to DiGiorgio without, as the Union contended, informing them of the strike. Time and again the Border Patrol was alerted and requested to raid the Farms as Wetback strikebreakers were detected by Union watchers. The Union also obtained a warrant for the arrest of a DiGiorgio employee on a complaint that he was recruiting strikebreakers in Texas. The Union persisted in demands for improvement in the housing on the Farms; state inspectors found surface discharge of sewage into the orchards, unsanitary latrines and boxcar quarters not fit for human occupancy.[15]

Violence struck at the Union organization. On the night of May 17 unknown gunmen sprayed bullets into the living room of a cottage where Jimmy Price was conducting a meeting of the strike committee. Price received a head wound, but he recovered and continued to lead the strike to the end.

On the side of the Corporation, there was a series of ordinary tactical moves. It provided Sheriff Loustalot and his deputies with parking facilities on the ranch. Patrol cars equipped with the weaponry of strike control such as tear gas secured the peace of the people of Kern County, which was public, and the property of Joseph DiGiorgio, which was private. From his vantage point on the premises the sheriff branded the picketing as "smacking of old-time I.W.W. methods."[16] The Sheriff, something of a linguist, also served as interpreter between the management and its *bracero* and Wetback replacements.

Within a month after the beginning of the strike the director of industrial and public relations of the Corporation, Robert DiGiorgio, set in motion the legal machinery for the eviction of striking employees who lived on the ranch. Their persons and household goods were deposited on the county roadside, where they waited among the puddles and the winter squalls until Union trucks took them to emergency quarters. Some of these families could have collected small sums to tide them over for it had been company policy to reimburse departing resident families for improvements on their cottages or apartments for which they had paid out of their wages. "In the case of persons who were evicted," said Robert DiGiorgio, "such arrangements were not made for obvious reasons."[17] The evictions were carried out under the supervision of the sheriff without any thought for the security of the private property of farm hands.

Early in January 1950 police charged seven Union pickets with malicious mischief. Some plum trees had been cut down during the night in the DiGiorgio orchards. Although there was no direct or circumstantial evidence to connect the union with the vandalism, on the complaint of the Corporation the pickets were held on bail of $15,000 each. A rock hit a DiGiorgio truck, and two Union men were jailed and held on easier terms—bail of $3,000 each. DiGiorgio employees who attacked pickets with chains and tools found justice more negotiable; they went free on $250 bail each.

These are only a few examples of Corporation strategy and local justice. Other moves of more substance and subtlety, in the long run probably far more damaging than evictions and high bail, were made.

In December 1947 a committee of eleven agribusinessmen from Kern County visited the Farms for a personal investigation of what the Corporation persistently described as a "labor disturbance." A former state treasurer of the Associated Farmers, Mr. Wofford B. Camp, now a cotton grower and seed processor, was one of the guiding spirits of the group, which called itself the Kern County Special Citizens Committee. They published an illustrated pamphlet, *A Community Aroused*. The illustrations included photographs of the model housing on the Farms. In considerable detail the pamphlet gave the operating losses incurred by the Corporation in providing housing, payroll data and the exact number of employees who reported for work on October 1. The pamphlet added the self-evaluation of the substantial citizens of the committee: "We are the pioneers who built Kern County . . . among the people who made America great." Among them were citizens who had protested the publication of the *Grapes of Wrath*, and they now denounced the National Farm Labor Union as "agitators, crack-pots and left-wingers and associates of known Communists."

But more than the community was aroused. The stir reached Jack Tenney, Co-Chairman of the State Senate Committee on Un-American Activities and his associate, Hugh M. Burns. Joseph DiGiorgio had said in the press on February 9: "We all know this agitation is Communist-inspired by subversive elements."[18] The

next day Burns announced: "We are interested in determining if
the farm labor trouble is Communist-inspired, as Joseph DiGiorgio
and others have charged."

Tenney subpoenaed Union officers to a cross-examination in
Los Angeles, and Burns held one hearing on the DiGiorgio Farms.
Neither found any evidence of Communist infiltration or control
at Arvin.[19] The investigation did establish, through the testimony
of Ranch Superintendent Newman, that around eight hundred
workers had joined the picket line on October 1.[20] The best the
investigators could do was to dust off an old charge that the National Sharecropper's Fund, a contributor to the Union's activities,
was a Communist front organization.

The assignment to prove that the Union was Un-Californian as
well as Un-American now fell to Robert E. Stripling, the chief
investigator of the House Un-American Activities Committee. He
arrived in Bakersfield early in June 1948, with a dog-eared dossier
on President Mitchell of the National Farm Workers Union. He
studied the strike but found nothing unusual. The Kern County
Special Citizens Committee in *A Community Aroused* had published, six months before, bits of the more quotable stuff from
Stripling's collection.

While Tenney, Burns and Stripling were investigating the Union,
the Corporation's attorneys were using the law to counter the
strike. Union pickets had surrounded a truck-load of DiGiorgio
potatoes at a produce terminal in Los Angeles and had also
attempted to stop shipments of wine. Under the National Labor
Relations Act, the Corporation sued for an injunction against the
NFLU, the Teamsters and the Winery Workers. The injunction
was granted by the Los Angeles Superior Court on Independence
Day, 4 July 1948. Subsequently the NLRB examiner dismissed the
action against the NFLU, on the ground that the Act did not cover
the farm workers.

Coincidently with these moves, the Corporation was making the
most of a document that Congressman Elliott had read into the
Congressional Record on March 22. This document was a petition of 1,160 employees who declared that they did not wish to be
represented by the NFLU. The statement had been prepared in
February 1948 and showed no date. Some of the "workers"
whose signatures appeared on the declaration were Max Newman,

ranch superintendent; Walt Palladino, foreman; and Lawrence Webdell, office manager. Congressman Elliott himself researched the attitudes of the employees on two visits to the Farms. Robert DiGiorgio disavowed any connection with the petition. He declared, "The first I knew was when it was presented."[21] He emphasized the spontaneous character of the declaration, and particularly pointed to its publication in the *Record* as evidence of its genuineness and credibility. The statement preceding the list of signers was in English. Many of them were Mexicans who could not read it.

The strike was now reduced to a series of maneuvers while the staying power of the Union weakened. Hasiwar's efforts to make contact with the Corporation were of no avail. Robert DiGiorgio continued to denounce the pickets as pawns of "outsiders" who wanted only "to make themselves the bosses of Kern County and eventually all California agriculture."[22] He insisted that "there never has been a strike at the Farm,[23] and that it was merely a labor disturbance. The difference between a disturbance and a strike was perhaps not as significant as the Corporation intended to convey. Strike or disturbance, the result was the same—the withholding of labor. "Labor," Ambrose Bierce once wrote, "is one of the processes by which A acquires property for B." The Union had disrupted one of the elements by which the Corporation acquired wealth. The others, it will be remembered, were water and freight.

If the disturbance was as mild as Robert would have had it, its effect on the Associated Farmers was not. They echoed the themes of the Corporation's campaign: that only a handful of employees walked out on October 1; that there were congressional statements on the record highly unfavorable to the Union; that there was no strike; that there were no legitimate grievances against that model employer, Joseph DiGiorgio. The Farmers adroitly suggested to the leaders of the California State Federation of Labor that they stop "allowing themselves to be used as suckers by a handful of out-of-state men who are using Communist front groups for publicity purposes."[24]

The erosion of Union funds and morale began to tell by the middle of 1948. The scene of action shifted by stages from the picket line to the courts, to the well of the House of Representa-

tives, to the Federal agencies and to the bureaucratic purlieus in
Sacramento. Enough tension and conflict was sustained in these
quarters to freshen continuously the news stories and magazine
articles that so incensed the Corporation. They could not replenish
the economic resources of the workers, so hundreds of them left
Kern County, some to return home, many others to scatter to
other farming areas of California. By November 1949 not a single
member of the Union was employed by DiGiorgio Farms. The
strike remained technically in effect and was reduced to the lone
picket who sat by the DiGiorgio packing shed.

NOTES

1. Securities and Exchange Commission. DiGiorgio Fruit Corporation. Charter and Articles of Incorporation.
2. *Fortune Magazine,* August 1946, p. 97ff, 12–13, November 1949.
3. *Hearings,* Subcommittee Number 1 of the Committee on Education and Labor of the House of Representatives. Hereafter cited
   as *Hearings.* Bakersfield, 12–13 November 1949. Bakersfield, California, p. 621, *Hearings. U.S. Senate Subcommittee. Violations of
   Free Speech and Rights of Labor.* Part 48 pp. 17634, 17648,
   17651.
4. Ibid., p. 17651.
5. *U.S. v. California Fruit Exchange et al.* Civil Action number
   2577-BH. Federal District Court of Southern California, 18
   November 1942.
6. *Hearings. U.S. Senate Subcommittee. Violations of Free Speech
   and Rights of Labor,* p. 17657.
7. DiGiorgio Fruit Corporation. *Annual Report* 1960.
8. Chambers. *California Farm Organizations,* p. 32.
9. Downey. *They Would Rule the Valley,* p. 189.
10. Ibid., p. 186.
11. *San Francisco Chronicle,* 26 July 1946.
12. *Hearings.* Special Subcommittee of the Committee on Education
    and Labor. National Labor Relations Act of 1949. House Reso-
    lution 2032, p. 1002.

13. Goldschmidt. *As You Sow,* p. 232.
14. *Hearings.* Bakersfield, 12–13 November 1949, p. 651.
15. Ibid., p. 663.
16. *Los Angeles Examiner,* 12 February 1948.
17. *Hearings.* Bakersfield, 12–13 November 1949, p. 657.
18. *Los Angeles Examiner,* 9 February 1948.
19. Senate Committee on Un-American Activities. *Fourth report. Un-American Activities in California.* Sacramento, 1948. p. 337.
20. Statements given before the Hon. Hugh M. Burns. 16 January 1948, p. 7.
21. *Hearings.* Bakersfield, 12–13 November 1949, p. 654.
22. *Bakersfield Californian,* 13 November 1949.
23. *Fresno Bee,* 14 November 1949.
24. Associated Farmers. News release. San Francisco, Calif., 2 February 1948.

2

POVERTY IN THE
VALLEY OF PLENTY

In the spring of 1948 the Hollywood Film Council (A.F. of L.) made a contribution to the striking farm workers. It produced and distributed a twenty-minute sound motion picture entitled *Poverty in the Valley of Plenty.*

Poverty was a sober documentary, simply pictured and narrated. Its location, the Valley of the Doleful, was only a hundred miles from the Valley of the Dolls; its tone, immeasurably far from the sex operas of Sunset strip. Among those who were considered to record the narration was the future governor of California, Ronald Reagan, then president of the Screen Actors Guild, sports announcer and actor.[25] The final choice was Harry W. Flannery, whose diction on the sound track carried with compressed vibration the story of the Oakie migration to DiGiorgio country. The Council was acting in the tradition set forth by Justice Jackson, in *Thomas v. Collins,* that "labor is free to turn its publicity on any labor oppression, substandard wages, employer unfairness and objectionable working conditions." These and other themes were being dramatized by the Kern County strike, and the Council proceeded to record them on film.

The documentary consisted of 57 scenes. It opened with panoramic shots of the southern San Joaquin Valley and the sunny poverty of Arvin, Weedpatch and other communities that surrounded the DiGiorgio Farms. Many of the shacks and hovels were homes of the DiGiorgio workers.

In the first 37 scenes the camera panned "the gorgeous sight" of the San Joaquin with close-ups of campsites "where the landscaping," Flannery narrated, "is done with junk." In this sequence the purpose was to set the stage for the last twenty scenes of the strike itself. The stress was on the industry and the corporation farmer, on agribusiness. Shooting near Arvin the camera crew picked up what Flannery described as "the homes of the farm workers." "These workers, toiling in a great industry," he went on, "are deprived of the rights and opportunities which are granted to all other industrial workers. . . . This cold-water shower . . . is used by twenty-five or thirty families." To wash their clothes, "women have to heat the water over an open fire." It would be ten years before the State of California would grant farm workers compulsory workmen's accident compensation, so Flannery could say. "There is no law requiring a farm corporation to carry compensation insurance for their employees." The narrator gave the setting the broad sweep of the southern Valley: "Beneath this divine canopy of cleanliness and purity . . . nine or ten people live in a one-room shack." The script also touched the raw nerve of the industry—the employment of Wetbacks. "Immigrant workers are smuggled across the Mexican border by headhunters employed by large farm interests. . . . Tools and equipment," Flannery went on acidly, "would be housed in a nice, clean, waterproof shed." He added the bitter reminder that "it was here that John Steinbeck got his inspiration and material for his book, The *Grapes of Wrath*."

Beginning with scene 37 the pictures and narration centered on the strike proper. There were the picket lines, the Union meeting, Jimmy Price speaking, the distribution of groceries brought from afar by labor caravans. Here and there on the sound track there were direct references to Joseph DiGiorgio and the DiGiorgio Corporation; he was "clever, shrewd . . . the largest grape, plum and pear grower in the world . . . the richest and most powerful of the corporation farmers." His Corporation "symbolizes bargaining on a big scale."

The allusions to Mr. Joseph and the DiGiorgio Fruit Corporation woven into the first 37 scenes proved the undoing of the film. They did not draw a sufficiently sharp line between the generalizations about the industry and the specific statements on the strike. This line, as the lawsuits proved, could be bent either way. It was to be given a name years later by the Corporation's attorneys, the firm of Brobeck, Phleger and Harrison of San Francisco. The name, taken from the legal rules on defamation, was Inducement,

Innuendo and Colloquium. It was on this line that Brobeck was to fight through not one but twenty summers.

To better gauge the tactical use and the damaging power of inducement, innuendo and colloquium as they will appear in subsequent chapters, here it is necessary to point out that the agribusinessmen, the Kern County Special Citizens Committee, felt vehemently that they themselves were the targets of the film. It was about them, they knew, that Flannery was talking when he said: "Farming is a big business; it has laws of its own, or I should say, the lack of laws to protect and benefit the greater number of people." This was a general charge against agribusiness, and so the Special Citizens understood it. The articulate public opinion of the area was incensed over the alleged falsehoods of the film. It was Robert DiGiorgio himself who made this plain when he testified: "The statements and representations in the film are grossly misleading, false and defamatory and discredit DiGiorgio Fruit Corporation *and all of the farmers of Kern County in the eyes of the public.*"[26] The italics are added to fix the point around which inducement, innuendo and colloquium were to churn in legal arguments. The emphasis which has been added to Robert's words was not, of course, intended by him. In later contexts, he no doubt realized how close he had come to fumbling with his most effective allies, inducement, innuendo and colloquium.

Poverty in the Valley of Plenty was sponsored jointly with the Hollywood Film Council by the Screen Actors Guild, the American Federation of Musicians, the California State Federation of Labor, the Los Angeles Central Labor Council and other affiliates of the A.F. of L. Prints were sold and screened throughout the country. It helped materially in raising some $87,000 in strike funds. Members of a subcommittee of the House Committee on Education and Labor saw it in Washington, on 16 March 1949. H. L. Mitchell, in presenting the film to the subcommittee, indicated the wide scope of its theme: "The DiGiorgio strike and the conditions under which agricultural workers live throughout the country."[27] A television station in Los Angeles broadcast it soon after the prints were released in March 1948.

As an organizing device, when shown to farm laborers the film was effective. As a fuse for the deep hostilities of the Special Citizens, it was much more so. The film closed with Flannery's words:

"These people have only one remaining hope to right the many injustices that have been inflicted upon them. That is to organize." To prevent such organization was the sole assignment of the Associated Farmers, for whom Joseph DiGiorgio raised funds.

But Flannery had gone further. He stirred sleeping passions by referring to the *Grapes of Wrath,* the suppression of which had once been attempted by Wofford B. Camp and Harold Pomeroy, secretary of the Farmers. Camp was the writer of the preface to *A Community Aroused.* "Poverty in the Valley of Plenty" was recalling passages in Steinbeck's classic that spoke familiarly to the tenants of Arvin, Lamont, Corcoran, Farmersville and a hundred other rural communities. It was the voice of Tom Joad repeating: "I been thinking a hell of a lot, thinkin' about our own people livin' like pigs, an' the good rich earth layin' fallow, or maybe a fellow with a million acres, while a hundred thousand good farmers is starvin'." And of Ma Joad, answering: "Tommy, don't you go fightin' them alone. They say there's a hundred thousand of us shoved out. If we was all to get mad the same way, Tommy, they wouldn't hunt nobody down."

But before the hundred thousand Joads could "get mad the same way," the eleven Special Citizens did. "Poverty in the Valley of Plenty" was their first target, and against it the Corporation filed the first of the nine actions for defamation, entitled

Complaint for Libel—the First /   No. 559 852
 In the Superior Court of the State of California
 in and for the County of Los Angeles
 DiGiorgio Fruit Corporation, a Corporation, Plaintiff,
 v.
 Paramount Television Productions
 Filed 16 May 1949.

The film had been broadcast over station KTLA in Los Angeles by arrangement between the Hollywood Film Council and Paramount Television Productions. The showing took place in May 1948. It was the television premier for *Poverty.* Thereafter the film was booked for exhibition in union halls, college campuses, churches, luncheon clubs, conventions and farm labor gatherings throughout the country.

The Corporation never had mixed feelings about the Union film.

To the DiGiorgios it was a package of unmitigated libels deliberately put together to destroy their business and tarnish their reputation. Nevertheless, for a full year they made no effort to challenge *Poverty*. The reasons for this delay can only be surmised. A suit for defamation by sound motion pictures presented novel legal problems. An injunction to prevent showing of the motion picture was considered and rejected. Some of the sympathetic exhibitors were potential defendants the DiGiorgio Fruit Corporation would not be anxious to sue, among them Fordham University, Robert DiGiorgio's *alma mater*. The Corporation had to complete its own detailed analysis of the contents of the film and to weigh carefully the collateral risks and advantages of a libel suit, including the publicity value of such a move.

A few days before the statute of limitations had run the DiGiorgios made up their minds. The first target was Paramount Productions. The complaint asked for $100,000 in special and $100,000 in punitive damages.

The Corporation demanded that certain corrections in the script be broadcast over KTLA. The station met these demands but the suit was not dropped. It remained inactive for exactly twelve months during which the Corporation's attorneys refined their strategy and bided their time. They had in hand, potentially, as many lawsuits as there had been exhibitors. The place, date and names of the next defendants were sensitive matters of strategy.

Although the filing of a lawsuit is in theory a respectful appearance before Justice and her court, this one was to be different. It was to be announced under the most advantageous political auspices. From what quarter they would come was indicated by the

Rumblings in the House. / In March 1949 a subcommittee of the House Committee on Education and Labor, under the chairmanship of Representative Augustus Kelly, held hearings in Washington on House Resolution 2032, a bill to repeal the Labor Management Relations Act of 1947. On the sixteenth H. L. Mitchell showed *Poverty* to the subcommittee.

Mitchell's appearance was a plunge into the roiled waters of the 81st Congress. The 80th, with 243 Republicans in control of the House, had passed the 1947 Act. Fred A. Hartley was installed as chairman of the Committee on Education and Labor. All but five of the committee members were unfriendly to organized labor.[28] Hartley's bill, House Resolution 3020, with the support of the Republican forces in the Senate under Senator Taft, became law over the President's veto. It was the major controversy pending before the House when the Democrats took control, with 262 members against 171 Republicans. The chairmanship of the House Committee on Education and Labor passed to Congressman Lesinski, its membership divided between sixteen Democrats and nine Republicans. Among them were names headed for the neon lights of American politics—John F. Kennedy, Adam Clayton Powell, Thruston B. Morton and Richard M. Nixon.

Lesinski's nominal majority of seven Democrats was misleading. The Dixiecrat coalition in the House worked in the committee to reduce that majority to a narrow balance between thirteen regular Democrats, three swingers and nine Republicans.[29] The three could tip the balance on any given vote of either the full committee or any of its subcommittees. Lesinski, like all committee chairmen, held the reins tightly on his slim majority. So did the chairmen of the satellite subcommittees, composed of three Democrats and two Republicans.

Mitchell's film showing was only one of a series of incidents which kept the issue of farm labor before the House during both the 80th and 81st Congresses.

On 22 March 1948 Congressman Alfred J. Elliott of California staged a full-scale attack on the farm labor Union and the strike. From the records of the House Un-American Activities Committee he retrieved some references to Mitchell as a former leader of the Southern Tenant Farmer's Union. Elliott presented the House with documentation to prove that the DiGiorgio workers were overwhelmingly opposed to unionization. This was the petition bearing over one thousand names, including that of the superintendent of the Farms. Elliott told the House: "Here is a case where communistic activities are connected with a program of picketing the DiGiorgio Farms." He concluded with a demand: "In all fairness to the State of California and the DiGiorgio Farms . . . I ask that a committee from the Committee on Un-American Activities, or a committee from the Committee on Education and Labor, go to California and make a thorough investigation to see what we can do to stop this picketing . . . because this type of picketing harass-

ment is Un-American. I hope the House will back me up in asking
for an investigation and correct this situation once and for all."[30]

On March 30 Chairman Hartley announced that his committee
would indeed investigate the strike. Mitchell promptly agreed to
co-operate, even though an investigation, goaded by Elliott's
unabashed demands to stop the strike, might be heavily biased.[31]

Hartley did not move, however, and the Republican defeat that
ousted him from the chairmanship left the decision up to Lesinski.
The Republicans from California would not let the matter rest.
Congressman Phillips spoke to the House on 24 June 1949, assert-
ing that "there is no strike on the DiGiorgio ranch with picketing
by people who ever worked for Mr. DiGiorgio." He referred to the
film that Mitchell had shown on March 16 of the previous year.[32]

Congressman Cleveland M. Bailey from West Virginia, whose
political base was the United Mine Workers of his district, and the
author of a resolution to repeal the Taft-Hartley law, answered
Phillips. "I can assure the gentleman," he said, "that this Congress
will have the facts on that situation in California if we have to send
a subcommittee out there. . ." There would be action, Bailey
promised, "in accordance with the information that the committee
reports." In the course of his remarks Bailey concealed his bias no
more than did Elliott. The DiGiorgio Corporation, he added, was
already fastening its tentacles upon the fruit and vegetable markets
of the world. It was an attempt, he charged, "bordering on the
edge of becoming a monopoly" which Congress would have to
defeat before it destroyed the American farmer.[33] For background
to these debates on the floor of the House, Congressman Thomas
H. Werdel, representing DiGiorgio's district, from time to time
inserted in the Appendix of the House *Record* Extensions of
Remarks highly favorable to the Corporation.

Thus matters stood when early in October Chairman Lesinski
decided to act on Elliott's demand. He did so in a complicated
manner that was to lead to important confusions.

The House had approved Resolution 4115, which authorized
Lesinski's committee to hold nationwide hearings on the effects of
Federal projects on public schools where civilian and military personnel were concentrated. Bailey was appointed chairman of Subcommittee Number 1 to conduct these hearings; but to avoid
duplication of travel and expenses, he was also instructed to hold

hearings in Bakersfield on the DiGiorgio strike. The authority under which this secondary assignment was given, however, was not delegated by the House under Resolution 4115 but under another House Resolution, Number 75. House Resolution 75 dealt with the general authority of Lesinski's committee to conduct thorough studies and investigations relating to matters coming within the jurisdiction of the committee. Lesinski made it clear that the Bailey subcommittee was to be primarily responsible for the educational problems of Federally impacted areas, as they were called. Another subcommittee, chaired by Congressman Burke, was to be primarily responsible for hearings and the report on labor-management relations. Bailey, rather than Burke, was assigned to the DiGiorgio strike simply because that was the way the travel schedules of the two subcommittees worked out.

Bailey set the strike hearings for November 12 and 13, 1949. Advance notice of several weeks was given both to the Union and to the Corporation. The scene, now shifting from Washington to Kern County, was prepared for the second

Complaint for Libel—the Second /   No. 566 888
In the Superior Court of the State of California
in and for the County of Los Angeles
DiGiorgio Fruit Corporation, a Corporation, Plaintiff,
v.
Harry W. Flannery, National Farm Labor Union, Hollywood
Film Council, Los Angeles Central Labor Council, et al.
Filed 8 November 1949.

The long delay in filing this suit was to pay large dividends, but it must have strained the patience of the DiGiorgios. To Robert the film was from the outset "a scandalous, libelous, scurrilous movie." Insofar as Mr. Joseph was concerned, it was something on the order of the *scandalum magnatum* of the thirteenth century of English law-defamation of magnates of the realm. The months, the years, were passing, and the lone picket still remained at the gates of the Farms, causing damage to the business, trade and repute of the Corporation.

The film, alleged Brobeck, Phleger and Harrison in complaint number two, was a libel which violated Section 45 of the Code of

Civil Procedure of California, namely, "a false and unprivileged
publication by writing, printing, picture, effigy or other fixed representation to the eye, which exposes any person to hatred, contempt,
ridicule or obloquy, or which causes him to be shunned or avoided,
or which has a tendency to injure him in his occupation." The libel
was a tort, that part of the common law which deals with twisted
conduct that violates another's rights to keep his mind at peace
and his body in one piece. Libel, from *libellus,* "little book," is
defamation set down in writing as defined in Section 45, to differentiate it from spoken defamation or slander. The violations
pleaded by DiGiorgio in its complaints are discussed in Chapter
VII in relation to the peculiar legal problems of libel by means
of motion pictures with sound.

Brobeck, Phleger and Harrison's complaint on behalf of Di-
Giorgio cited showings of the film in Washington, D.C.; Berkeley,
California; New York City; Los Angeles, "and numerous other
places throughout the United States." It prayed the court for a
million dollars in general and a million in punitive damages. It set
forth at least fifteen specific charges of libelous untruths about the
Corporation, to wit: that it was unfair to its employees; that it
denied them rights and opportunities granted to all other industrial
workers; that it refused its employees accident insurance protection; that it robbed its employees of normal American rights;
reduced them to the status of serfs; provided them with rude habi-
tations unfit for human use; exacted $26 a month rent for hovels;
forced nine and ten people to live in one shack; compelled them to
heat water over open fires; payed them eleven hours wages for
twelve hours of work; denied them compensation for loss of limb;
refused them workmen's compensation for physical injury; denied
them adequate medical care; deprived their children of decent
educational opportunities; and that the Corporation participated
in smuggling Mexican nationals into the United States through
intermediaries called head hunters.

All these, the complaint alleged, were tortious and immoral
actions directly attributed in the film's pictures and sound track
to the Corporation. The length of the list of allegations and their
variety were in themselves something of a precedent in libel suits.
Even so, it was not to be understood as a complete list. This was
because of the nature of the medium—a sound motion picture.

The DiGiorgio attorneys inserted paragraph VII in the complaint, which read:

> Because the words, sounds and pictures are contained on a motion picture film and sound track, and are inextricably connected and interdependent for their meaning and effect, it is impossible to set them out in this complaint.[34]

The legal strategy behind this language was a bold one. Section 45 of the Civil Code rested on the traditional cases of libel, which for five hundred years or more had dealt with words printed or otherwise inscribed. The general rule as to defamation in this form was that "the complaint must set out the particular defamatory words as published."[35] Where the pleader must, from the nature of the case, resort to a verbal description of the defamatory matter "as where movements, postures, or pictures are used," a modification of the rule was to be allowed.

Poverty was a statement in visual images, not in "writings." These images could not be set forth in a written complaint. The words that accompanied the images were spoken. If both were defamatory there was libel in the images and slander in the words. Did the images make the spoken words libelous, or did the spoken words make the images slanderous? A test of the rule was in the making. In 1963 some legal opinions were still holding that "the great weight of authority supports the view that in the absence of any statutory provision to the contrary, a libelous statement must be reproduced verbatim."[36]

These doubts were not reflected in paragraph VII of the complaint. On the contrary, it advanced a legal theory to the effect that in a libel using the medium of a motion picture with sound track, it was not possible to reproduce exactly in the complaint either (a) the pictures or (b) the verbal sounds or (c) the words signified by those sounds. The medium by its very nature combined these elements into an inextricable mix from which neither words nor sounds nor pictures were any longer separable. It was a bold rush into the nebulous and DiGiorgio's lawyers carried it off with complete success.

The traditional rule about specific setting forth of words, to which Brobeck paid such scant attention, was intended to give defendants clear notice of the exact language they were supposed to defend themselves against, or to justify. Gilbert and Nissen, the attorneys for Flannery and the unions, made an effort to protect their clients in this quarter. They filed a demurrer on the ground that the usual rule of pleading in libel must be followed. Superior Court Judge McKesson ruled on the demurrer on 9 January 1950, holding that because of the difficulties involved Di-Giorgio's attorneys need not describe the allegedly libelous scenes in greater detail. An appeal from this ruling was never taken.

The co-ordination of the case for the plaintiff in this second libel action called for close and careful teamwork. Robert DiGiorgio was assigned to the team by the Corporation by virtue of his position as labor relations and publicity director. A junior associate of Brobeck, Phleger and Harrison, Malcolm Dungan, was responsible for the research and the legal documents. It was Dungan who prepared the complaint filed on November 8. Five days later Subcommittee Number 1 opened

The Bakersfield Hearings. / In the 80th Congress the workload of the House was distributed among more than one hundred subcommittees.[37] These *ad hoc* subcommittees, usually composed of three majority and two minority Members, are traditionally appointed by the chairman of the standing committee. The chairman of the subcommittee is always a member of the majority party. To him the chairman of the standing committee entrusts a portion of the great power with which he is vested by the rules of the House and the seniority system. The first skirmishes of the battles on the floor of the House take place on these subcommittees. To every Member of the House his assignment to a standing committee is crucial; his appointment to a subcommittee can make the difference between obscurity and repute among his colleagues. His votes on a subcommittee can deflect the runnels of congressional decision, attach his name to some current national issue, attract the notice of the news media and give him solid credentials with those who co-opt the future favorites of power.

As a member of a subcommittee, the congressman is the drudge of the House. He promptly learns that the subcommittee system is the alternative to anarchy in the business of the House, the practical answer to chaos. If he is a minority member, and short on seniority, he may have to serve time under a cross-grained, wily, unreasonable arbitrary veteran of the opposition, perhaps wondering at times why anarchy and efficiency must at times be reconciled with senility.

When this daily round of hard work and menial obscurity can be broken by an investigation, the big moment of the congressman arrives. Investigations are authorized by the rules of Congress.[38] There were some six hundred of them between the 1790s and the 1940s. Originally intended to provide Congress with the means for gathering facts for legislation, to check on the executive branch and to inquire into its own internal affairs, the investigative process always manifested a fourth power—that of molding public opinion. The brief but scandal-propelled prominence of Senator Joseph P. McCarthy proved, indeed, that such a power could be the principal use of a congressional investigation. As Taylor observed, "in skillful and unscrupulous hands, a legislative investigation is truly a most potent and versatile engine of destruction."[39] Congressman Elliott's demand for an investigation of the DiGiorgio strike "to put an end to it once and for all" was plainly in the McCarthy style.

Chairman Lesinski had announced publicly on 22 July 1949 that an investigation would be made and hearings would be held near the scene of the strike. In a letter of authorization dated October 7, Bailey, as chairman of Subcommittee Number 1, was "authorized and directed to investigate conditions to provide for the education of children . . . residing in localities overburdened with increased school enrollments resulting from Federal activities . . . as outlined in H. R. 4115." Bailey was "further authorized and directed to conduct a thorough study and investigation of labor-management relations at the DiGiorgio Fruit Corporation known as the DiGiorgio Farms in DiGiorgio, California." At the completion of the study and investigation Bailey was instructed to "prepare a report to the Congress."[40]

Bailey called the Subcommittee to order at ten o'clock on the morning of 12 November 1949, at the Bakersfield Inn. It was a charming setting for a hearing on a labor disturbance. The bougainvillea that November still hung in small cascades of lavender over the red-tile roofs of the guest bungalows. The crowns of the palm trees raised their graceful green sprays around the blue waters of the swimming pool. Around them and between the luxuriant hedges and shrubs the cement paths curved and were lost in the private retreats of the caravansary.

Chairman Bailey presided at a large table at one end of the hearing room. To his left sat the Hon. Richard M. Nixon, to his right the Hon. Tom Steed. Congressman Thruston B. Morton and Congressman Leonard Irving, the remaining two members of the subcommittee, did not attend the hearings. The majority clerk, Frank Boyer, and the clerk for the minority, John O. Graham, completed the official panel. A court reporter sat next to the witness chair recording the proceedings.

In front of Bailey and his colleagues was the audience of some hundred persons, the seating arrangement neatly dividing their partisan interests. The majority of those present were representatives and spokesmen for large-scale farming, an enlarged cast of the Special Citizens of Kern County, joined now by influentials like Robert Schmeiser of the Associated Farmers, whose connections formed the network of agribusiness of California.

With a quorum verified—Bailey, Nixon and Steed—the chairman explained that the proceedings would be formal under the rules of the House. In addition to hearing the oral testimony, the subcommittee viewed two films, *Poverty in the Valley of Plenty* and a company production called *The DiGiorgio Story*. Robert DiGiorgio received the congressmen at the ranch on the second day of the hearings, at which time employees of the Corporation were interviewed and examined on their opinions of the strike. The Hon. Thomas H. Werdel, representative of the host district, drifted in and out of the sessions. He was not a member of the subcommittee.

During the noon recess of the twelfth in the patio adjoining the hearing room copies of the complaint of the DiGiorgio lawsuit against Flannery et al. were served on H. L. Mitchell, Henry Hasiwar, Jimmy Price and Ernesto Galarza. The complaint was a mimeographed document of nine pages with the summons attached.

Formally, the subcommittee hearings were in the control of a Democratic chairman, Bailey, supported by a Democratic colleague, Steed, and under the partisan watch of the Republican minority in the person of Nixon. Of the two absentees, Irving and Morton, only Morton was to play a role in future events.

Werdel, seated at the head table by congressional courtesy, had been elected to Congress in 1948. A lawyer with a corporate practice in Bakersfield, he served several years in the State legislature.

His partner was Vincent DiGiorgio, a relative of Mr. Joseph's. A tall, heavily-fleshed man, Werdel did not enjoy using his influence openly, but preferred to bring it to bear in quiet ways. He did not testify at the hearings, but rather attended them as an observer, without being heard at all and being noticed as little as possible. His political ambitions were tied closely to the America First party and to the well-financed approval of Kern County's Special Citizens. On their platform of honesty, economy, loyalty and the ordinary virtues[41] Werdel stood. In speeches in the House, he denounced strikes as "periodic interference with the family income," and he stood up to "the bureaucratic Cossacks riding through the halls of Congress" who opposed his bills to discipline the trade-unions.

The junior Democrat on the subcommittee who heard testimony and visited the Farms was Tom Steed, from the fourth congressional district of Oklahoma. Born Thomas Jefferson Steed on a farm near the town of Rising Star, he was a newspaper reporter, editor and automobile salesman. He was elected to the House in 1948, and modestly recognizing his unexceptionalness he dropped the Thomas Jefferson and became plain Tom Steed, the representative for a district of small family farmers, the American tillers of the soil who were a continent and a social class apart from agribusiness. Steed listened to the testimony with just enough alertness to avoid involvement in issues which would be meaningless—and perhaps alarming—to his constituents. For him attendance at Bakersfield was one of the drudgeries of a junior committeeman.

In contrast Nixon was in fine fettle for his role. He had graduated from Whittier College, near Los Angeles, in 1934 and from Duke University Law School in 1937. After service in the Navy and as government attorney in Washington, he was elected to the House in November 1946 from the twelfth congressional district of California. His election majorities in the district were impressive if not phenomenal—56 percent in 1946, 86 percent in 1948. Although he rated only number 44 in Republican seniority in the 81st Congress he was climbing rapidly above his contemporaries. He owed this to his appointment to the House Un-American Activities Committee, where he gained solid footing. He was appointed chairman of a subcommittee to find out whether Whitaker Chambers or Alger Hiss was lying under oath, and became known as a particularly active conservative. His successes were notable, as with Alger Hiss; his failures went almost unnoticed, as his unproductive assignment to Robert Stripling to "make a record" on the National Farm Labor Union, Local 218.

Sitting next to his antagonist, Bailey, Congressman Nixon cross-examined Union witnesses with the practiced courtesy that had already attracted favorable notice, questioning the spokesmen and friends of the Corporation sympathetically to underscore the points they made. Beneath Nixon's well-brushed wavy dark hair, his nimble, alert mind was at work. He sat forward in his chair and frequently darted glances at that portion of the room where the Special Citizens sat. Among them were the strongest and most influential supporters of the Nixon-for-Senator movement. They were watching their man in a crucial test and he was doing well. Here, for them, was their political model who, by his own defini-tion, "owes it to himself and to the system" to "use his abilities and his experience to the fullest." He was, moreover, at that critical moment a freshman congressman beckoned by the appeal of "the power and the glory."[42]

The Union stated its case first. H. L. Mitchell, its president, stoop-shouldered and outwardly flaccid, was one of the most dura-ble defenders of the farm laborers in the nation. Once more he reviewed the evils of the corporation farming system, arguing single-mindedly for equality in bargaining power. Hank Hasiwar, the director of the strike, recited the grievances, the efforts to negotiate, the boycotts, and the misfortunes of the Union with the National Labor Relations Board, the state agencies and the courts. C. J. Haggerty was a character witness for the strikers, conveying to Nixon, principally, that no union endorsed by the State Federa-tion of Labor could possibly be suspected of Communism. The Union submitted six copies of a brief. The thirty-page statement of the Union's case included a chronology of the principal events of the strike to the date of the hearings.

Jimmy Price, president of Local 218, closed for the Union. Price cautioned the congressmen that "maybe you won't hear some of the fancy words some of these people use . . . I haven't got no high education." Price went on to detail the complaints of the DiGiorgio strikers: men who moved from a temperature of 32 degrees in the cooling rooms of the packing shed into the broiling heat of 112 degrees outside; the lack of hot water and bathing facilities in some of the DiGiorgio housing; toilets in such shape that "sometimes you could get in there, sometimes you couldn't"; the firing of an employee who asked for a raise in wages of five cents an hour; no overtime, no unemployment insurance, no social security, no paid vacations, no regular hours.

Nixon tried to lead Price into a more favorable review of DiGiorgio's labor relations:

NIXON: What did you earn when you first came?
PRICE: I believe it was twenty-five cents.
NIXON: That was ten years ago?
PRICE: Approximately.
NIXON: Now it is eighty cents?
PRICE: Eighty cents. Yes.
NIXON: That's a little more than three times as much.
PRICE: Groceries is more than that.[43]

The Corporation's principal witness was Robert DiGiorgio. He reviewed the notable accomplishments of Mr. Joseph, the many benefactions of the Corporation to the community, the sensitive awareness of its management to the welfare of its workers, their complete negativism toward the Union, the total ineffectiveness of the strike. He testified that he would never consent "to have outsiders come in and tell us whether we will or will not have an election."

But above all Robert's testimony was a sustained attack on the Union film, *Poverty in the Valley of Plenty*. He detailed the alleged canards, misrepresentations and falsehoods he and his associates read and heard in the film. To impress the subcommittee with the seriousness of the matter, DiGiorgio put into the record official notice that the Corporation had just a few days before filed a libel action against the Union and other sponsors of the motion picture. To drive home his denunciation of the film, he introduced correspondence between Governor Warren, Mr. Joseph and Congressman Werdel which had been exchanged previous to the hearings. He also asked Bailey for permission to file an answer to the Union's brief. Bailey acceded, informing DiGiorgio that the record would remain open and that supplementary documents should be forwarded to the majority clerk, Frank Boyer.

Some prominent agribusinessmen testified to the high prestige and the solid reputation of the DiGiorgios. Gregory Harrison, the Corporation's attorney, flatly rejected the Union's offer to produce more than eight hundred signed authorization cards of DiGiorgio employees. To the Union's complaint of discrimination under the National Labor Relations Act, Harrison replied that "Congress need not purchase compliance with the laws of the United States on the basis of privileges and gratuities."[44]

A minor witness for the Corporation was Lawrence Webdell, office manager of DiGiorgio Farms. Webdell had previously told newspapermen that he knew of no DiGiorgio employees who lived in the run-down houses that marred the surrounding communities. For the subcommittee, he did estimate that some eight hundred of DiGiorgio's permanent employees lived in homes in the neighborhood. Webdell also accused H. L. Mitchell of forcing his way into the home of a non-union employee. Alexander Schullman, the Union attorney, protested and demanded that the committee "use its power to have somebody held for testifying falsely concerning that situation." Nixon's face darkened a shade in the slanting afternoon shadows of the room as he answered ominously, "There is likely to be a lot of that before this hearing is over, and not only about Mr. Mitchell." The punishment of perjurers, however, was not the main business of the hearings, so Nixon dropped the subject.

Webdell's weak feint did not sidetrack the proceedings. Robert DiGiorgio tried more insistently. He arranged for the screening of the Union's film as well as for that of his own. A print of *Poverty* was introduced as evidence and became a part of the exhibits before the subcommittee. This served no purpose of the Union, whose presentation was made by live witnesses and supported by documents which Brobeck refused to accept.

It did serve DiGiorgio's tactical aim, which was to convince the subcommittee of these propositions: that the charges in the film were directed exclusively at the Corporation; and that they were false, scurrilous, vicious and scandalous. It placed the film and its sponsors, not the labor-management relations at the Farms, on trial.

Bailey did not step into the snare. He viewed both films unperturbed, admitted them as evidence and went on with the proceedings. Steed gave no hint, on the official record, that he was any more interested in the motion picture than Bailey. He asked no questions on any aspect of it.

Nixon's reaction was positive. Before the film was screened he had gathered from a private briefing that the producers of the film "were very careful . . . to point out that most of these pictures were taken on the ranch,"[45] but the showing did not confirm his previous judgment. He agreed that the sound track "did not say" that the shacks were on the Corporation's land, but in any case, he asserted, "the implication was clear."

Another statement which the film did not make was that "there is no compensation on DiGiorgio" for injuries suffered on the job. Nixon attributed this charge to the film also by implication and marked another count of false witness against the Union. He was to leave Bakersfield with "no doubt in my mind whatever as to its implications."[46]

Although Nixon swiftly saw these implications, he did not detect one that intruded itself into the record by way of DiGiorgio's testimony, one which raised a legal issue of some delicacy.

Both Robert DiGiorgio and Nixon were attorneys. Robert had informed the subcommittee, with emphasis, that the Corporation had just filed a suit for defamation against the producers and sponsors of *Poverty*.[47] The film, therefore, was on trial before the Superior Court of Los Angeles County. It was to be presumed that DiGiorgio, his attorneys and Nixon were familiar with Canon 20 of the Proposed State Bar rule on civil procedure during trial. This canon, approved by the California State Bar, declared that "A member of the State Bar whether engaged in private practice or public employment shall not, directly or indirectly make . . . any press release statement or other disclosure of information, whether of alleged facts or opinion, for publication or other release to the public in any newspaper or other documentary medium, or by radio, television or other means of public information relating to any pending or anticipated civil action or proceeding . . . calculated, or which may reasonably be expected, to interfere in any manner or to any degree with a fair trial in the courts or with due administration of justice."[48] In the *Times-Mirror* case (1940) it had been held that one of the duties of the courts was "to give every suitor . . . assurance that no . . . hostile influence shall operate against him while his cause is under consideration."[49]

It was an old doctrine, confirmed by often-quoted authorities like Odgers, for whom there was nothing more pernicious "than to prejudice the minds of the public against persons concerned as parties in causes."[50]

The witnesses for the Union at the hearings had, without benefit of counsel, considered the point and concluded that neither in their testimony nor in the Union's brief would the charges made in the DiGiorgio complaint be refuted. It was decided to reserve the defense for the court proceedings and to rest for the time being on brief declarations as to the intent of the film. To Nixon's question "Do you intend for the picture to leave the implication that those houses were on DiGiorgio Farms?" Mitchell replied: "No, I don't think that was even intended or certainly not stated in either the picture or the sound track."[51] Mitchell's direct challenge was evaded by Nixon, DiGiorgio and DiGiorgio's attorney, Harrison.

On Sunday November 13 Bailey closed the hearings. "It will not be known," he announced, "what our recommendations will be in this matter until we have gone over that record and studied the testimony and given it due consideration." By "that record" he meant the testimony that the official reporter at his side had been busy taking in shorthand. Her notes would be typed up; delivered to Boyer, the majority clerk; sent to the Government Printing Office in Washington; printed, and the volumes delivered to the committee chairman who would release them. It would be upon review and study and due consideration of that document that the report required by Lesinski's instructions would be issued.

This, at any rate, was the formal course laid down by custom and the rules of the House for such important particulars. In this instance it was avoided. Four freshman congressmen—Nixon, Morton, Steed and Werdel—the Special Citizens, Joseph DiGiorgio and other members of the Corporation strained at the slow pace of House procedure. To them it was an obstacle course to be avoided, so the congressmen produced the

Nixon-Morton-Steed-Werdel Report. / At the close of the session of the House on 9 March 1950, Congressman Werdel was recognized by the Speaker. He asked for and was given permission "to extend his remarks in the Appendix of the *Record* and include a majority report filed by the subcommittee on which he serves."[52]

The right to extend remarks "affords Members the opportunity to explain their attitude on pending questions and so give constituents a basis on which to approve or disapprove . . . and apprises the country at large of local sentiment."[53] By virtue of this rule, serious and informative matter additional to the proceedings on the floor can and often does come to public attention.

Extensions of remarks have become a form of high congressional courtesy that can also be put to uses less practical though not less expensive. Congressmen permit one another to extend their remarks in the Appendix, to escape having to listen to them on the floor of the House. It is a device even more frequently used to please in print, at public expense, a constituent who has composed an otherwise unpublishable poem, a recipe for bean soup, an editorial that shook Toonerville to its foundations or a public address that was never delivered. Since every Member of the House will have occasion to extend his political views or to circulate the whimsies of friends or constituents, unanimous consent for an Extension of Remarks, such as Werdel was given on March 9, is a routine matter.

There is not a Member of the House but who at one time or another could and would use the Extensions in such inoffensive ways. Undoubtedly also it was agreed with Speaker Champ Clark that it was preferable to let the speeches and articles be printed rather than be compelled to listen to them. It was "a mass of worthless matter which composes nearly one-half of the Congressional set" of records.[54]

The worthless matter was allowed, but only on the condition that it occupy a separate and unequal, segregated and inferior place among the Congressional papers. Thus the standing rule of the House is: "I. Arrangement of the daily *Record*. The public printer will arrange the contents of the daily *Record* as follows: First, Senate proceedings; second, House proceedings; third, the Appendix." That the Appendix did not contain the proceedings of the Chamber was further emphasized: "When either House has granted leave to print (1) a speech not delivered in either House, (2) a newspaper or magazine article, or (3) any other matter not germane to the proceedings, the same shall be printed in the Appendix."[55]

Long the target of criticism from Members and the public who complained both of the trifling subjects in the Extensions and the

expense of printing them, the House never brought itself to the
point of abolishing the practice entirely. It did, however, ease its
conscience and the public purse somewhat by discontinuing the
publication of the Appendix in a bound volume for permanent reference. This was done through a resolution adopted by the Joint
Committee on Printing on 22 June 1953, excluding all extraneous
matter and excessive bulk "from the permanent form of the *Congressional Record.*" The last bound volume of Extensions was
Number 99, Part 12, 2 July 1953 to 18 August 1953, 83rd Congress, First session. The closest thing to a valedictory were some
insertions in that last volume entitled "Death Stalks the New Deal,"
"The William the Silent Award", and "It Tolls for Thee." Thence-
forth the congressional oddities would appear but once in the daily
edition of the *Record*.

The rules of the House of Representatives permit congressmen
to order reprints of their Extensions of Remarks, in quantities of
not fewer than one thousand copies, ordered and paid for by the
interested congressman. The order goes to the Government Printing
Office while the type of the daily edition of the *Congressional
Record* is still in the forms, and the reprint is arranged as a mailer
or flier. The congressman adds an appropriate headline. The most
trivial contents of an extension gain something in elegance from
the format of a reprint. The standard running head gives the source
as the "Proceedings and Debates" of Congress and the Great Seal
of the United States of America is stamped on one corner of the
front page. Above it there is a legend: "Not printed at government
expense." At the top of the first column there appears the name
of the Honorable Member of the House whose Extension of
Remarks follows.

Congressman Werdel, soon after the publication of the Nixon-
Morton-Steed report in the Appendix, ordered reprints and delivered them to the Corporation. They were captioned "Congressional
Committee Bares Facts on Alleged DiGiorgio Ranch Strike." Like
all such prints it was intended for wide distribution. Many copies
undoubtedly would come into the hands of citizens who would not
know that Extensions of Remarks are not proceedings in the
House, nor are they taken from debates on the floor. None but the
most expert in congressional procedure would know that the seal
and the running head were as appropriate as a notary's seal on
a menu.

This borrowed dignity in fact gives reprints much of their appeal. It also provided, in the case of the DiGiorgio Fruit Corporation, an appearance of credibility, officialism and authenticity.

The Corporation enlisted these assets in a continuing though confidential distribution of the Nixon-Morton-Steed reprints. Copies were given out as Werdel delivered them fresh from the Government Printing Office. The distribution, by mail and by hand, continued for nearly fifteen years.*

Werdel's Extension was printed in the daily edition of the *Congressional Record* of 10 March 1950 in the Appendix. It consisted of some forty-four hundred words of close print filling nine columns. The contents were divided in two parts. The first six paragraphs in column 1 were devoted to Werdel's own prefatory remarks, and the last section, to the text of what Werdel called "the report." This text was preceded not by a letter of submittal from the chairman of the subcommittee to that of the full committee but by the letter of authorization which Bailey had produced in Bakersfield four months before—an unprecedented departure from House custom. Werdel himself said in his preface that the report was not yet in print, which meant that it was not yet in form for official submission to the House.

In his preface Werdel said he wished to enlighten the House about a false and libelous film that had been fabricated by one Harry W. Flannery and his associates "for thirty pieces of silver."

---

*Robert DiGiorgio, Deposition. 16 December 1964, p. 16. The Corporation's use of the Werdel reprint from 1950 to 1966 illustrated with uncanny accuracy the comment of the Court in *Winrod v. McFadden,* 67 Fed. Sup. 251, decided in 1945: ". . . the publisher could, with impunity, print a large number of extra copies of an issue containing libelous matter, retain them on hand and from time to time through the years mail them to members of the general public. The original publication may have been forgotten, but the continuous mailing of same by the publisher year after year would reiterate and emphasize the libel and could possibly after repeated mailings cause more damage to the person against whom the libel was directed than the original publication." The Werdel reprint contains five libelous charges against Union officials: bearing false witness, deliberately fabricating falsehoods for 30 pieces of silver, collecting hundreds of thousands of dollars for a nonexistent strike, committing fraud and perverting the processes of the Congress of the United States.

Werdel went on to say that the fabrication had been used "to collect hundreds of thousands of dollars from workingmen throughout the country to finance a purported strike that did not exist." The authors and sponsors of *Poverty*—for that was the name of the film—were "corrupt men deliberately bearing false witness." They had perpetuated a fraud "to the advantage of a handful of men." They had committed "a disservice to the legitimate American labor movement."

Werdel then introduced the "report" which, he asserted, had been prepared by Bailey's Subcommittee Number 1 based on the Bakersfield hearings. "I am including the report in the *Record*," he explained, "inasmuch as it may be several weeks before it is distributed in printed form by the subcommittee. It follows."[56]

What followed was a devastating attack not only on the film but on the National Farm Labor Union, the striking members of Local 218 and their officers.

External evidence was not necessary to bring out the contradictions and inconsistencies within the document itself. It said that the DiGiorgio employees had no grievances, yet it listed them. It said first that there was no strike and then that the strike "at least theoretically continues to the present time." It said that there was no picket line, and then it declared that the picket line "may be regarded as a relatively peaceful one." It based the authorization for the investigation first on House Resolution 2032 and then on House Resolution 75. It stated that no Union witness testified to anything which even approximated the charges depicted in the film, and it also stated that officials of the Union testified that the film gave a true picture of DiGiorgio Farms conditions. It referred to evidence received which "shows that a strike of any serious proportions in agriculture would choke off interstate commerce in necessary foodstuffs" and then it pointed out that the picket line had failed to affect the operations of the fruit corporation. It cited evidence proving that "the sole issue is recognition" and then referred to "much testimony" concerning other issues.

The rapporteurs concluded that "insofar as it [the film] purports to represent conditions existing on DiGiorgio Farms . . . [it was made] and was presented to the committee in disregard of the truth." The major charges set forth in the DiGiorgio complaint filed on November 8 were found to be true. The horrendous housing in which employees were forced to live; the cold-water showers; the open fires; the failure to pay wages for a full working day; the rent for washing machines; the lack of workmen's compensation; the smuggling of Wetbacks—these conditions did not exist on the DiGiorgio ranch. The film "said" they did. "No one could doubt that these charges were levelled straight at the corporation. . . . All of these representations are false."

Although frequently referring to evidence, the report lashed the Union and its film on the basis of "unmistakable innuendos" as well as on words explicitly "said" in the sound track. There was not, for the Union, any escape from this crossfire of congressional logic seemingly based on documentary evidence as well as on inferences.

In vain Mitchell and Hasiwar denied that the primary target of the film was the Corporation, and affirmed that it was intended as an attack on conditions prevailing throughout the industry. The report waived this aside, adducing that "the educational director and the western representative insist that the film is a true picture of the DiGiorgio Farms." Although there was no evidence in the record to this effect, there was, in their judgment, ample proof that the film was "a shocking collection of falsehoods almost wholly unrelieved by any regard whatever for the truth and the facts."

As to the strike itself, the Union men fared no better. There was "no strike, no grievances, no pickets." The subcommittee considered the testimony given by Price and other Union witnesses irrelevant, extraneous matter with no more merit than "afterthoughts and makeweights."

The report rounded out its indictment of *Poverty* and the strike with these words: "The processes of the Congress of the United States have been perverted and misused by the National Farm Labor Union in order to furnish a sounding board for its claims. The committee should certainly not be without power to prevent the recurrence of this kind of abuse of its functions and impositions upon its energies."

The rapporteurs were the Hon. Richard Nixon, the Hon. Thruston B. Morton and the Hon. Tom Steed, so identified by their names in print in that order at the bottom of Werdel's Extension in the Appendix.

This typographical detail was to become a major issue in the

years to come. Werdel stated in his preface that the report had
been "signed." The names in print were for the time being the
closest to holographic evidence that he could produce.

Werdel also characterized it as a "majority report." "I recommend as the majority report," he wrote, "of the subcommittee . . .
to all the Members of the House" what he was about to insert in
the Appendix.

It was also Werdel's intention to give the insertion in the Appendix every appearance of an official report, an official document of
the subcommittee, and of the full Committee on Education and
Labor. It was for this reason that he extended himself in the prefatory remarks, which are usually a laconic sentence or two by the
extending congressman. Only the unwary could be impressed, not
the Members of the House, who were thoroughly familiar with the
character of official House reports and the surplusage that they
themselves often put into the Appendix.

A detail that would not have escaped the critical congressional
eye was the document that Werdel used to introduce the fear-
some report. Immediately after the title—Agricultural Labor at
DiGiorgio Farms, California—he had inserted the letter of authorization from Lesinski to Bailey of 7 October 1949. House reports,
when submitted, are prefaced by a letter of submittal, which con-
cludes the assignment as unmistakably as the letter of authorization
begins it.

In response to pressure from his electors, Werdel had evidently
given an informal twist to the process by which reports are prepared and submitted, the process which Bailey had explained in
Bakersfield. Nixon recalled that Werdel had often asked about the
progress of the publication of the hearings and the promised
report.[57] Referring in his prefatory remarks to his district, Werdel
wrote: "Public opinion in the area of the DiGiorgio Ranch is
incensed over the falsehoods embraced in the said moving picture
and narration. . . . That area is desirous of immediately correcting
the infavorable publicity resulting from the libelous action." Whose
opinion Werdel was referring to, and the degree of its indignation,
had already appeared in the visit of the Special Citizens to the
Farms and the subsequent publication of *A Community Aroused*.

The publication of Werdel's Extension of Nixon, Morton and
Steed took the Union completely by surprise. There had been no

correspondence or discussion between its officers and the staff of the subcommittee since the Bakersfield hearings. On March 11 Congressman Shelley of San Francisco gave the Union its first information regarding Werdel's action. Mitchell then talked with Walter Mason, lobbyist for the American Federation of Labor. Together they met with Bailey, who promised to answer Werdel. Union officers telegraphed Werdel inviting him to repeat his charges off the floor of the House, an invitation which Werdel ignored; he kept a safe distance within the aura of constitutional privilege which surrounds all congressmen.

Thus protected, the report began immediately to produce drastic effects. It settled like an invisible noose around the lone picket at the DiGiorgio gates. A few violent yanks of publicity and some twists in private negotiations lifted the picket, her box, her sign and her umbrella completely out of sight.

NOTES

25. *Oakland Tribune,* 26 February 1948.
26. *Hearings.* Bakersfield, 12–13 November 1949, p. 644.
27. *Hearings.* House Resolution Number 2032, 999–1004.
28. MacNeil. *Forge of Democracy,* p. 159.
29. *Congressional Quarterly.* Vol. III, 1947, p. 180.
30. *Congressional Record.* 22 March 1948, pp. 3287, 3288, 3293.
31. *Congressional Record.* Appendix. 29 March 1948, p. A-2058.
32. *Congressional Record.* 24 June 1949, p. 8396.
33. Ibid., p. 8396. *Congressional Record,* 26 September 1951, p. 12175.
34. Complaint for libel. *DiGiorgio Fruit Corporation v. Harry W. Flannery et al.* Number 566888, 8 November 1949.
35. 53 C J S sections 255–256.
36. 33 American Jurisprudence, section 237.
37. Miller. *Member of the House,* p. 145.
38. *Jefferson's Manual and Rules of the U.S. House of Representatives.* 81st Congress. Section 739.

39. Taylor. *Grand Inquest,* p. 15.
40. *Hearings.* Bakersfield, 12–13 November 1949, p. 541.
41. Kern County Werdel Delegation Committee. Bakersfield, California. 1952.
42. *San Jose Mercury,* 13 October 1968.
43. *Hearings.* Bakersfield, 12–13 November 1949, p. 700.
44. Ibid., p. 682.
45. Ibid., p. 557.
46. Ibid., p. 656.
47. Ibid., p. 644.
48. Proposed State Bar Rule. Canon 20. "California Civil Procedure During Trial." California State Bar Association, p. 59.
49. 98 Pacific 2d., 1039.
50. *Odgers on Libel,* p. 324.
51. *Hearings.* Bakersfield, 12–13 November 1949, p. 546.
52. *Congressional Record.* 9 March 1950, p. 3157.
53. *Cannon's Procedures in the House of Representatives.* 81st Congress, p. 315.
54. *Tables and annotated Index of U.S. Public Documents.* Government Printing Office, Washington, D.C. 1902, p. 12.
55. "Laws and Rules for Publication of the Congressional Record." *Congressional Record.* 9 March 1950, A-1938.
56. *Congressional Record.* Daily edition. 81st Congress, second session. February 27–March 10, 1950. Bound volume number 96. Appendix, pp. A-1479–1947.
57. Richard M. Nixon. Deposition. 7 January 1963, p. 29.

3

VINDICATION AND
SOME FRINGE BENEFITS

The release of the Nixon-Morton-Steed report by Werdel in Washington and publication of extensive quotations from it in the national press brought enormous satisfaction to the Di Giorgios. On March 11 the *San Francisco Chronicle* printed the substance of the sweeping indictment and what the Corporation thought about it.

"In San Francisco officials of the corporation expressed satisfaction saying the report substantiated the position taken by the chairman of the board, Joseph DiGiorgio, in refusing to deal with the Union, and confirmed his statement that his employers were satisfied with wages and working conditions." Robert later recalled that "my uncle was very proud of that report and the clearing of the Corporation's name and justification of its position."

The event, in the eyes of other leading agribusinessmen, was one to be remembered. Recalling it two years later, W. B. Camp, outstanding Special Citizen of Kern County, said: "Almost single-handed and alone [Joseph DiGiorgio] defied the racketeers who sought to control American agriculture."[58]

To the DiGiorgios vindication was the keynote of Werdel's Extension of Remarks, and they appreciated, with a keen sense of public relations, the fringe benefits which accompanied it.

To begin with, it was no ordinary denunciation of their foe, the National Farm Labor Union. It was, by all appearances, no less than a *congressional* arraignment issued in the printed pages of the *Congressional Record*. No common jury of ordinary citizens had spoken, or a judge sitting on a superior court bench in any one of three thousand counties. It was the Federal power, in whose name

57

congressional committees wielded what Edmund Burke called "the thunder of the state." The Corporation could not desire more political advantage than this.

To make certain that this would not be overlooked, the Corporation noted with emphasis Werdel's prefatory remarks. Six times in his preface he had called it a report, a majority report of three of the five members of Subcommittee Number 1. No one could, certainly no one should, doubt the legitimacy and the finality of these credentials.

With them the Extension of Remarks was well on the way to winning a respected place in the national archives. Twice it appeared in the Index of the *Congressional Record* as a "report." According to Anne Morris Boyd, an expert on government documents, the proceedings and reports of Congress "are among the most important historical documents of the government."[59] Future scholars, coming upon this one and only text, would pay it the respect due an important government record. Vindication would become history.

As to the film itself the document left no doubts. *Poverty* had been tried and convicted. In the text of the putative report the motion picture was denounced as a concoction of deliberate falsehoods. In Werdel's preface there was the finding of law that the film was libelous. Notwithstanding the sworn testimony of Mitchell and others, *Poverty* was judged as purposely "designed to represent the living and working conditions at DiGiorgio Farms." To be sure, the Court of Appeals of New York State had declared that "the public has learned that accusation is not proof," but the case[60] was not cited by Werdel.

The document also contained a tactful invitation to the American labor movement to disavow an affiliated union whose members were capable of doing it so much harm. "The film," the Extension of Remarks said, "is a disservice to the legitimate labor movement . . . responsible labor leadership will not join with it . . . the cause of labor is not aided." Taking its cue from the Extension, the *San Francisco Chronicle* editorialized: "The fact remains that the tactics employed by the Union in this instance are tried and true Communist tactics," violating "the American doctrines of integrity, sincerity and fair play."[61] The document itself reinforced this charge. Even though Nixon and his investigator Stripling had found no Communist connections at Bakersfield, Nixon, Morton and Steed came to the conclusion that "The processes of the Congress of the United States have been perverted and misused by the National Farm Labor Union." In the climate of McCarthyism, perversion and subversion, misuse and abuse, were not far apart.

They were brought even closer by the publicity that followed the appearance of the document on March 10. Already the Hiss case had proved what McCarthy had so amply demonstrated—that without publicity an indictment by information through a congressional investigation was like warm beer drunk in a deserted bar, a sudless, unappreciated solitude. Werdel set the wheels of public relations moving from Washington.

The simple appearance of the Extension of Remarks in the Appendix assured an international circulation of some forty-five thousand copies. The official mailing list of the Government Printing Office included hundreds of public libraries, colleges, embassies, government bureaus and private subscribers throughout the world.

National correspondents in Washington do not usually breakfast over the Appendix, but on March 10 some did. On March 11 the *Bakersfield Californian,* no sympathizer of the strike, carried a story with extensive quotations and two glaring inaccuracies. It said that Werdel had on the previous day "read the majority report of the subcommittee on the floor of the House," and that Werdel himself had also signed the report. "The Union," the *Californian* went on to say, "received a stinging setback this week." The *Los Angeles Times* of the same date also quoted from the most excoriating passages. The *San Francisco Chronicle,* in the news story of the eleventh taken from the same wire press services, noted that "the report concentrated much of its fire on the film" and called it the product of "an extensive, first-hand investigation." The metropolitan dailies also reported an item that was to interest the DiGiorgios to an extraordinary degree. This was Bailey's comment, published on the day the report was released, that he would release a "minority report" in a few days.

This was in the heat of the news. In the cool follow-up, the agribusiness press reproduced long excerpts analyzed in approving editorials. The *Bulletin* of the Associated Farmers of March-April 1950 copied most of the text of the report with the headline "Farm

Labor Union Raised Money to Support Nonexistent Strike by Use
of Filmed Falsehoods."

By these accounts the Nixon-Morton-Steed text was a great
publicity success. Marion Plant, one of the 57 attorneys of Brobeck, Phleger and Harrison, commented in court on the notoriety
achieved by the report on its appearance. Robert DiGiorgio was
asked in one of the many lawsuits that hounded *Poverty*: "And
you sought that type of publicity . . . in order that persons would
have a view of the Corporation that you desired them to have?"
To which he answered: "Naturally."[62] The Institute of Propaganda
Analysis listed seven important devices in the art of molding public
opinion. Number four of these devices was "quoting a conspicuous
individual or group of individuals." Of the three to whom the report
was attributed at least one was already well known to the American
public.

An important side effect for which the Corporation could well
claim credit was the exoneration of corporate farming as an industry from the strictures of *Poverty*. As Mitchell and Hasiwar had
testified, and as the pictures and narration of the film itself clearly
showed, the industry's labor relations were the principal target of
the Union. Flannery opened with the words: "This is the San
Joaquin Valley . . . In these four counties the thirteen largest
owners possess 20 per cent of the land." Two-thirds of the motion
picture dealt with "corporation farmers" and the "agricultural
industry." This explained the indignation of the Special Citizens
of Kern County.

The report made it clear that the miserable dwellings of the farm
workers were not on DiGiorgio's Farms, but it did not locate those
hovels anywhere. For propaganda purposes they did not exist.
Mitchell's invitation to the subcommittee, to look at agribusiness
itself as the economic system within which the Corporation had its
being, was declined. The Special Citizens had reason to be grateful to Joseph DiGiorgio. Not inappropriately, they could para-
phrase Nixon's words about the Hiss case. He had succeeded in
preventing injustice being done to a truthful industry and was now
on the way to bringing an untruthful union to justice.[63]

These were indeed solid satisfactions for the Special Citizens.
For the Congressmen there were undoubtedly others. One of these
was the receipt by Congressman Steed of a crate of fresh DiGiorgio

asparagus on his return to Washington sometime after the hearings. The vegetable was at that time on the unfair list of central labor councils throughout the country. A careful and courtly man, Steed neither returned the gift nor did he accept it personally. Instead it was placed on the table in the reception room of his suite on Capitol Hill and his staff and visitors were invited to help themselves. The record does not show whether this was a special civility to Congressman Steed or whether his associates also were remembered in kind.

So far as Congressman Nixon was concerned it would not have mattered much. He was on the way out of the House and into the Senate. In a farewell eulogy, Congressman Ford said of his colleague: "We in the House will remember his great contributions."

The most valuable of these services, however, was not visible from the well of House where Representative Ford spoke. It was in fact a short legal document which had been quietly filed with the Superior Court in and for the County of Los Angeles six months before. This was the

Judgment for One Dollar / which ended DiGiorgio's suit against Flannery et al. While the stage was being set for Werdel's progress in Washington, the Corporation's complaints for libel moved slowly through the courts in California. The Paramount Television Productions suit was in abeyance. Attorney Robert Gilbert had been overruled on the issue of specific wording of the complaint against Flannery et al. Discovery proceedings by Brobeck's attorneys were sporadic, even leisurely. Flannery's deposition was scheduled for 15 March 1950. Mitchell's was taken in January. Galarza's had been postponed.

In March Brobeck won another victory. Gilbert's effort to plead language to the effect that the film "truly and faithfully portrays and depicts conditions as they exist in the San Joaquin Valley with which the film is concerned" were rebuffed by the court. "Said language," argued Attorney Harrison, "is sham . . . and irrelevant." He would and did have it that *Poverty* was about DiGiorgio Farms only. The specific language that established this vital reference, the court had already held, Harrison did not have to spell out.

The officers of the National Farm Labor Union were strongly in favor of an aggressive defense in the lawsuit. Werdel could be stripped of his immunity and forced to throw light on the origins of his Extension of Remarks. The Union's complaints could be documented by dozens of witnesses who had not been heard by the subcommittee. Alexander Schullman, the Union's volunteer attorney, was convinced the Union had a favorable legal position. Mitchell pointed out to the Secretary of the State Federation of Labor, C. J. Haggerty, that "it might be better to fight that libel suit than run the risk of similar actions on every hand."*

The Federation had supported the strike in its early stages. The first contribution by the Federation to Local 218 in the sum of one thousand dollars was made three days after the strike started. In the customary manner, all of the Federation's affiliates in the state were notified of the strike and urged to help. The Federation offered to pay the legal expenses of defending against an injunction with which Brobeck had threatened to prevent the showing of the film in Delano.

After 28 months, by mid-March of 1950, the strike was in serious difficulties. Its funds were exhausted. There was only token picketing. An injunction had been issued in favor of the Corporation for violation of the secondary boycott provisions of the National Labor Relations Act. The Corporation had dismissed all Union members and sympathizers. There was pending a $2 million lawsuit against the Hollywood Film Council and the important and influential Los Angeles Central Labor Council. The cost of legal defense, in the opinion of the Hollywood Film Council, would be "tremendous." An apparently legitimate congressional committee report had condemned the film as a scurrilous libel, and the indictment received nationwide attention.

In the light of these adversities Haggerty and other officers of the State Federation made the decision: the lawsuit and the strike

---

*Letter. H. L. Mitchell to Alexander Schullman. 3 May 1950. Also, "And it may well be a measure and device hereinafter employed to stop you at every turn since all that will be required will be a lawsuit for libel and some other lawsuit against you, and even though your economic action is justified, you will cease picketing and fighting economically." Letter from Attorney Alexander Schullman to H. L. Mitchell, Dated 21 April 1950.

must be settled. Mitchell's letter went unanswered and his prophetic warning passed unheeded.

If there had been prospects of a serious confrontation between the organized labor movement of California and agribusiness over the condition of farm workers, they had, by the early spring of 1950, disappeared. Mitchell and his fellowworkers sensed the dilemma. The strike had been called too soon or too late—too soon if an immature labor movement was not ready to face the issues of power revealed by the encounter; too late if the leadership of organized labor had already reduced those issues to the practical demands of ministerial unionism. It soon appeared that the strike had been called too late.

In either case Local 218 was breaking. Price's appeal of April 1949 for funds to pay attorneys and pickets was poorly received. Mitchell was working alone in Washington, with one secretary. By December there was not enough in the Union treasury to pay even for incidental legal services. Schullman was replaced by the attorneys who represented the other defendants in the lawsuit, Gilbert, Nissen and Irvin.

Early in February discussions among the principal defendants and the State Federation of Labor on the possible settlement of the suit were under way. The DiGiorgio attorneys were approached. They were instructed by Mr. Joseph "that they were not to consent to any settlement unless the defendants agreed to a judgment against them in the suit, thus confirming the libelous character of the film, or unless all other matters in issue were disposed of at the same time."[64] Brobeck demanded a judgment of one dollar against all the defendants; removal of the film from circulation; a stop to the picketing; and reimbursement to the Corporation for attorney's fees and costs. Attorney Harrison advised Gilbert of his understanding as of 3 April 1950: "We do understand that, though this is separate and apart from the libel action herein concerned, the NFLU and its Local 218 intend to discontinue the strike . . . picket lines and possible secondary boycott." Mitchell tried, without success, to obtain a guarantee that the Corporation would reinstate the striking Union members.

By the first week of May, when the Nixon-Morton-Steed report had made its impact, the pressure for a settlement from the State Federation on the Union was operating in full force. On May 5

Mitchell was notified by Gilbert that immediate withdrawal of the pickets was desired by both the State Federation and the Los Angeles Central Labor Council. Mitchell finally yielded. On 8 May 1950, he telegraphed instructions to Hasiwar to end the picketing. In further compliance with the agreement that had been reached between the attorneys for the parties, Mitchell sent a letter to Joseph DiGiorgio advising him of the action to terminate the strike. Meticulous to the end, Malcolm Dungan, one of the numerous Brobeck, Phleger and Harrison legal team, insisted that Hasiwar also sign the letter.[65] The Department of Employment of California took note officially that the strike had ended on May 8.

On May 23 the agreement was concluded between the NFLU, the Hollywood Film Council and Harry W. Flannery on the one hand and DiGiorgio Fruit Corporation on the other. It called for the destruction of all prints of the film, dismissal of the suit against all defendants without costs and a stipulation for judgment to be executed separately. A judgment assessing damages of one dollar against all defendants was entered. H. L. Mitchell signed on behalf of the NFLU; Robert DiGiorgio for the Corporation. The agreement further provided:

> 6. The Corporation will, before undertaking any legal proceedings with respect to any third party or parties arising out of or connected with the film, advise the unions in writing by notice to their counsel, Mssrs. Gilbert, Nissen and Irvin, . . . so that the unions may use their best influence to induce such third party or parties to refrain from exhibiting and to deliver up copies of said film, and the Unions shall be allowed a period of thirty (30) days from the date of receiving notification as above described to induce said third parties to take such action. . . . It is understood that this action on the part of the Unions is in the interest of good faith and in the event the unions fail to induce such third party or parties to refrain from exhibiting and deliver up said film, after using reasonable efforts in attempting to do so, the Unions are not to be deemed or held liable in any respect or regard.

Gilbert's legal interpretation of these terms was given to Mitchell in a letter dated 30 November 1954. He wrote: "As you recall, the sole parties to the settlement agreement are the Film Council,

Harry W. Flannery and your national Union. Such parties are expressly made immune from liability for acts of third parties, not authorized or ratified by them, under paragraphs 6 and 7 of the May 23, 1950, agreement."[66]

The suit against Paramount Television Productions, which DiGiorgio had been in no hurry to prosecute, was dismissed upon the signing of the agreement. The State Federation of Labor notified all its affiliates of the legal settlement, indicating that they should refrain from showing the film, destroy all prints and notify the Federation attorneys of such actions.[67] The Hollywood Film Council did likewise, adding a note that was both apologetic and hopeful: "The film was already old and dated and the same amount of money necessary to meet the tremendous expense involved in defending such action could be used to turn out a new and timely film of current interest and importance."[68] Such a film was never made.

These transactions, completed sixty days after the publication of Werdel's Extension of Remarks, were remarkable achievements for the Corporation. The strike was crushed; the picketing was at an end; the Union had confessed judgment for falsehoods and defamation; and *Poverty* was legally dead. Above all the State Federation of Labor had withdrawn its support of the most determined organizing effort among agricultural workers in two decades.

That DiGiorgio had been diligent behind the scenes these drastic events proved, but it was not clear why the Corporation should have been intent to bring legal, congressional and propaganda pressures to end a labor disturbance that, according to the March 9 document, had produced no grievances, no strike and no pickets. The explanation lay in the fact that there were indeed grievances, there was a strike and there was picketing. The Werdel Extension of Remarks itself admitted all this.

There were other pressing reasons why the Corporation wanted to get rid of the lone picket at its gates. Picketing kept the strike legally and technically in effect. DiGiorgio's products remained on labor's unfair lists. Consumer boycotting was going on in various parts of the nation, sporadically but irritatingly. Newspaper men and magazine writers continued to publicize Local 218. Mr. Joseph, who considered himself labor's best friend, was not improving his image before the pubic. A small company of veteran

strikers continued to talk loudly of union organization throughout Kern County. With a strike technically going on, the Corporation could not contract for Mexican *braceros* for employment
at Arvin. Nor would the Wetbacks, in the face of the vigilance of
the Union and the Border Patrol raids, be as likely to hire in at the
Farms. Importantly, this situation also prevented referrals by
the Farm Placement Service in Bakersfield to DiGiorgio without
notification of the existence of the strike.

To all these reasons there must be added one of another order.
In spite of the setbacks and the tactical defeats, Local 218 had
shown the staying power of an emerging type of sophisticated farm
laborer. Against great odds, when organized into a union, the
white, brown and black men of the NFLU had shown the capacity
to draw the world's leading food grower, processor, shipper and
auctioneer corporation into a prolonged and notorious confrontation. The fact that this could be done with a very small treasury
nourished their faith and strengthened their hope. It was to break
this hope, symbolized by the picket, that the Corporation committed its energies from 7 November 1949. So rich a catch as Brobeck, Phleger and Harrison were able to deliver to Mr. Joseph on
23 May 1950 had been made possible by

The Perfect Web. / Werdel's Extension of Remarks was, on
the first view, an artifice of sturdy stuff. It was legitimized by the
delegation of power set forth in Lesinski's letter of authorization,
quoted in full by Werdel. It spoke frequently and convincingly of
"evidence" of which it was the summation. Its authors were three
congressmen who constituted a bi-partisan majority of a House
subcommittee. There was no rebuttal to its sweeping charges anywhere in the *Congressional Record*. Its main thrust was against
what it called a false and libelous film which it said had been con-
ceived in deceit and perpetrated in fraud and whose contagion
defiled everything that the Union had said on its own behalf.

Werdel's prefatory remarks, coupled with his request for unanimous consent as taken down in the *Record* itself, gave the entire
text the character of a privileged statement—words spoken by
Members of the House in the course of proceedings. It appeared
in a government print that carried the Great Seal of the United
States, which gave it an even more impressive stature.

The angry tone of the report hardly invited a close and temperate inspection. It was also, on the surface, an official finding that the farming industry of the nation had been brought to near ruin by the caprices of a handful of selfish men. For that reason the report placed itself squarely on the side of tradition—the exclusion of farm workers from federal law for the protection of the rights of workingmen.

All this had the air of a hard, compact product of the legislative, constitutional process in the House of Representatives. There was a House resolution; there had been hearings; here was the report. These had been preceded by two years of appearances before subcommittees, debates on the floor of the House, lengthy insertions in the *Congressional Record* and numerous extensions of remarks in the Appendix.

Under such favorable signs the effectiveness of the document was not surprising. Its future usefulness was not, for the same reasons, to be underrated. It would turn out to be not a weapon but an arsenal in the hands of the Corporation.

It was so nearly perfect that its weakness passed unnoticed on first reading. Lesinski had instructed Bailey and his four colleagues to conduct "a thorough study and investigation" of the DiGiorgio labor-management controversy. Bailey did not send investigators to Kern County in advance of the hearing, nor did his staff research the assignment in Washington. Boyer, the majority clerk, arrived in Bakersfield a day ahead of the congressmen. There had been an investigator in the area, but he came, not from Subcommittee Number 1, but from Nixon's Un-American Activities Committee. There was no appropriation for this inquiry, no special counsel, no personnel technically expert in labor-employer conflicts. Nor were there advance interviews with witnesses, or requisitioning of files— there were none of the usual preparations for a thorough study and investigation of an important issue before Congress.

On the scene the subcommittee was no more diligent. None of the congressmen responded to the Union's offer of proof that it represented a majority of DiGiorgio employees on 1 October 1947. They did not question Sheriff Loustalot on his role as counselor, advisor and interpreter to the *braceros* he helped induce back to work. Some of the DiGiorgio housing had been condemned by state inspectors but the subcommittee did not check these reports on the spot; whether DiGiorgio employees lived in shacks such as those shown in *Poverty* could have been determined while the subcommittee was on a field tour with Robert DiGiorgio. The testimony received at the ranch from employees, which was later to be cited in the Nixon-Morton-Steed report, was not taken down by the official reported, as all other testimony was.

None of this laxity could be laid to a lack of experience in the conduct of thorough studies and investigations by House committees. Steed, to be sure, was a freshman in the House, but Bailey was a veteran. Nixon was already expert in these matters. "We succeeded in the Hiss case," he wrote later, "for three basic reasons. First, we were on the right side. Second, we prepared our case thoroughly. Third, we followed methods with which few objective critics would find serious fault." On the second count, Subcommittee Number 1 fell short of the high standards of the Hiss case. On the third, the record was to remain inconclusive for many years. And on the first, Nixon's rocketing career showed that he was still on the right side.

It was not the Union but the friends of DiGiorgio who were most disappointed with the performance of the Subcommittee. The *Bakersfield Californian* published by Walter Kane, a member of the Special Citizens Committee, chided the subcommittee for its "swift passage" and observed that "this junket" deserved "more time and study than the subcommittee is willing to devote to it."[69] Bailey had cut the hearings short by one day in order to get on with his main assignment, the investigation of education in Federally impacted areas.

The Corporation's private complaints, if it had any, were probably not as acerbic. It had had an opportunity to brief Nixon in advance on what it objected to in *Poverty,* and principals and attorneys for the Corporation had met previously with Congressman Werdel and with Camp, a member of the Special Citizens Committee.

As to Bailey, he said and did little that would clarify his conduct of the hearings. It was, after all, Congressman Elliott's investigation in the sense that it was his candid demand more than a year and a half past that led Lesinski to act. Further, Bailey's Subcommittee Number 1 was primarily responsible for an educational report, not for one on labor-management relations. He was under no persuasion from the A.F. of L. lobbyists in Washington, and he may have sensed, if he did not learn, that the State Federation was ready to negotiate a settlement. Bailey, an old labor hand, could recognize a dying strike. Under these circumstances even a hurried stopover in Bakersfield could be a more than disproportionate outlay of congressional time, money and energy. This would suggest, if it did not explain, why Bailey on his return to Washington put the DiGiorgio assignment so low on his agenda, from which Werdel took it to add to the Appendix.

In sum, the perfection of the web was due not so much to its craftsmanship as to its utility. It got results that satisfied even the exacting and impatient Joseph DiGiorgio.

The web, taken figuratively, was a mesh of decisions, legal actions, deployments, understandings and moves that were calculated to prevent unionization of the Corporation's field and shed workers. Only a little of this mesh would ever show in the historical record.

By the necessities of the case, nevertheless, this little was embodied in a writing which became a print of a report made public for the first time in the Appendix of the *Congressional Record.* The complicated net of which it was a tiny part had some of the qualities that John Marshall had attributed to corporations—artificiality, invisibility, intangibility and perhaps even immortality.

NOTES

58. *Proceedings.* Commonwealth Club, San Francisco, California, 4 April 1952.
59. Boyd. *U.S. Government Publications,* p. 79.
60. *Campbell v. New York Evening Post.* 157 NE 155.
61. *San Francisco Chronicle,* 15 March 1950.
62. Robert DiGiorgio. Deposition, 16 December 1964, p. 13.
63. Richard M. Nixon, *Six Crises,* p. 39.
64. DiGiorgio Fruit Corporation. *Stockholder's Report,* 1950, p. 1.
65. Letter Gregory Harrison to Louis A. Nissen, 3 April 1950.
66. Letter. Robert W. Gilbert to H. L. Mitchell, 30 November 1954.
67. California State Federation of Labor. *Bulletin,* 14 June 1950.
68. Hollywood Film Council. Circular letter, 12 June 1950.
69. *Bakersfield Californian,* 12 November 1949.

PART TWO

4

TEN YEARS:
STRATEGY OF RESISTANCE

The Lessons of the Strike. / Mitchell's telegram of 8 May 1950 ordering the end of the strike marked the beginning of the end of Local 218. Its members began to disperse in the spring of 1948 when it became obvious that the strike would be a long one. Many found farm jobs in Kern County. Many more drifted northward into the Central Valley keeping an eye on work opportunities in the growing industries of the coastal cities. By the time of the Bakersfield hearings in November 1949 the Local was a rearguard of the more or less mobile strikers who refused to give up until Mitchell made the end of their hopes official. Unlike the termination of other unsuccessful strikes, the one at DiGiorgio Farms did not result in a grudging return to work under the old conditions. It meant the scattering of nearly a thousand men and women who had challenged the Corporation, and the destruction of the base that the Union needed in California.

In the tradition of California's farm labor struggles, this should have signalled the end of agricultural union activity for many years. DiGiorgio's victory normally would have begun another long lull in the organized protests against the power of corporation farming. That it did not was the result of the assessment by the Union of the DiGiorgio experience. In the short view, the loss of the strike was a disaster that could well have banished the National Farm Labor Union from California. In the long view, it was merely a bitter episode in a historic process that had begun long before the NFLU came on the scene, and that would continue after its demise in 1960.

In this assessment the major assets and liabilities are to be noted.

To begin with Local 218 had shown the staying power of farm
laborers who had settled out of the migrant stream and into relatively stable community life. They had joined, supported and led a
union campaign that lasted more than three years. Individual
workers came and went, but the Union survived the seasonal
depressions when packing sheds were closed, harvesting was over,
pruning and cultivation had not begun and the slump of wintry
weeks had taken possession of the land.

This continuity was being achieved with an ethnic diversity of
men and women to whom integrated unionism was a new and at
first dubious experience. The DiGiorgio work force, most of whom
signed union cards, was composed of Filipinos, Mexicans and
southern whites. From Bakersfield and surrounding communities
the Union drew a black membership of potato and cotton harvesters. In the fields the crews were organized by labor contractors
along racial lines; and where, as in the cotton fields, the work force
formed and dissolved haphazardly every twenty-four hours, the
mingling of the races did not reduce the distance between them
that contractors and employers encouraged. In the Union meetings
this distance was shortened by a deliberate effort to overcome the
barriers of prejudice and language. The high morale of Local 218
showed in every phase of the strike.

A promising sense of community was beginning to overcome
these barriers. Local 218 became the center of political organization in rural Kern County. It registered citizens of all colors and
began to teach them how to continue in the battles of the polls the
battles of the picket lines. At the political meetings candidates in
Arvin and Lamont saw faces and heard questions that came out
of the long-dormant precincts of the countryside, now filling with
new voters. The Union's political handbills provided information
heretofore denied and encouraged a new sense of identity and of
importance in community affairs.

A process of discovery of fresh leadership among the rank and
file was taking place. During the strike unfamiliar roles were
pressed upon men and women who accepted them with a sham-
bling reluctance and a shy speech to the effect that "I hadn't
oughta do it fer I ain't got no high edgication." The Union forum
was soon plentifully supplied with able conversationalists if not

orators. When there was a momentary loss of speech or theme, the "arragators" who doubled as lay preachers would rise and give the union doctrine the flavor of the old-time religion.

At this core of organization, with Galarza in charge as director of education and research, the Union maintained a program of information, discussion, analysis and techniques of group action suitable to the requirements of the strike. There was a strong mental appetite among many of the members to understand the social forces that for all their concealment by the mists of "high edgication" were bearing down on Local 218. Into these dim, outer margins the Union laid a course of guidance and instruction. The curriculum was not the facts of work and life, which the workers knew better than the Union officials. It was the meanings of these facts when related to one another in patterns that had not been noticed before. A talk on inflation was judged a success if someone said: "I get her. You could win the strike, but the groceries will take more from you than you'll ever get from Die-George."

Taught to appreciate the meaning of routine details in the daily work experience, the members of the Union became the eyes and ears of a research operation such as agribusiness had never been exposed to. However remote the places where agribusiness planned its strategies to manipulate the labor market, in the end these strategies took concrete shape in Wetback pools, *bracero* crews and the hundred ways in which the domestic workers were harassed and displaced. Union intelligence was simple. It consisted of listening to the members, checking their reports, assembling these in outlines for discussion by study groups, and equipping the members to look more closely and carefully and to report again and again. These were the ultimate sources of the press releases and reports that the Union issued in its nationwide propaganda which provided a protective shield for Local 218.

So far as the labor movement was concerned Local 218 was the connection with local central labor councils and organized workers in other trades and crafts. Over this circuit the DiGiorgio strikers travelled in delegations, explaining the strike, soliciting support, observing the institutional mechanics of American trade-unionism and staking out contacts for future organization throughout the state. Whether the raw energies of the new union were

being funneled slowly and imperceptibly into the accepted molds
of business unionism, or merely taking temporary shelter in them,
remained a disturbing question.

The settlement of the lawsuit, the termination of the strike and
the legal execution of *Poverty in the Valley of Plenty* were more
disconcerting to the Union than the setbacks it had suffered during
the strike. To the members the confrontation with DiGiorgio and
corporation farming was a progressive one. The longer the Union
survived the more agribusiness had to display, one by one, the
weapons of its power. The taint of communism and the raids of
vigilantes were, by 1949, discredited as forms of union-smashing.
Injunctions, evictions and police surveillance were still respectable
but unwieldy and undecisive. It was now the era of public relations, Wetbacks, *braceros,* lawsuits, citizens committees, legislative
investigations and political defamation. As devices of class interest
they were, in the end, merely devices. Beyond them were widen-
ing social fissures—the increasing numbers of a rural proletariat,
the withering of the small farm economy, the addition of the Mexican poor to the market where the American poor sold their labor,
the bitter controversies over the control of water.

This was the route that agribusiness, led militantly by Joseph
DiGiorgio, was determined to defend. It was the course from
which the California State Federation officials turned aside on 23
May 1950 with the settlement of *DiGiorgio v. Flannery, et al.*
Local 218 and the NFLU in some fashion had begun, quite haphazardly but persistently, to give to farm labor strikes in California
a context they had not previously had. This context, as it turned
out, was beyond the limits of prudence from the point of view of
the State Federation. It broke off its support of the strike, declined
to test its adversary to the limits of his powers and negotiated the
settlement that crowned the Nixon-Morton-Steed report.

The depression in which these decisions left the NFLU was
hardly an advantageous point from which to view the future. The
braceros were moving in ever-increasing numbers into the major
farm production centers; they would reach a peak of 265,000 in
September 1959 in California alone. Thirty-six out of the fifty-
eight counties in the state would give them preference over domestic workers.[70] The underground of smugglers and contractors
maintained a ready reserve of Wetbacks. Menial field jobs were

being reduced as fast as the universities and laboratories researched
and perfected new varieties of vegetables and new machines for
harvesting them. Freeways were beginning to slice through the
farm communities where labor had pooled and put down roots.
The dispersion was beginning to show a marked trend of migration to the coastal cities, mainly to Los Angeles and the San Francisco Bay area. The consumer boycotts of DiGiorgio products had
been scattered throughout the nation and had proved as ineffectual as the unfair lists of the central labor councils. Most importantly the Union possessed no leverage of its own in Washington
near the seats of executive and congressional power.

Although the losses were severe the gains had not been insig-
nificant. Men and women trained during the strike found jobs and
homes in practically every major farm area of the state. They were
defeated but not discouraged. Wherever they moved they made
new connections for union work. They had begun to see their
familiar problems in new dimensions and they opened new sources
of information to the Union. By avoiding major strikes the Union
would not again be caught in a crisis that its precarious connections
with the State Federation could not help it to survive.

Moreover, it was plain that no Local of the NFLU could bear
the costs of a prolonged effort to organize one of the largest
corporation farms. As yet, organized labor was not disposed to
budget for such costs, to approve aggressive actions and to dig in
for decisive struggles. At any rate, the NFLU was not judged the
right instrument for such important work.

It was also clear that unless the *bracero* and Wetback tide
was turned back domestic farm worker's efforts to organize were
doomed in advance. To reveal the extent and depth of this tide,
to chart its movements, and to document the drastic erosion that
it left in its wake on wage standards and job opportunities for
resident farm workers; this was the task the Union undertook in
the aftermath of its defeat in Kern County.

The strategy of resistance was to engage the corporation farms
where the pressures of displacement, harassment, wages, discrimination and preferential hiring of *braceros* were greatest. In each of
these actions the devices of the industry with respect to the control
of the alien labor supply would be forced to reveal themselves.
Relayed into the information service of the NFLU in Washington

the issue of *bracero* contracting could be kept fresh before the public and Congress. The aim was twofold: the repeal of Public Law 78, and the detailed disclosure of the Wetback traffic. The immediate goals were to be job protection, resistance to wage cuts and the disciplining of farm labor contractors who, as the middlemen of corporation farming, ran its more distasteful errands.

The defects of this strategy were clear. The time schedule of ten years to bring about the repeal of an obnoxious law had a touch of utopianism. The scene of action was a farm belt six hundred miles long and two hundred miles wide. Harvest strikes could stop a wage cut or hold the alien labor invasion at bay, but they would not produce contracts or union recognition. Veteran trade-unionists would observe the jigsaw movements of the Union and conclude sadly that there was a pointless pathos to the behavior of their brothers in the fields.

The point of the campaign, however obscure even to the most sympathetic, was there. It became sharper through the decade until in 1964 it broke Public Law 78 and contained, although it did not dry up, the Wetback flow.

To these ends the Union maintained its system of volunteer organizers giving them continuously what could be called practical field training. The dispersion of the DiGiorgio strikers was turned to achieve ends that with plenty of time could be attained. In pursuing those ends the survival of the National Farm Labor Union did not have a very high probability. The tactics of resistance were improvised over a decade in a series of

Skirmishes with Agribusiness. / The first of these took place in the Imperial Valley where, in July 1952, the Union organized a strike of melon pickers. The central issue was the wholesale displacement of domestic workers by *braceros* and Wetbacks. The Imperial Valley Farmers Association supplied the *braceros* and winked at the illegals. Its principal customers were some of the most powerful corporation operations in agriculture, American Fruit Growers, Arena Imperial Company and The Maggio Company, carrot king of the industry.

This action was erroneously publicized as the "Wetback strike of the Imperial Valley." The Union pulled back, after three weeks, when by concerted action between Mexico City and Washington the valley was flooded by five thousand *braceros* who were rushed in to meet the "labor shortage" declared officially by the State Farm Placement Service.

While the Imperial strike was on, the Union had occasion to renew its contacts with the DiGiorgio Fruit Corporation. Borrego Valley, a desert development of the company, drew its manpower from the Imperial Valley Farmers Association. Because of its isolation it had not been noticed for its employment of alien labor and the low-level wage system which such labor made possible.

Concurrently with its preparation for the Imperial Valley strike, the Union took part in the work stoppage of six hundred Filipino grape pruners centering in Delano. Some *bracero* crews had been moved into the area, and more were scheduled to arrive. A wage cut from $1.00 an hour to 90 cents was announced by the growers. After a short but tense encounter a series of informal accommodations restored the wage level without loss of dignity by the employers.

Although not directly confronted by the Filipinos, the DiGiorgio Fruit Corporation must have watched the short strike with some interest. Its Sierra Vista ranch was in the strike area, scarcely an hour's drive from DiGiorgio Farms.

In the mid-summer of 1952 the Union followed the Imperial melon pickers to the Los Baños area, where cantaloupes and watermelons were grown in abundance. Through the packing sheds of Los Baños the golden avalanche of fruit moved by rail and by truck to the great metropolitan markets. Preferential hiring of *braceros* and Wetbacks was undermining the crew system of the domestic workers and the established wage schedules. In a quick move planned under a bridge and relayed by volunteers to half a dozen camps, picking was stopped for two days. The Los Baños police and the highway patrolmen were at a loss to locate the nerve center of the stoppage. When they did the packers and growers were ready to negotiate.

Between 1952 and 1955 the drift of farm workers dislodged by *braceros* from the southern counties increased. Families long settled in Imperial, Riverside and other border areas stopped temporarily in the southern pocket of the San Joaquin Valley, moving northward to the rim of the Sacramento basin. The Union followed them in their retreat, the issue often being not jobs and wages but housing. In the town of Patterson shelter had to be found for Mexican families who were removed from a labor camp to make way for *braceros*. In the Salinas Valley small Locals were established to teach local farm workers simple techniques of resistance to the adverse effects of Public Law 78. In Sacramento and Stockton the migrant pools of transients called "skid rows" were watched by Union volunteers. Crews of domestic workers who were denied work in the fields by employers already plentifully supplied with *braceros* were led to local farm placement offices to press grievances and to picket.

In the spring and summer of 1955 Union workers turned their attention to DiGiorgio operations at opposite ends of the state. In Borrego Valley, they found alien workers occupied in harvest tasks for which they had not been certified, including the operation of equipment. Six hundred miles to the north, they collected check stubs and statements of earnings that showed noncompliance with contract terms at DiGiorgio's famous Dantoni and New England orchards.

These orchards were located in the Peach Bowl of California, where the apron of the Sierras begins to level off into flood plains of legendary fertility. In and around Yuba City the farm labor market was firmly in the control of the Northern California Growers Association, which operated a bank of several thousand alien contract workers. DiGiorgio's vice-president was a member of the board of directors of the Association. The Corporation drew manpower from the bank for its peach and pear operations.

By this time the Union's paid staff in California had been reduced to one man, Galarza. Under his direction the Union's volunteers turned their attention to the fruit orchards of Yuba. Their field checks, reported by Galarza to the press during the summer of 1957, documented severe harassment of domestic workers. They found the usual package of malpractices in the administration of the *bracero* system. In orchards throughout the area including DiGiorgio's, domestic workers were turned away because Mexican nationals had already been contracted. The Association operated a side business of cashing worker's pay checks for a commission. This "Casa de Cambio" functioned inside a stockade known by the Mexicans as *El Corralon,* a derivative of *corral,* where cattle and other stock are secured. The contract violations were laid before the U. S. Department of Labor, to the consternation of Rhodes, the Association manager. The Union also brought the matter of *El Corralon* to the attention of the Mexican ambassador in Washington. The money exchange business was discontinued, the open privies were screened and shaded benches were installed in the corral.

No major grower's association escaped the attention of the Union's volunteers in the eight years following the end of the DiGiorgio strike; and none failed to contribute to the growing weight of evidence against Public Law 78. By the end of 1957 the large growers were casting about for Hawaiian and Japanese substitutes for the Mexicans. The Associated Farmers gave this proposal their enthusiastic support.[71] Sanborn, a DiGiorgio vice-president, was appointed member of a committee of farm employers to promote it, and again DiGiorgio was met by Galarza's complaints of unproved labor shortages, biased wage determinations and other technical camouflage issued by government agencies. Enough opposition was thus organized to cool the interest of the Federal agencies in Asian labor and by the end of 1959 Sanborn and the Associated Farmers abandoned their efforts in that direction.[72]

In fact it was becoming clear that the continuing reports of the Union of the foreign labor program were more than isolated instances of oversight or negligence. The accounts, widely distributed by Mitchell out of Washington, were a reliable diagnosis of evils present throughout the system. Most of these were operational devices, such as the so-called determination of the prevailing wage, approved by law and applied by normally honest bureaucrats possessed of meager economic insights. In 1958 the Department of Labor began to acknowledge, in the face of accumulating proof, that the system was tainted with graft.* It was becoming more difficult for champions of Public Law 78 to keep the good image of the system intact.

---

*"An extremely serious situation has arisen causing deep concern to both the United States and Mexico . . . in a number of instances employers have been paying amounts to various persons for facilitating and furnishing of *specials* (*braceros*). Both governments will take immediate corrective measures to stamp out the traffic." Circular letter. Bureau of Employment Security, U.S. Department of Labor. Dated 17 January 1958.

It was also becoming more uncomfortable for government enforcers to overlook the contract violations which the Union continued to turn up. One of these incidents set a drastic, if belated, precedent. The D'Arrigo Company was certified to employ 137 *braceros* in the fields of Santa Clara County. One of these aliens was set to painting a house in violation of the contract. A formal complaint by the Union led to an investigation and the withdrawal of the certification. A joint determination of May 1959 by the Department of Labor and the Mexican Consul found that the employer and the Progressive Growers Association "are engaged in a course of conduct of knowingly and willfully violating" provisions of the migrant labor agreement between Mexico and the United States.

The keystone to the *bracero* system was the Farm Placement Service of California, which had the power to declare local labor shortages and determine the prevailing wage to be offered to contracted *braceros*. The chief of the Service was Edward F. Hayes, who was also counselor to corporation farmers and advisor to the State Board of Agriculture, the official beachhead of agribusiness in the state government. Hayes, in professional matters, was a man who loved with strength and hated with determination. His sympathy for the corporation farmers was unconcealed; his opposition to agricultural unionism was personal and bitter. His management of the agency which opened the gates to hundreds of thousands of *braceros* did not survive the Union campaign. In August 1959, Hayes's superior, John E. Carr, publicly acknowledged that "mismanagement of the farm labor program does exist."[73] Carr promised: ". . . those who richly deserve it are going to get it." For Hayes "it" meant removal from his post. He resigned to become the manager of the Imperial Valley Farmers Association, one of the labor agents for the DiGiorgio Fruit Corporation.

Just as the DiGiorgio strike uncovered the interlockings of the corporation with agribusiness, so the Union's campaign against the alien contract labor system unfolded the wider influence of the industry on public policy, and its connections with government agencies and Mexican-United States diplomacy. These connections were forced into the open by the resistance of the Union. And even though at the end they were still but dimly visible the outlines could be discerned, and they were the profile of

California's Rural Power Structure. / Social power systems put together by men tend to look from the outside more enduring, formidable and seamless than they are in fact. Were this not so the history of mankind would have been even more tragic. Power, in order to lengthen the span of its abuses, must present an awesome front. The facade must give the impression that behind it something exists that is impermeable, cohesive, overmastering, some mystic joining of dominant wills able to polarize, paralyze and pulverize.

The ideal form of power is a pyramid, for then it has no rear open to observation or attack. The peak of the pyramid is a single bartizan from which the whole of it can be watched and guarded. If this watchtower can be crowned with a temple or a sacrificial stone, power can also become holy. It can then lay claims as the creator and custodian of moral values.* Its secrets cannot be reported, even by systems analysts. Indeed, the object of its public relations is to make the world believe that it has no secrets. No particular power system will concede to Justice John Marshall that "power wherever reposed is abused." An existing system of power, by its own pleading, is always an exception to that rule.

In sum, men can suffer if they underestimate or overestimate the powers that rule over them. Either mistake will impair enlightenment and understanding, the only powers that can dissolve the myths on which power rests.

This analysis is appropriate to the ill-matched contest between California's agribusiness and the National Farm Labor Union between 1950 and 1960. Outwardly corporation farming appeared so impressive that even the California State Federation of Labor declined a match with it of more than one round.

This was, as the National Farm Labor Union demonstrated, an overestimate. Agribusiness in the late 1950s was a loose alliance of corporations, growers, shippers, processors and distributors with common interests in particular crops, in the control of the field

---

*"Each age is characterized by its dominant social institution. There have been ages in which the church was dominant; ages in which the military was dominant; ages in which political entities (as in the days of kings) were dominant. The institution that sets the style and pace of the 20th Century is the Corporation." *Kaiser Aluminum News,* Vol. 25, number 2, 1967, p. 3.

labor market and in state and federal legislative advocacy. Around
them were the modest operations of thousands of small growers,
who leaned heavily upon the influence and the financial solidity
of the larger companies for protection and support. The rural
political and social structure was not unlike that of the English
countryside in the eighteenth century. There were the agricultural
landlords, the larger corporate farmers, the small family farmers,
the local congressman, the County Supervisor, the sheriff, the
manager of the farm labor association, the supervisors of the Farm
Placement Office, the president of the county unit of the Associated
Farmers. Somewhat on the edge of local affairs yet a part of the
élite were the directors of the corporation branches of financial,
utility and service corporations—the Pacific Gas and Electric Company, the Bank of America, the Southern Pacific Railway.

The three-billion-dollar industry polarized these diverse elements
into working arrangements to promote their common interests, but
these arrangements did not produce a monolithic control of its
members from within. The peers who made the decisions were independent, successful and influential, and of them Joseph DiGiorgio
was the prototype. Within the political aristocracy of agribusiness
there was the democracy that rests on economic independence.
Its effectiveness came from an excellent system of internal communications, adequate staff, a variety of agencies to divide the
labors of propaganda and lobbying, many retainers and managers
in the fields, and the most expensive if not the best of legal advisors.

This was the structure that gave itself a synthetic name, agribusiness. The name was attended by the necessary public relations
myths: the grass-roots character of the business; the perennial
shortage of domestic workers; the competitiveness of the labor
market; the dire need for alien labor; the savings to the consumer
secured by the use of such labor; and the harsh vigilance of government enforcement agents in the observance of laws, agreements
and contracts.

Hagiolatry was avoided by the peers themselves. This was left
to the house organs of the industry, like the *California Farmer,* in
which it was once written about the farmer: "He is in partnership
with God and Mother Nature . . . He personifies free enterprise."
No names were mentioned, but since the DiGiorgio Corporation
was advertising itself as The Jolly Farmer, complete with straw hat

and overalls, it did not shun, though it did not claim, a share in this partnership. Vice-president Sanborn avowed on behalf of the Corporation its loyalty to the principles and positions of contemporaries like the California Grape and Tree Fruit League "because we feel our interests are identical."[74]

Joseph DiGiorgio was not only a subscriber to but a financial sponsor of these principles. In return for his support of the Associated Farmers, the organization defended him up and down the state. The President of the Farmers visited DiGiorgio Farms during the strike, later issuing charges of Communist infiltration of the Union. Between agricultural strikes, the Farmers maintained a quiet vigilance of the labor scene. When the workers struck, the Farmers would mobilize their informers, their publicity and their official connections on behalf of the beleaguered associate.

The main gears of the system were the local farm labor associations. DiGiorgio belonged to at least two. Topping them in another loose structure was the California Farm Labor Association on which Sanborn represented DiGiorgio. In Sacramento the rural coalition was firmly in control, behind the scenes, of the Farm Placement Service. With the Department of Labor it had efficient means for both immediate and remote influence, if not control. Sanborn sat as a member of a private cabinet which advised the Bureau of Employment Security in San Francisco. The Bureau was a direct line to the Department of Labor in Washington, which accommodated the growers by creating the private cabinet and by avoiding rulings on Public Law 78 not previously discussed with its members.

The whole of this informal but highly efficient arrangement was reinforced by the legislative contacts of agribusiness in Sacramento and Washington. In Sacramento these contacts propelled the Tenney Committee to investigate the Union. They produced friendly testimony from Governor Earl Warren. In Washington they aroused the interest of Congressman Nixon and obtained the services of Mr. Stripling of the House Un-American Activities Committee. They secured through Congressman Elliott a demand for the investigation of the strike. They influenced the Nixon-Morton-Steed hearings and conclusions.

These matters the Union volunteers learned and pondered during the ten years of the resistance. It was a process, however, that

utterly exhausted its men and its skimpy treasury, the epilogue to
the fulfillment of a mission. It was also the prologue to the

Death of a Union. / In the course of the long and crippling
struggle the Union was not only discovering the role of agribusiness
in a broader scheme of things; it was also appraising, over the long
term, the place of agricultural workers in the world of organized
labor. The signs were not encouraging.

To begin with, the poverty of field laborers placed a low ceiling
on the dues structure of the Union. The dues were at most two
dollars a month, and they were lowered during the three or four
winter months when work slackened or stopped completely. With
a small membership it was evident that the Union would have to
rely on subsidies for a long time to come. It was engaged in an
elephant hunt armed with a pop gun, and when it failed year after
year, its credit in the world of organized labor declined. Funding
sources outside of labor were meager. Mitchell and Galarza, in
their unending rounds of conventions and councils, came to be
regarded as the poor relations of labor.

Those in the labor movement who gave the matter close attention, and they were not many, came to a candid understanding of
why this was so. Corporation farming was moving steadily toward
mechanized operations. The hoe was being replaced by complicated
devices of rods, gears and blades that thinned and trimmed and
weeded. Water was being moved more economically through aluminum pipes, replacing the irrigator and his shovel. Fruits and vegetables were being packed in ungainly rigs that moved on their own
power across the fields, small packing sheds on wheels that, like
the cotton picker, were to take the jobs of thousands of workers.

Not only was technology decimating the field labor force, it was
also posing some important issues of union politics and jurisdiction.
The machines which took over in the fields moved on wheels, the
traditional symbol of jurisdiction of the International Brotherhood
of Teamsters. Also, the United Packinghouse Workers of America
viewed with alarm the shift of packing operations from the sta-
tionary buildings in town to the movable rigs. Mechanization meant
the elimination of the low-level ill-paid tasks, and the formation of
a considerably smaller but more highly skilled labor force. It was
the technological process, which was in the hands of management,

that was weeding and pruning out the problems of organization and union financing, making agricultural labor increasingly suitable to the trim and cut of established union management. The National Farm Labor Union had few if any credentials for the new era that was dawning over the fog-drenched fields of Salinas and the tamed deserts of the Central Valley. It could survive only as an élite remnant of the few who were chosen for work, not as the pleader for the many who were rejected.

There was still a place for the Union as a pleader, founded on the intense emotional sympathy that it had aroused on behalf of the rural underdogs among America's better offs. The nation was told of the brutality and the misery of the deep South, the deprivation amidst the affluence of the far West, the poverty in the valleys of plenty. Organized labor, too, trembled with indignation in unison with millions of citizens. The plucking of this woeful string in the conscience of the republic was not, however, something that necessarily had to be done by the National Farm Labor Union. It could as well become a permanent sentimental crusade of labor's leadership. When this was recognized, the end of the NFLU was in sight.

It was hastened by the conclusions that the Union drew, and expressed publicly, from its experience between 1950 and 1960. It called for the dismantling of the Farm Placement Service and the formation in its place of locally based, co-operative labor pools. It proposed drastic reforms in the administration of the immigration law and the operations of the Border Patrol. It was, of course, insisting on a wage structure comparable to that of other industries. The appropriation of the water resources of the state by corporation farming was stressed as a major menace not only to rural but also to urban California. Far in the background, the Union pointed out, was the economic policy of the United States with respect to Mexico, which took no notice of the trends that policy abetted and which were slowly preparing a population and economic revolution along the border.

There was no room for these considerations in the official strategy of labor at the time, and very little more in its ideology. To insist on them threatened the existing relationships between DiGiorgio Fruit Corporation and agribusiness and the numerous unions with which they had established acceptable terms of collective bargaining. Furthermore, it was within these relationships that the legislative priorities of both labor and agribusiness had to be determined from time to time. From this point of view the agenda which the NFLU was proposing was clearly irrelevant.

Probably very little of this was present in the thinking of the highest levels of organized labor. It was rather a drift of slow appraisals and of intermittent decisions over many years, which concluded in February 1959 with the decision of the AFL-CIO to create the Agricultural Workers Organizing Committee. This decision was put into operation in April, when the AWOC opened organizing headquarters in Stockton. Its director, Norman Smith, was a former organizer of the United Automobile Workers. The AWOC became a fully chartered affiliate of the AFL-CIO in June 1960. It promptly opened offices in a number of Central Valley communities through the heart of DiGiorgio country. By the spring of 1960 the NFLU had been thoroughly displaced by the AWOC, and that following summer its charter was surrendered to the Amalgamated Meat Cutters and Butcher Workmen of America.

Agribusiness watched these developments with much interest and some puzzlement. From them an organizing campaign emerged and rapidly gained momentum. Few could know, in its first stages, that like Local 218 and the NFLU, it would become snagged in

The Durable Web. / In compliance with the agreement of 23 May 1950, neither the NFLU nor any of the other parties to the agreement showed *Poverty in the Valley of Plenty* again. Mitchell had bought two prints and these were destroyed. All purchasers received notice both from the Hollywood Film Council and the California State Federation of Labor to do likewise. So far as the Union was concerned *Poverty* was resting in peace and would continue to do so at least as long as the writ of the Superior Court of the State was in effect.

The Corporation, however, did not bury with the film its lively possibilities for its continuing pursuit of farm labor organizers. The report was again brought to the attention of the House in 1957, when another subcommittee of the House Committee on Education and Labor held hearings in Fresno, California, on labor-management issues. Before this subcommittee, and on behalf of the Corporation, appeared Vice-president Sanborn. Arguing for the continuation of exemption of farm labor from the Taft-Hartley Act, Sanborn submitted to subcommittee chairman James Roosevelt a copy of the Werdel reprint. He testified, "I have here a copy of the *Congressional Record* setting forth the report of that House committee on Education and Labor, Subcommittee Number 1." The report, he explained, "was introduced in the House of Representatives, Thursday March 9, 1950."[75] The reprint not only refreshed the memory of Congressman Roosevelt and his colleagues as to the thoroughly established policy of Congress of exempting farm labor; it also reminded them of the deprecation of the Union in Werdel's prefatory remarks and in the accompanying report.

At about the same time, or somewhat before Sanborn's appearance in Fresno, the reprint had been put to effective use in rebutting evidence that the Union had gathered on the exploitation of *braceros* hired by the farm labor associations. This evidence was published in a booklet entitled *Strangers in Our Fields*.

Strangers raised a storm of indignant protest among Special Citizens and agribusinessmen throughout the state. As advisors to the Department of Labor, they assigned staff members of the Department and of the Farm Placement Service to the task of compiling a rebuttal.[76] The preparation of this document was entrusted to the chief of farm placement, Edward F. Hayes. His research turned up several copies of the reprint, which were provided by Sanborn from the Corporation's files. To the final product, a lengthy memorandum detailing the exaggerations and misrepresentations of *Strangers,* Hayes attached a copy of the reprint. "The investigating congressmen," he commented, "denounced the Union for its misrepresentations. The enclosed copy of the *Congressional Record* will give you some insight to the person we are dealing with. He is one of the persons referred to in the first column on page 1." Hayes was referring specifically to Ernesto Galarza, who was the educational director of the Union, and generally to those who according to Werdel had produced *Poverty* "for thirty pieces of silver, more or less," and who "then used the fabrication to collect hundreds of thousands of dollars from workingmen throughout the country to finance a purported strike that did not exist."

Hayes's memorandum was never published. It was used as the basis of a demand addressed to the Secretary of Labor that

Strangers be suppressed. It was, in truth, an inglorious and obscure incident in the long duel between the Corporation and the Union. Sanborn acknowledged that he had given Hayes copies of the reprint, but he denied any connection between it and the Hayes memorandum. In one of many depositions, attorney James Murray examined him on the point:

> MURRAY: In fact, don't you know from your own knowledge
> that a rebuttal to *Strangers in Our Fields* was made,
> to the Secretary of Labor?
> SANBORN: I do recall that.
> MURRAY: Who was responsible for that rebuttal?
> SANBORN: I don't know.
> MURRAY: DiGiorgio had nothing to do with it, directly or
> indirectly?
> SANBORN: I don't believe so.[77]

The durability of Werdel's reprint was now well established. Its usefulness would depend on circumstances, and it would be relevant as long as there were union organizers in the fields. The document branded them as a class on alleged evidence that had long ago been sifted and accepted by four congressmen. It was well on the way to becoming what in the law is called an ancient document —a writing that eventually becomes credible only because it has passed unquestioned.

In the spring of 1960 the Corporation had more than a hundred copies of Werdel's reprint on hand. The supporting documents were on file in the law offices of Brobeck, Phleger and Harrison. They included the 1950 agreement, the confession of judgment for one dollar, the printed volume of the Bakersfield hearings, a carbon copy of the reporter's transcript, the mimeographed 1949 complaint and a print of the film. These and many other papers were, in the context of the past, only the obituaries of the dead *Poverty*. Sanborn and Hayes had proved that, in the context of subsequent events, the reprint and its backlog of records could still be brandished over the heads of persevering unionists.[78] In the spring of 1960 such a context was in the making.

NOTES

70. *Merchants of Labor* contains a detailed historical and critical treatment of the *bracero* program and its effects on domestic agricultural labor.
71. *San Francisco Chronicle,* 8 June 1967.
72. Minutes. Regional Foreign Labor Operations Advisory Committee, February 1957.
73. *San Francisco Examiner,* 3 August 1959.
74. *Hearings.* Subcommittee of the Education and Labor Committee. U.S. House of Representatives. Fair Labor Standards Act. 85th Congress, first session. 1957, p. 2399. Hereafter cited as *Hearings.* Fair Labor Standards Act, 1957.
75. *Hearings.* Fair Labor Standards Act, 1957, p. 2403.
76. Farm Placement Service, California State Department of Employment. *Bulletin,* number 75, 5 September 1956.
77. Bruce W. Sanborn, Jr. Deposition. 2 December 1960, p. 36.
78. Agricultural Workers Organizing Committee. *The Organizer.* 21 April 1960.

5

WON'T YOU COME
INTO MY PARLOR?

The Agricultural Workers Organizing Committee. / The base of the American labor movement in the 1950s was in the International unions that had emerged out of the struggles of half a century. Like the teamsters, garment workers and butchers, they began in violent campaigns of raw self-help. As they consolidated their gains and accumulated resources they saw the necessity of extending the boundaries of unionism. In the steel, automobile and other basic industries millions of production workers remained outside those boundaries. "Organize the unorganized" became the standing order of the 1930s. The Internationals created and financed the means to that end—the Organizing Committee. It was such a committee, the Agricultural Workers Organizing Committee, that the Executive Council of the AFL-CIO set up in the spring of 1959 to operate initially in the fields of California.

The circumstances were somewhat different from those that had existed in the manufacturing industries that had been organized through such committees. In California there was already a union duly chartered by the Executive Council, the National Farm Labor Union. Theoretically, it was vested with the closest to a divine right that any American union can possess—a jurisdiction; but practically, it had failed to organize agriculture. In deference to that jurisdiction, yet unwilling to give the NFLU directly the financial muscle it needed, the AWOC was assigned to do the job. It was to transfer to the NFLU the new Locals of agricultural workers if, as and when they were consolidated. The professionals were stepping in.

Appointed to head the AWOC was Norman Smith, a scarred

veteran of the Automobile Workers Organizing Committee, the predecessor of the United Automobile Workers of America. He was drafted from his job as foreman in a steel mill in California to bring his experience and talents to the task. He was a man for the part, heavy, solid and tough. He weighed some 250 pounds and dressed in a rumple of floppy pants, slouch jacket and open-collared shirt. His powerful shoulders sloped into a bull neck, matched by a jaw that was often unshaven but never charitable. He scrutinized men and places with blue eyes that swiveled suspiciously, as they should in a man who has been suddenly trapped by finks and goons and beaten savagely. His heavy eyebrows beetled like small barbed wire entanglements; Smith liked it when people told him that John L. Lewis had eyebrows like his.

Director Smith hired several of the NFLU volunteers as the core of his field staff. From September 1959 to 16 January 1960 Ernesto Galarza served on the organizing staff of national AFL-CIO headquarters in Washington and was assigned to help Smith, but with no official title. This indirect connection between the NFLU and the AWOC was broken when Galarza resigned from the AFL-CIO staff. By that time Smith had rented a roomy barn in downtown Stockton for his headquarters and deployed a team of field representatives over most of the Central Valley. A revolving fund of several thousand dollars a month was replenished from Washington as his campaign progressed.

Smith's diligence drew the respectful attention of the corporate growers he was preparing to challenge. "The campaign is being conducted in a very hard-headed and businesslike way," the *Western Fruit Grower* reported in October 1959. "You can count on them for a maximum effort to prove it."

The proof was appearing in many parts of the Central Valley. By the spring of 1960 the AWOC had opened organizing posts in Lodi, Linden, Yuba City, Strathmore, Modesto, San Jose, Patterson, Tracy, Riverbank and Los Palos. In these areas Director Smith enlisted many of the men and women who had served in the ranks of the NFLU. Their detailed knowledge of the industry and their long acquaintance with the local work force enabled the AWOC in a few months to appraise its task and assemble a staff.

For a test run Smith took two hundred Union marchers to Sacramento where they camped on the lawn of the capitol in protest against the preferential employment of *braceros*. His men stirred the cherry pickers around Lindsay and served demands upon the contractors to negotiate a standard wage. At four in the morning his teams mixed with the transients on the Stockton and Sacramento skid rows. In his brand-new Impala sedan, Smith and his lieutenants travelled the high levees of the San Joaquin delta, the fortress of the asparagus department of agribusiness. He scowled at corporate lobbyists in legislative hearings and picked up the quarrel with the Farm Placement Service that the NFLU had begun.

It was not long before the AWOC turned its attention to the DiGiorgio Fruit Corporation. A valley-wide organizing campaign could hardly miss the Corporation's holdings spaced between Bakersfield and Yuba City. Smith sent his organizers into the Peach Bowl, looking over DiGiorgio's Dantoni and New England Orchards and uncovering violations of the Public Law 78 on the way. By early summer the AWOC and the Northern California Growers Association were facing each other. DiGiorgio joined other large fruit growers in creating the Tri-Counties Agricultural Committee. Pickets appeared in Yuba City and Marysville. Smith secured an order from the Secretary of Labor against the referral of workers to the struck orchards and the hiring of *braceros* in the area. The Tri-Counties group went to court. Resistance to the AWOC had by now become a major assignment of Vice-President Bruce Sanborn.

The action in the fields was more than sufficient to inform the Corporation that the AWOC was off to an aggressive organizing drive. Smith nevertheless made certain that his efforts were not hidden. He hung a huge canvas sign across the front of his Stockton headquarters advertising his place of business. A local radio station regularly carried "The Voice of Agricultural Labor." A bulletin of the *AWOC Organizer* supplied farm workers and anyone else who cared to read it, including the watchful growers, with detailed reports of current activities. Through the *Bulletin* and by means of letters to other unions, public officials and employers, Smith delighted in announcing not only what he had just done but also what he was just about to do. In March 1960 Smith disclosed his plans for the summer well in advance. "We shall go to work in Salinas as soon as we can get in there." With the AWOC the press had no need to attribute news to "unusually well informed sources." The Communist *People's World* and the non-Communist

San Francisco News agreed on the significance of the AWOC; they said, "The most concerted drive to organize America's farm workers since the 30s" and "The Central Valley is about to become a battlefield."[79]

The Corporation noted these forecasts and watched the trend of events. Sanborn regularly collected the releases and bulletins of the AWOC and passed them on to Robert DiGiorgio. When the AWOC threatened DiGiorgio's supply of peaches and pears in the north, Sanborn himself made an unusual appearance in the newspapers. Along with his Tri-Counties associates he denounced Secretary of Labor Mitchell for denying them *braceros* and accused him of having "an inordinate interest in unionizing farm workers."[80] Sanborn challenged the Secretary's authority and Brobeck secured a court order reversing the decision of the Farm Placement Service to stop referrals of domestic farm laborers to the picketed orchards. Sanborn told the press on 18 July 1960, "The Union organizers have certainly lost this battle since DiGiorgio and other fruit growers are now in a position to get the assistance they need."

Court orders, injunctions and bureaucratic partisanship were familiar employer tactics in the agrarian struggle. Smith was familiar with them and knew that they had been used effectively during the decade of resistance of the NFLU. What he did not know when he lost the legal skirmish in Yuba was that DiGiorgio had added a technique to its strategy—a libel lawsuit with a demand for heavy damages backed by a report of a congressional committee. It was a weapon, however, that the Corporation could not unlimber at will. It required a false step on the part of its antagonist, and this step was taken with

The Resurrection of Poverty. / Smith walked into quicksand innocently enough. His director of publicity and training, Louis Krainnock, kept a small library of labor films which were shown at meetings of farm workers. At a labor convention he learned of a film that was mistakenly referred to him as *Poultry in the Valley of Plenty*. Krainnock reported to Smith that this was a film on the earlier struggles for organization in the Central Valley. He wrote to the United Auto Workers for the film. It was delivered sometime in March and was shown regularly at Union meetings.

As Krainnock explained the film, it was an object lesson in how not to organize a corporation farm. This was understandable, since the entire AWOC operation was to be a demonstration of the professional approach, unhappily lacking in the NFLU. The film was not used as a propaganda piece against the Corporation except as it was depicted as a part of the agribusiness system. If DiGiorgio employees saw *Poverty* in 1960 it was by accident rather than design.

At some of the exhibitions Smith added his personal commentary to the narration on the sound track. He recognized in the documentary the same chronic poverty that he found around him on his rounds. His letters to the growers, like Hasiwar's, also went unanswered. The *braceros* and the Wetbacks that Flannery had quietly described had not ceased bearing down on wage levels and pre-empting jobs. Smith's organizing fervor, always warm and frequently hot, went up a degree or two whenever he viewed the film.

From early April through May and June *Poverty* was screened to farm labor audiences and new staff members. One of the first showings was on April 6 in Stockton. One of the last was in Woodlake on May 12. Between these there were presentations in Strathmore, Marysville, Olivehurst, Empire, Riverbank and Wesly. There were probably many others, for Smith testified later that *Poverty* "was out and being shown almost every night."

The audiences were not large. The Woodlake showing was attended by 35 to 40 persons. It was a fitting introduction, accompanied by bucolic music, for the short speeches that Smith called his "pitch."

That the film served the purposes of the organizing staff well enough was evident from its full bookings. It did not raise funds for the AWOC, which was adequately supplied from Washington. Unlike the showings of 1948 and 1949, *Poverty* was not shown to labor conventions or sympathetic urban audiences. Krainnock was in the habit of pointing out that it was a dated production and that some of the legislative goals of farm workers had been attained or brought within reach.

The print which Smith obtained from the UAW was not the only one in existence. The Corporation kept at least one in its files. It had been shown privately to the staff of the Farm Placement Service in Sacramento. Since the chief of the Service, Hayes, had obtained copies of the Werdel reprint from Sanborn for his attack on the booklet *Strangers in Our Fields,* he was familiar with its background. This private showing to public servants may or may not have come to the attention of the Corporation. Whatever the case, no legal action ensued.

For a sound motion picture film that was supposed to have been so thoroughly eradicated, the modest revival that *Poverty* was enjoying was surprising. Stray prints kept appearing. The UAW can be supposed to have shelved it in a secure corner of its headquarters in Detroit as a memento of a cause Walter Reuther had espoused. The Corporation had received due notice to turn over its print or prints to the Hollywood Film Council for destruction, but it had never done so. DiGiorgio may have kept one or more prints as a kind of trophy, to be shown when profits and spirits were sagging, or perhaps for more practical reasons.

There were, then, those who continued to view and use *Poverty.* It was a curious turn. Only those who had condemned it could view it openly; those who had sponsored it and agreed with it could show it only at grave peril. Norman Smith was among these, although he did not realize it.

He was to find it out soon enough. During the week after the Woodlake showing of *Poverty* on 12 May 1960, the Corporation, undoubtedly smarting from Smith's pickets and his candid promises of more to come, was quietly at his heels. It was the busy week of

DiGiorgio's Hot Pursuit. / The *Valley Labor Citizen* was a labor newspaper of about fourteen thousand circulation published by the Fresno County Central Labor Council. In its May 6 issue it carried a casual bit of farm labor news, in which an organizing meeting of the AWOC was reported. The paragraph included the statement that "Films were shown on the DiGiorgio strike in 1947."[81]

The weekly was mailed to subscribers on May 7, and the obscure item was delivered in San Francisco on or about May 10, and it then came to the attention of Robert DiGiorgio. He promptly relayed the clipping to Brobeck and associates, with instructions to investigate the matter. DiGiorgio could reasonably guess that the report referred to the old Hollywood Film Council documentary. Legal liabilities lurked somewhere behind those few printed words; his guess had to be supported by hard facts if those liabilities were to be pursued.

It was in situations such as this one that the Associated Farmers proved valuable to its members. The Farmers maintained a state office and county branches in the principal agricultural areas. Services to members included checking on reported union activities, advising on tactics during strikes, co-ordination and exchange of information, lobbying, and appearances at legislative hearings. The *Bulletin* and the press releases issued by the Farmers provided the medium by which the sharpest attacks on unionism could be published without attribution to a specific employer. It was the business of the Farmers to investigate and report to their contributors any matters that affected the labor market.

In May 1960 the secretary of the Associated Farmers of Orange County was William R. Callan. DiGiorgio approached the state office of the Farmers in San Francisco, which in turn assigned Callan to the investigation of the film showings. Although a staff member located nearer the scene of the AWOC activities was available, Callan was probably chosen because he would be unrecognized so far from his home base. Also, as a registered investigator with experience in insurance claims he was legally licensed to make investigations related to libel.[82]

Within forty-eight hours after the Corporation had turned over the matter to its attorneys, Callan was in the Strathmore area, where Union activity had been reported. He was instructed to determine whether the film that was being exhibited was in fact *Poverty in the Valley of Plenty;* who was showing the film, the names of witnesses present and the relationship of the NFLU and the AWOC to these presentations. These inquiries were undoubtedly considered to be adequate by the Corporation, since it relied solely upon Callan's reports for the actions that were to follow.

Callan's first stop on May 12 was the office of the AWOC in Strathmore, a farming community southeast of Fresno. He collected some Union leaflets and the information that the film had been shown in Stockton. He also learned that there would be a showing that evening in Woodlake, a nearby town. That afternoon he recruited some local growers who attended the Union meeting that night with him. They saw the screening of what was indeed the genuine *Poverty in the Valley of Plenty,* heard Krainnock give his usual talk and took note of others who were present.[83]

The confirmation was telephoned by Callan to San Francisco and he was invited to report there immediately. On May 13 or 14 Brobeck, using the Corporation's own print of the film, screened it for Callan. This precaution was taken to double check the fact that the AWOC was using the proscribed film.

On May 15 Callan returned to the Central Valley to verify some other important items. The principal ones were to find out what present connection there was between the AWOC and Galarza, and to identify the assistant director of the AWOC. This Callan proceeded to do on his way back to his home in Santa Ana. In the week from May 12 to 18 he travelled several hundred miles by automobile, visited several AWOC offices, talked with union organizers, consulted farmers, gathered a quantity of leaflets and press releases and bulletins and made at least two verbal reports to the Corporation. On the last two days of the week only two additional steps remained to be taken. These were the filing of a complaint for libel on behalf of the Corporation, and the publication of a press release relating to the lawsuit. These matters were handled by Brobeck, and Callan withdrew from the scene.

On May 17 Attorney Malcolm Dungan, for Brobeck, Robert DiGiorgio and Bruce Sanborn, Jr., met with the Corporation's public relations director, Albert O'Dea, who was supplied with a copy of the complaint, a copy of the Werdel reprint and general information on the 1950 controversy and the settlement. On or about May 18 the press release was drafted, and the final text was checked by the attorneys, submitted to Sanborn, approved by him, and released. Naming Norman Smith, H. L. Mitchell, Ernesto Galarza and several others, it charged them with exhibiting *Poverty* in violation of the 1950 agreement, as well as of a court judgment. Quotations were given from the Nixon-Morton-Steed report and from Werdel's prefatory remarks, "a shocking collection of falsehoods . . . fraud perpetuated by a handful of men . . . a deliberately fabricated falsehood . . . almost totally unrelieved by any regard whatever for truth and facts . . . a disservice to labor." The release characterized the recent presentations of *Poverty* as "a malicious flaunting of a judgment arising from a similar suit in

1950 in the Superior Court, Los Angeles County." The Corporation, it continued, "regards the continued showing of this propaganda film as a compounding of bad faith . . . a flagrant violation of the company's right to a good reputation."

Further, the release was at pains to emphasize that "there was no labor question involved in the present action." And to convey the idea that the Corporation had been forced into the disagreeable business as a matter of self-defense, Sanborn concluded: "We have no alternative to this lawsuit."[84]

Three additional statements in the release should be noted. It was said that only "some" of the persons participating in the exhibitions of the film had consented to the 1950 judgment or had agreed to discontinue showing the motion picture. DeWitt Tannehill was identified as the assistant Director of the AWOC. The congressional report was identified as one that had been issued in November 1949.

The indignant and scandalized tone of the release, added to the importance of the issues and the prestige of the aggrieved Corporation, made for a second round of extensive publicity. The headlines in the metropolitan dailies announced the lawsuit and the stories picked up the more lurid charges quoted directly from the prestigious congressional report. Few of the daily and weekly newspapers in metropolitan and rural California failed to carry the release. Their readers totalled a circulation of more than two million. The stories originating in San Francisco were fed into the national networks of the press wire services.

As the story passed over the city desks and through the hands of rewrite men, it gained in impact what it lost in truth. The *Stockton Record* had it that "the film was banned by court action ten years ago and union officials violated this order by re-issuing the film."[85] The *San Francisco Chronicle* on May 19 invented a ruling by the Superior Court of Los Angeles ordering the destruction of all copies of *Poverty*. The *California Farmer* had more time to check the facts, but simply published the *Chronicle's* version on 18 June 1960.

The Corporation's technique of trying its case concurrently in both the court of public opinion and the courts of justice and of impeaching before trial the intended defendants as liars and defrauders was not a new one for the plaintiff. On 8 November

1949 it had filed an almost identical suit; a week later it had asked a congressional subcommittee to sit in official judgment on the issues of that lawsuit; and in the early part of March 1950, with that lawsuit still before the Superior Court of Los Angeles, it now publicized the conclusions of four congressmen that the film was libelous and that it was a "shocking collection of falsehoods almost totally unrelieved by any regard whatever for truth and facts."

It could not have been supposed that these were mistakes of amateur litigants. Robert DiGiorgio and Bruce Sanborn, Jr. were attorneys. Brobeck and associates were reputed by the *Bakersfield Californian* as among the best lawyers in the state. Nor could it be thought likely that they were using innocent instruments to their purpose, for Werdel and Nixon also were members of the Bar. In the system of due process of the law, men's fortunes and lives turn on two fateful hinges. One is the authenticity of the physical evidence and the other is the credibility of witnesses. The DiGiorgio press release had the effect of jamming the pin of both these hinges so that they could turn only in one direction. The authenticity of the Nixon-Morton-Steed report was again avowed. The defense was again implied to be unreliable and untrustworthy.

Ordinarily the practitioners of the law give time and thought to considerations of this order, not only because there are undertones of professional ethics, but because they can lead to practical difficulties if a court should decide that this kind of publicity interferes with the rights of the accused and obstructs the administration of justice. The tendency in the American courts in the 1960s was in this direction.

Considering the events of the week preceding the release of May 18 and the drafting and filing of the complaint concurrently, these preparations gave the impression of haste and of eagerness to litigate. From the point of view of the Corporation the chance could not help but appear clean, promising and exciting. By subjecting the officers of the AFL-CIO, the State Federation of Labor and the staff of the AWOC to the discovery powers of subpoenas, interrogatories and depositions, it would give DiGiorgio's lawyers the opportunity to pry into Smith's operations. It might even help derail the AWOC organizing campaign. These were drastic matters and they were no doubt weighed accordingly. Yet they were

arranged very swiftly and the Corporation began its pursuit of the
Union with the filing of a

Complaint for Libel—the Third /   No. 71841
In the Superior Court of the State of California
in and for the County of San Joaquin
DiGiorgio Fruit Corporation, a Corporation, Plaintiff,
v.
Norman Smith, H. L. Mitchell, Ernesto Galarza, National
Agricultural Workers Union, Agricultural Workers Organizing
Committee, et al.
Filed 18 May 1960

The complaint was formally entered on the eighteenth in Stockton. It charged that defendants wickedly and maliciously published
Poverty in the Valley of Plenty in Woodlake and certain other
places. Publication, the technical legal term for exhibiting or showing, had taken place in some of the communities that had been
visited by Callan. Except for the names of the defendants, places
and dates, the complaint was almost identical with the one Dungan had prepared in November 1949. Dungan added in 1960:
"The falsity of said statements and representations has been increased and exacerbated by the passage of approximately twelve
years since the film was made." The Corporation asked for a million dollars in actual damages and a million in punishment of the
numerous offenses for libel as set forth.

The general demurrer is the first resort of defending lawyers to
test the strength of a complaint. It is a pleading to the effect that
the complaint is insufficient and inadequate to sustain a cause of
action. A demurrer, when sustained, closes the case in favor of the
defense. When denied the case proceeds and the way is open for
discovery proceedings. These are the legal devices by which the
attorneys of the opposing parties can draw from their antagonists
as much information on the case as their ingenuity and skill can
contrive. They are the deposition, the interrogatory, the subpoena
and the demand for admission of the genuineness of certain facts
and documents.

On behalf of defendants counsel filed a demurrer on May 27.
In a supporting memorandum the defense argued that the show-

ing of the film was privileged, that is to say, not subject to legal complaint. The grounds of privilege were that *Poverty* had been exhibited in connection with a labor dispute, namely, an organizing campaign. California court decisions allowed both parties to such disputes limited rights to publicize their side of the controversy. The demurrer was denied.

On 11 July 1960 the taking of depositions by Brobeck's associates began in the suite of Brobeck, Phleger and Harrison in San Francisco. A deposition is something like exploratory surgery. The witness is under subpoena and on oath. Every word he says, a shake of the head when he responds silently to a question, is written into the record by the reporter who sits at the elbow of the examiner. His own attorney is present to parry objectionable questions, to pick arguments with the rival attorney in order to give his client a breathing spell over rough ground, and to advise the witness not to answer. If the witness has been served with a *subpoena duces tecum,* he must bring with him the documents or things described in the subpoena. Neither judge nor jury is there to unnerve him, but the deposition can be lengthy, and the duration itself can wear him down.

On the morning of July 11 Norman Smith was the deponent and Malcolm Dungan was the examiner. Dungan sat at his desk, the anchor of a semicircle of parties to the case, attorneys and the witness. He was a plump, unhurried man tending to an early rotundness. He beamed as he extracted admissions from the glowering Smith. Dungan pivoted easily in his chair, aiming his questions with precision. He tilted and leveled as if finding the range to his target. His voice, sonorous and well modulated, delivered the questions with a touch of relish. It was not the voice of a lawyer who would ever browbeat a witness. The walls he occasionally glanced at were lined with lawbooks. Through a window behind his shoulder the city of San Francisco and its sunlit bay completed the picture of a professional who sat high in a nearly perfect world.

Smith, on that occasion, was a worried, angry witness but not a scared one. He had not known of the litigation of 1950, of the agreement, of the Werdel Extension of Remarks or of the judgment. Dungan handed him a copy of the Werdel reprint and Smith read it for the first time. The attorney explained to Smith that this was the last copy of the document in Brobeck's files. Smith had brought with him and delivered to Dungan the print of the film which had been used in the AWOC showings. There were to be other depositions, but with this one Dungan was left in possession of the marrow and the meat of his case.

Proceedings of another kind were developing as to Ernesto Galarza. James Murray, representing Galarza separately in the case, filed a declaration by his client that he had had nothing to do with the showings of the film; that he had resigned from the AFL-CIO staff in January; that he had in no way violated the agreement of 1950. On the basis of this declaration Murray filed a motion for summary judgment, another technical method by which unfounded complaints can be judged before trial. Dungan delayed agreeing to a definitive date for the hearing of the motion for summary judgment. From August 16 it was moved to September 6, then to September 13.

Dungan's reason for delay, given in a letter to Murray dated August 29, was that his firm was preparing counter affidavits and a memorandum to the court. Murray never received these documents. He went to Stockton on September 13 prepared to argue his motion. Instead he was surprised to find that his client had been dropped from DiGiorgio's action by a different route, that of

Dismissal. / Dungan's letter of August 29 with the information that the affidavits and memorandum would be ready by September 5, now appeared to be a tactic to gain time. Either he had not made up his mind to move for a dismissal, or he had made that decision and did not want to discover it to Murray. At any rate, on motion of the plaintiff, on September 13 the complaint of May 18 was dropped as to all and each of the defendants named in it.

The Corporation did not issue a press release explaining the withdrawal of the complaint. Such a statement would have cleared the names of two defendants who had been unjustly charged with flouting a court judgment and violating an agreement of long standing. It would have also compromised the dignity of the Corporation. In the dismissal there was the tacit admission that it had had no facts, as to some of the defendants, on which to base the extraordinary chastisement of the May 18 press release.

By refraining from an apology or an explanation, DiGiorgio also avoided further attention to the credibility of its prime witness, the

Nixon-Morton-Steed report. The citations from that source in the release had not been necessary to explain the suit filed on May 18. They had no bearing on the current showings of *Poverty* as to the alleged legal wrongs of which the Corporation was complaining. Now that the reliability of the Corporation's authority as to one part of the release was put in question by the dismissal, the chance was posed that other passages might prove as vulnerable. Did the dismissal imply that the charges Sanborn had levelled indiscriminately against every one of the defendants were backed by a document of questionable authenticity? It had no legal obligation to admit this, although it may have been appropriate as a matter of manners or morals. The tactical reasons for shunning a public correction were overriding.

The Corporation's goal was prosecution of the AWOC and toward it Brobeck, Phleger and Harrison moved with some deliberation and much speed.

NOTES

79. *People's World*. San Francisco, Calif. 6 June 1959; *San Francisco News*, 15 June 1959.
80. *San Francisco Chronicle*. 31 July 1960.
81. *Valley Labor Citizen*, 6 May 1960.
82. *Business and Professional Code*. State of California, section 7502.
83. William R. Callan, Deposition. 18 September 1963.
84. Press release. DiGiorgio Fruit Corporation. San Francisco, Calif. 18 May 1960.
85. *Stockton Record*. 19 May 1960.

6

THE TRIAL OF
A DEAD DOCUMENTARY

The filing of legal papers is one of the routines of the practice of law that large firms delegate to junior apprentices, and solo practitioners have to attend to themselves. In a metropolitan judicial district the county clerk's office will receive and file hundreds of thousands, perhaps millions, of sheaves in the course of a year. To dismiss a complaint, like every other detail of litigation, requires the filing of a notice. This Brobeck's agents did on September 13 in the office of the county clerk in Stockton. At the same time they filed the fourth

Compaint for Libel—the Fourth /   Number 72635
In the Superior Court of the State of California
in and for the County of San Joaquin
DiGiorgio Fruit Corporation, a Corporation, Plaintiff,
v.
American Federation of Labor and Congress of Industrial Organizations, Norman Smith, United Packinghouse Workers Agricultural Workers Organizing Committee. et al.
Filed 13 September 1960.

From the list of defendants Mitchell, Galarza and the NAWU had been stricken. The notable addition to the new list was the AFL-CIO. This had a two-fold significance. First, it lined up with the minor targets the major one, the parent body in Washington, D.C. Second, it joined a party with the financial ability to pay $2 million in damages. Against Smith, Krainnock and Tannehill, the Corporation stood to win a moral victory but hardly so much money.

The text of the allegations of the fourth complaint was identical with that of the third. There were fifteen charges of libel, all of them based on the film—the denial of rights granted to all American workers, miserable living quarters, lack of compensation for injuries, unpaid work time, extortionate rents, overcrowding in housing facilities and other egregious, immoral and unlawful practices. Again Brobeck charged that these practices were directly attributed in the film's pictures and words on the sound track to the Corporation; and again Flannery's recital of these evils as faults of an entire industry operating not under the particular patch of the heavens over DiGiorgio Farms but "beneath this divine canopy" of the San Joaquin Valley, was ignored.

The libels, Brobeck again noted, had been exacerbated and increased by the passage of nearly twelve years since the production of the film. What had been wickedly untrue in 1948 was far more so in 1960.

Since damages were at issue in the amount of $2 million it is worth remarking that in neither its third nor its fourth complaint did the Corporation allege injury to its reputation as an employer. "At all times prior to the defamatory publications," the complaint read, "plaintiff has had a good reputation in its occupation and business as a producer and marketer of agricultural products." Local 218 had called over eight hundred witnesses to the picket line to testify that its reputation as an employer was at least open to debate.

Once more Brobeck pleaded: "Because the words, sounds and pictures are contained on a motion picture film and sound track, and are inextricably connected and interdependent for their meaning and effect, it is impossible to set them out in this complaint."[86] In these words there was wrapped a theory of libel by sound motion picture to the effect that the blend of defamation resulting from pictures seen and words heard simultaneously was a fusion that no man could again separate into its components. If the court could be persuaded to accept this theory, the most could be made of the argument that the film referred to the Corporation and to no one else. The words alluded to miserable housing, corporation farming, the Corporation, Joseph DiGiorgio, the agricultural industry, conditions of serfdom, DiGiorgio Farms. Implications, purports and inferences diffused themselves into every word and picture of the film. Defamation spread through the whole of it.

Taken literally, Brobeck's plea in paragraph VII of the complaint, that it was impossible to set forth words as well as sounds and pictures, would have made it difficult indeed to set forth in writing a "cause of action." Having pleaded thus Brobeck proceeded to do the impossible. In paragraph V of the compliant it was said: "In the film defendants by word, and picture have depicted, represented and published of and concerning plaintiff false and defamatory matters which are hereinafter more particularly alleged." The effect of paragraphs V and VII was that the Corporation had it both ways: it set forth the particular alleged libels, by quoting the specific language, and it also pleaded the impossibility of identifying separately the words or the pictures that pinned these libels to the Corporation unequivocally.

Attorneys for defendants, Charles P. Scully and Nels Fransen, pressed the issue in demurrers arguing that the complaint was vague, ambiguous and uncertain. The demurrers were overruled by the court. As in 1950, when Gilbert and Nissen had objected on the same grounds, Brobeck was excused from setting forth on behalf of his client the particulars which connected the alleged libels to the Corporation directly and specifically. It was a crucial ruling.

In the course of these maneuvers it became clear that Brobeck intended to try the film on charges of nefarious and malicious misrepresentations both as to conditions as they existed in 1948 and in 1960. Time and again the plaintiff's argument stressed that the film's charges related to conditions existing "now and heretofore."

The time of production of the film—1948—was admitted by Brobeck—some twelve years past. What it said and pictured was what Flannery had narrated and the camera's eye had seen in the wintry, grey light of February of that year. There was only one way to update the film, and that was for Smith or Krainnock to explain, on showing the film, that the pictures and words described conditions as of 1960. Both Smith and Krainnock did the opposite. They noted the obsoleteness of the film and referred to changes in the legal status of farm labor in the intervening years.

In successfully arguing against the demurrers, Brobeck cited section 45 of the Civil Code of California as the legal basis of the action. The essentials of this definition are as follows: it is a false publication; it brings contempt and hatred upon the libeled person; it is a writing or other fixed representation to the eye. It differs from slander in that the latter is a fleeting representation to the ear and is not a writing but a saying.

Of additional significance was the fact that what Brobeck alleged was libel *per se*—direct libel, so to speak, a writing which on the face of it is defamatory "without the necessity of explanatory matter."[87] An allegedly libelous publication which did require explanations outside itself, which in order to stand up had to be propped with references to other writings or facts than those appearing on its face, became libel *per quod,* or indirect libel. The great advantage of libel direct over libel indirect for Brobeck was that in libel direct damages did not have to be proved.

The pleadings following the filing of the complaint and preceding the trial only added to the discomfitures of the defense. It did not help its case to argue that the allegedly defamatory matters in the film were true, which Brobeck took to mean true to the Corporation. Brobeck subpoenaed from Smith in July 1960 the print of the film which the AWOC had used. The defense did not see it again until the trial in November 1961. Attorney Fransen, defending Smith and the AWOC, attempted twice to recover the film for examination. He saw it only when DiGiorgio's attorney produced it from his brief case to offer it in evidence in the courtroom.

As motions, demurrers and answers were presented to the court, the case became singular in one respect. Neither side cited any previous decisions in libel actions based on motion picture films with sound track. The litigation in this area, beginning in the 1930s, was not abundant but it was significant. It contained the elements of Brobeck's theory of the inextricable mix set forth in paragraph VII of the complaint. These important precedents Brobeck chose to ignore. The citations it invoked and which won the case were taken from the school of Gutenberg, not from that of Cecil B. DeMille. These were the preliminaries to

The Trial. / With the Hon. George F. Buck presiding, and without a jury, the proceedings opened on 14 November 1961. Charles

P. Scully and Victor Van Bourg appeared as counsel for the AFL-CIO, Nels Fransen for Smith and the AWOC. Marion B. Plant was chief trial counsel for the Corporation.

Scully and Fransen opened with a torpedo aimed not at the plaintiff but at the Bench. Upon the case being called they offered an affidavit of prejudice against Judge Buck, declaring their belief that he "is prejudiced against the party" and therefore unable to conduct "a fair and impartial trial." As he listened to the argument that he should disqualify himself, Judge Buck's complexion turned a shade rosier. When counsel had finished, he reached under the Bench for a law book, read section 170 of the Code of Civil Procedure, and denied the motion on the ground that it had been unseasonably presented. Plant tallied without a blink of satisfaction his first score.

Plant was an elder member of the Brobeck staff. His face was deeply creased from the tensions of innumerable court battles. His temper was that of ice that melted at the edges only when he recited with satisfaction the libels of which his client had been the victim. Loath to waste energy he applied it effectively and economically. It was difficult to team this methodical professional with the impetuous, scrambling investigator, Callan.

The foundations of Plant's case were solid. They consisted first of all of numerous documents that had been carefully preserved in Brobeck's files since 1948. Among them there were maps, photographs, congressional hearings prints, an agreement, a judgment, an Extension of Remarks, reprints, a documentary film and financial reports. Twenty-four exhibits were introduced in evidence for the plaintiff. They included, it is to be noted, a special delivery registered letter which Brobeck, Phleger and Harrison had sent to Gilbert and Nissen, their adversaries of 1950, on 18 May 1960.

Plant called fourteen witnesses. Not included among them was William Callan, whose investigation had updated Plant's formidable collection of ancient documents.

Documents and testimony were emplaced as Plant's strategy unfolded. This strategy was to charge the film with libel in 1960 as well as in 1948; to underscore its wicked, malicious character; to prove that its target was the Corporation and no one else; to invoke the subcommittee report and to qualify it as authentic and official for use as evidence.

Plant's first witness was Attorney Charles Emmett Lucey, of Washington, D.C. Under instructions from Brobeck, Lucey had presented himself at AFL-CIO headquarters and there had consulted a bound copy of the Appendix of the *Congressional Record* of 9 March 1950. He then inquired of the Clerk of the House of Representatives and the Committee on Education and Labor. They were unable to find an original, signed report of Subcommittee Number 1.[88] Lucey had also been instructed to search for a minority report and found none. Finally, Lucey repaired to the Library of Congress where he again consulted the bound volume of the Appendix of 1950, identical to the one he had read at the AFL-CIO library.

Now there occurred a slip in the trial that only an expert hand could contrive and only an expert eye could detect.

Plant's Exhibit Number 20 in evidence was a photocopy of the Werdel Extension of Remarks as it appeared in the volume at the Library of Congress. The certification of this source was duly notarized by a Library official and submitted in compliance with the usual rules of evidence as to public documents. Plant questioned Lucey on the point:

PLANT: Have you examined the volume of the *Congressional Record* from which the pages shown in Exhibit 20 are taken?

LUCEY: I have.

PLANT: And where did you examine that volume and when?

LUCEY: I examined it at the AFL-CIO headquarters in Washington, D.C. on October 30, of this year. . . . I called at the AFL-CIO. . . . an employee . . . brought out the *Congressional Record,* the bound volume.

PLANT: Now, the volume which she brought out contained the pages of which Exhibit 20 is a copy?

LUCEY: It did, yes.[89]

There was no question that the printed pages consulted by Lucey at AFL-CIO headquarters and at the Library of Congress were identical. But that was not his testimony. The pages of Exhibit 20 submitted by Plant were not copies taken from the volume brought out by the AFL-CIO's employee. They were copies of the volume brought out by the Library of Congress clerk.

Lawyers have slugged through towering arguments over the admission of evidence. Plant had his Exhibit 20 accredited on the testimony that it was a copy of the print that the AFL-CIO employee had produced, when the fact attested by the certification was that it was a copy of the print produced by the congressional librarian. Attorney Fransen objected but on different grounds. He observed that the reproduction was taken from the Appendix. Scully pointed out that it was merely an Extension of Remarks and not a complete report. But Plant insisted on his vital point and the court upheld him. "The objections are overruled and the exhibit may be received," ordered Judge Buck.

Plant had made a number of important gains. First, he had in evidence that the AFL-CIO was in possession of the Werdel Extension from which he could argue that Smith, an official of that labor organization, could have informed himself about the scandalous character of the film. Second, the Extension was credentialed as an account of the official proceedings of the House entitled to admission as evidence in a court of law. Third, the authorship was assigned to a responsible committee of Congress. Fourth, the statements contained in the Nixon-Morton-Steed report could be cited as testimony as to the truth of what had happened in 1948. And fifth, it allowed Plant to quote the clinching language of the three congressmen that the film was "a shocking collection of falsehoods, almost totally unrelieved by any regard for the truth and the facts."

In effect Plant was calling Nixon, Morton and Steed as his witnesses by way of Exhibit 20, without exposing them to cross-examination by Scully and Fransen. This was prudent, for none of the three had read the script of the film; Steed had asked no questions about it at the Bakersfield hearings; and Morton had probably never seen it. As members of the subcommittee they had received the motion picture in evidence, but had not reviewed it in Washington as they were pledged to do through their chairman, Bailey. Nevertheless, there was now before Judge Buck their testimony to the effect that "The union film also represents that living conditions on DiGiorgio Farms consist of disreputable, filthy shacks and that the living standards of the occupants are substandard and squalid." The critical words "on DiGiorgio Farms" were now securely in the trial record.

Plant's strongest witness was Lawrence Webdell. He had investigated the background of *Poverty* in 1948. Officially employed as office manager at DiGiorgio Farms he had helped in the circulation of the petition of February 1948 against Union recognition, signing it himself as one of the "workers." His office collected the cancelled checks and other confidential Corporation documents which eventually appeared in *A Community Aroused*.

Plant guided Webdell through the catalogue of alleged libels and elicited from him testimony to the effect that the Corporation provided swimming pools for its workers, served them good food, maintained medical services, kept sanitary toilets and showers and supplied hot and cold running water. According to Webdell, the Corporation did so in 1960 and had done so in 1948. When Plant asked him if conditions on the ranch were substantially the same in 1960 as they were in 1948, Webdell answered, "Yes." Webdell also countered the rumor about DiGiorgio hiring Wetbacks through headhunters. In that scene of the film, he testified, one of the actors was a Union organizer, Louis de Anda. The Corporation, he said, had co-operated with the Border Patrol when it made periodic "surveys" of the ranch and arrested illegals. Webdell also testified that he did not know of any DiGiorgio employees who lived in the repulsive shacks shown in the film, even though half of them during the peak season lived in Weedpatch, Arvin and other locations pictured in *Poverty*.

With Webdell still on the witness stand, Plant now introduced in evidence more than a dozen photographs of housing conditions on DiGiorgio Farms. These pictures were taken sometime in 1947 by Cal Williams, a Bakersfield commercial photographer. Some of them appeared in the illustrated section of *A Community Aroused*. They had reposed in the administrative files of the Farms ever since. Like the copies of cancelled checks the photographs were supplied to the Special Citizens Committee by the Corporation and their custody was within Webdell's jurisdiction.[90] Plant removed the labels from the back of the prints since his offer of evidence was limited to those matters which served the interests of the Corporation only. No attorney ever does otherwise. But the label on one picture refused to come off. It identified the photographer and dated all the pictures at the time the Special Citizens were preparing *A Community Aroused*.

Plant now called Norman Smith to the witness box. A quick

triangulation could give an observer the drift of the trial: Plant
examined from his seat behind counsel's table, leaving it only when
he had to hand the witness a document for identification. He
handled it with fingers finely formed for brush work or molding
but now scuffed from bouts with antagonists such as the one now
before him. Smith filled the witness chair with his usual disarray
of garments bulging out of shape to give a restless man working
room. Out of his ample flesh and bones four frail Plants could
have been produced, still an insufficient number to exhaust the
scorn that Smith mixed with his rumbling answers. Above them,
Judge Buck in his black robes listed slightly in his black uphol-
stered chair. Now and again his eyelids would narrow as if the
glare of the November sun slanting through the windows of the
court room made it more difficult to see what was taking place
before him.

Plant drew from Smith that he had never been on the premises
of DiGiorgio Farms. He had not asked anyone about the proscribed film. Some itinerant workers had told Smith that the Di-
Giorgio camps were better than average. As a foundation for the
charge of malice the examination went as follows:

> PLANT: Now, in this standard talk that you gave where the
> picture was shown did you make any reference to
> corporate farmers as trying to put the smaller farm-
> ers out of business?
> SMITH: Yes.
> PLANT: Did you make any reference to robber barons?
> SMITH: I did.
> PLANT: And what did you say in that respect?
> SMITH: That corporate farmers were robber barons, that they
> were putting the little people out of business.[91]

When Plant pressed Smith as to why he did not investigate
conditions at the Farms before showing the film, the attorney, as
sometimes happens in trials, received some unwanted testimony.
Smith said he did not make an investigation because the film did
not say that the unsanitary facilities, the ramshackle housing and
the other conditions complained of were on DiGiorgio property.
Smith repeated this answer and Plant could not shake him from it.
Whereupon counsel moved that it be stricken from the record.

The court allowed the answer to stand, and Plant took this reverse fully aware of its import. Smith, as a viewer of the film, was saying under oath that it did not refer to conditions on the ranch. Plant had no live witnesses who would testify that it did. Smith was not contradicted as to the allusions and references of the film by any adverse witness present in court. His only adversaries on the point were Nixon, Morton and Steed, testifying by means of a certified photocopy of certain pages from the Appendix of the *Congressional Record*. It was now a question of the weight of Smith's opinion against that of the paper labelled Exhibit 20.

Before leaving the stand Smith also testified that he had not known of the film before the AWOC showed it and knew nothing of the details of the congressional investigation or the litigation of 1950.

The film was introduced in evidence by Plant and screened for the court, the same print that Smith had surrendered under subpoena more than a year before and that Fransen had been unable to locate.

Along with the film Plant introduced a printed transcript of Flannery's narration on the sound track. It was reproduced for its first public appearance from the original typewritten shooting script prepared in Hollywood. Plant said, "My main reason for putting it in is so when it comes to the court, the court will find it convenient to refer to it to refresh his recollection of the film."

Plant had drawn the text of the narration from the DiGiorgio files after more than ten years. In March 1949 Joseph DiGiorgio sent a copy to Governor Earl Warren with the request that he refute some of the statements contained in it. Governor Warren's comments were forwarded to Congressman Werdel. The narration was not presented to the subcommittee at the Bakersfield hearings.

Plant completed his documentation with the addition to the record of two more exhibits, a printed volume of the 1950 hearings and the text of the agreement of 23 May 1950 that ended the strike. Carefully limiting his offer, the attorney explained that the volume was to be taken to establish only that the subcommittee had been in Bakersfield.

The defense called only one witness to the trial, a Corporation official named David B. Shippey. The six arguments of the defendants were: that the representations of the film referred to

Joseph DiGiorgio and not the Corporation; that they were true; that the Corporation was without a reputation that could be damaged; that the film was not libelous *per se;* that it was privileged as a piece of propaganda in a labor dispute; and that the AFL-CIO did not act through any agents in the showings of *Poverty.* Counsel denied that the Wetback scene placed the actors on the DiGiorgio ranch and insisted that the intent of the scene was to attack not the Corporation but a practice common throughout commercial agriculture. Nowhere did the film say, argued Van Bourg, Scully's associate, that the shacks were on DiGiorgio property. The attorneys also argued strenuously that the 1950 agreement provided their clients with a protection that the Corporation had ignored—the thirty-day notice to third parties before the Corporation would take legal action against future showings of the film. Scully directly charged DiGiorgio with violating this clause of the agreement.

These arguments availed the defense nothing. Judge Buck sustained the formidable catalogue of alleged libels and found that the allegations in the film did refer to DiGiorgio Fruit Corporation and were defamatory by word, sound and picture. He awarded plaintiff $100,000 in general and $50,000 in punitive damages. Judgment was entered on 6 February 1962.

The Findings of Fact and Conclusions of Law signed by Judge Buck were another legal accolade for Brobeck's team. Plant had scaled down his prayer for damages to "something in six figures" and got it. The defamatory character of *Poverty* was officially declared by a court of law. The Nixon-Morton-Steed report was accorded the status of a genuine congressional report adopted by a responsible committee of the House. It was now a matter of court record, witnessed by four congressmen, that certain union organizers were liars, perpetrators of fraud and subverters of the processes of Congress. Plant had only one more hurdle to overcome. That was

The Appeal. / Notice of appeal was filed on 15 February 1962 and the case went to the Third Appellate District Court in Sacramento. Its decision was handed down on 30 April 1963. The judgment of the lower court was sustained except for the award, which was lowered to $10,000 for damages and $50,000 as punishment.[92] The reduction of the monetary award was the only consolation that Smith, the AFL-CIO and other defendants could find in the decision. Justice Schottky, who prepared it with the concurrence of his two associates, fulfilled Brobeck's best expectations by upholding Plant's findings and Judge Buck's decision.

Although more than one half of the scenes in *Poverty* related to conditions in the corporate agricultural industry as a whole, the alleged libels were taken to refer to the DiGiorigo Fruit Corporation exclusively and not to agribusiness as such. Plant himself had argued in support of the well-established rule that a libelous publication must be considered in its entirety.[93] A major part of that whole was the film's strictures against an entire industry. Plant had himself located the repellant housing in the neighboring communities, and it was uncontradicted that these were the dwellings of farm workers. Smith testified that the target was the industry. Mitchell, also in the record before the court, had made this clear and Hasiwar had reiterated these declarations. Nixon in the same printed record of the hearings introduced by Plant had observed that the film did not actually say that the shacks were on DiGiorgio Farms. But in the report which he approved along with Morton and Steed he had changed his opinion. Exhibit 20 and its authors prevailed in the mind of the court.

The appellate court cited over twenty cases bearing on the issues but did not include any of the precedent decisions on libel by motion pictures with sound track. This was unusual, because by 1962 there were settled cases which dealt precisely with libel by sound motion picture. The rules in these cases, or the issues they left unresolved, were overlooked.

Also, the appellate court held with Judge Buck that the case was one of libel direct and stated: "It is to be noted that an article libelous on its face, or libelous *per se,* is actionable without proof of special damages.[94] Now, an "article" legally defined is "a literary composition on a specific topic, forming an independent portion of a book or literary publication, especially of a newspaper, magazine, review or other periodical."[95] Judge Buck had found no "article," and an appellate court is not legally capable of finding new facts not discovered below. However, since it was abundantly clear that the controversy was over a motion picture film with sound track, the foundation of the decision on an "article" was surprising. Even so, the decision passed in this form into the digests of the law.[96]

The Schottky decision reinforced the strength of Werdel's Extension of Nixon, Morton and Steed. The three constituted "a responsible committee of Congress." Scully suggested to the court that this was merely a characterization of that committee and not a valid authority for legal conclusions but the court did not change its opinion.

There was another curiosity in these proceedings. At the trial in Stockton Plant submitted a photocopy of certain pages of a bound volume of the Appendix in which Werdel's Extension of Remarks appeared. Exhibit 20 was there complete, including Werdel's prefatory remarks. But Plant's responding brief filed in Sacramento carried an Appendix which set forth the text of the same report, but without the prefatory remarks. The deletion of these remarks was not noticed by the appellate court. Cases had come to disaster by the misplacement of a comma; this one did not falter with the removal of more than three hundred words.

With the removal of the prefatory remarks went the date of the report. The Nixon-Morton-Steed text proper carried no date, and Plant identified the report as one that had been presented in February 1950. The court accepted this as a correct statement of fact, although there was no record of any report being presented in February. Now 9 March 1950 became simply the date on which the text of the report had appeared in the Appendix.

The appellate court had before it the printed text of Flannery's script as submitted by Plant. It heard the same words from the sound track when it saw the film. The court gave weight to the "the words of the sound track as spoken."[97] It did not make reference to the same words as printed. Defamation by speech, it will be recalled, is slander; by writing, libel.

One other aspect of the decision remains to be considered:

Scully and Fransen in their pleadings before trial had raised the defense of privilege—the use of the film as propaganda in an organizing campaign. They cited principally the classic case of *Emde v. San Joaquin County Central Labor Council*,[98] which dealt centrally with the qualified privilege of publicizing of facts in a labor dispute.

Plant, instead of denying that the suit had arisen out of a labor matter, contended that the privilege had been lost because the film did not state facts but was a deliberate falsification of them. The implication that there was a labor dispute woven into the litigation was left dangling. Plant, apparently not recalling how pointedly Sanborn had denied this in his press release, referred to the AWOC organizing campaign and pointed out that the film had been used as a piece of propaganda to recruit farm laborers. The court tied down Plant's loose end. Referring to a previous case, the decision declared that DiGiorgio's libel action arose out of a labor dispute in a contest between industrial combatants.[99] It then proceeded to agree with the Corporation that the qualified privilege had been lost.

The reasoning of the court led to still another difficulty. For now the situation was this: Sanborn had declared in his release of May 18 that there was no labor question involved in the suit. Plant now argued that there was, the court concurring. Fortunately, this was nothing more than an exercise in logic. Sanborn's release could not embarrass Plant, since it was not in evidence in the Stockton trial. Plant's pleadings could not embarrass Sanborn, since they were not reported in the newspapers. The same facts served contradictory purposes, proving again that truth is a many-splintered thing.

As to damages, the appellate court was less responsive to the plaintiff. Plant had said that the film "was likely" to do the greatest damage in preventing the Corporation from finding workers. Because DiGiorgio did not market its products under its own name, the trade name had not been libeled. But since the court had ruled that it was a matter of libel direct, the Corporation had no burden to establish damages by proof. The appellate court reduced the general damages from $100,000 to $10,000 observing that "while a corporation has no reputation in a personal sense to be defamed by words, such as those imputing unchastity . . . language which casts aspersions upon its business character is actionable." The damages in punishment were allowed to stand at $50,000 as not excessive or, as the court was at pains to make clear, "the result of passion or prejudice."

In June 1963 Scully made one more effort to repair his defeat. He filed a petition with the State Supreme Court for a re-hearing, which was denied. The Corporation was left in possession of the

field in a labor dispute, of the print of *Poverty,* of valuable information about the AWOC and its operations, of $60,000 and of

The Workable Web. / The Stockton lawsuit and the resulting
appeal showed now just what elements on the side of the Union
the Corporation had been able to combine into an effective anti-
union weapon. Using the public exhibition of *Poverty,* the organizing campaign and strike, the timid moral support for the Union
adversary from its trade-union allies, and ineffectual legal defenses
against the Corporation's complaints, DiGiorgio could bring to
bear its elaborate documentation, a team of lawyers who were
familiar with the subject, the precedent of a successful action in
1950, the prestige of a responsible committee of Congress, the
certified testimony of three Members of the House and the pressures of publicity.

There was an important difference, however, between the 1950
success and that of 1963. The 23 May 1950 settlement had been
reached through private negotiations, and the perfect web in which
the strike had been strangled had not been tested. The dominant
consideration then was the avoidance by the State Federation
of Labor and the Hollywood Film Council of the financial costs of
such a test. The Stockton judgment was, contrarily, a product of
adversary proceedings in a court of law. DiGiorgio had to place
in the record the documents and testimony essential to its case.
These did not meet a severe test of opposition either in Stockton
or Sacramento. Nevertheless, the lawsuit and what it produced in
the way of a public record made it possible to at least begin the
examination of DiGiorgio's composite of law and facts.

The weakness of the Corporation's web began to become evident. To begin with, the Corporation was now committed to a
report that carried three different dates. Sanborn had identified it
in the May 18 release as a report issued in November 1949. Plant
told the court that the date was sometime in February 1950. His
Exhibit 20 was from the Appendix of 9 March 1950. This was
then amended to a report without date when Plant eliminated
Werdel's prefatory remarks from his exhibit for presentation to the
appellate court. To all of which the following difficulty must be
added: The Werdel Extension first appeared in the daily edition of
the *Congressional Record* dated March 9, on pages A-1923 to

A-1926. The certified copy which Plant converted into his Exhibit 20 was photocopied from pages A-1817 to A-1820 of the bound volume of the Appendix printed in May 1950.

There was also a discrepancy so slight it went unnoticed by the court. Nixon, Morton and Steed reported that "The subcommittee came to Bakersfield." They were presumably writing in Washington, but either the three, of one accord, situated themselves in Bakersfield to give their report perspective or the original ghost author was in fact writing in Bakersfield or somewhere else in California. Congressman Nixon especially had the skill to track down seemingly trivial slips of this kind, for he always sought to clarify each and every problem with documentary proof.[100]

Most important, the text of the Nixon-Morton-Steed document, Werdel's preface aside, nowhere said it was a report. Werdel had divided his text neatly. At the end of his own remarks he again identified the report and added: "It follows." Werdel did not pretend that his conclusions were a part of the report itself. If later DiGiorgio was to confuse the two, presenting them jointly in court exhibits and press releases as integral parts of a congressional subcommittee report, the fault was not Werdel's.

In the course of the Stockton trial the foundations of Werdel's rhetoric began to slip. Plant made a major effort to accredit the Appendix as a record of the official proceedings of the House and as such admissible as evidence. The effort could succeed only as it relied on ignorance, not on the law and custom of the House. Proceedings are only and exclusively what is taken down by the official reporters which by law "shall be printed in the *Congressional Record*."[101] Nothing is a proceeding, for legal purposes, which is not in some relation to the business before the legislature.[102] It is these rigid tests which have at times raised the issue of committee reports as official proceedings of the House and therefore of their right to constitutional privilege.[103]

But not even the strict definition of proceedings was enough to give the *Congressional Record* the credentials for admission to a court of law as evidence. This high privilege is reserved for the *Journal*, which by constitutional command must be kept both by the Senate and the House. The *Journal*, which records the acts but not the reasons and opinions behind them, is the official record of the proceedings. Extracts from the *Journal*, certified by the Clerk of the House, "shall be received in evidence in the Courts of the United States."[104]

Plant's Exhibit 20 met none of these requirements.

There were two other problems in the case. One was in reference to the 1953 agreement, which bound DiGiorgio to give thirty-day's notice to third parties who showed the film, such notice to be given through the 1950 union counsel, Gilbert, Nissen and Irvin. Plant introduced in evidence, anticipating this defense, the registered letter that Brobeck, Phleger and Harrison sent to Gilbert precisely on 18 May 1960, the day the Stockton suit was filed. The receipt for the letter showed that it was received in the Beverly Hills post office on May 20 at 6 P.M. Gilbert read the letter on the first available business day thereafter, May 22. The letter was in compliance with the terms of the agreement relating to notification, but that was as far as compliance went.

It will be recalled that Sanborn had stated in his release of May 18 that the Corporation had no recourse but to sue. Yet there was another choice.

Sanborn's release said that some of the alleged exhibitors of *Poverty* knew of the old agreement and judgment. Therefore, some were not aware of it. Smith bore this out in his Stockton testimony. The purpose of the agreement was to caution the uninformed, as well as to avoid unnecessary litigation in the future. The notice, had the Corporation waited for the thirty days to run their course, would have brought the whole matter with its many risks to the attention of the AWOC and the AFL-CIO. It would have compelled the National Agricultural Workers Union to demand from Smith the surrender of the UAW print of the film for destruction. It would have produced a demand from Gilbert and Nissen to the AWOC and its associates to desist from further showings and to deliver the film. The Hollywood Film Council would have been alerted to the danger of a repetition of the 1950 episode. These would have been effective pressures on Smith which he could not have ignored. The showings would have ceased and there would have been no lawsuit.

Brobeck's action in writing to Gilbert precisely on the day the suit was filed effectively prevented any of these things from happening. The justification offered was simple. According to Callan's investigation, Galarza and Mitchell were jointly responsible for the showings, and this disqualified them as third parties, making them instead joint tort feasors. Upon this ground Plant stood before Judge Buck against the arguments of Scully and Fransen. Judge Buck agreed and the appellate court did not consider the issue sufficiently important to discuss it in its decision.

Some important aspects of the matter were brushed aside. Sanborn had acknowledged that some of the defendants did not know of the 1950 settlement. This included Smith and his associates, the AFL-CIO, Krainnock, Tannehill and several other defendants. None of them could be sued for violation of an agreement to which they were not parties; nor could they be charged with contempt of a court order of 1950 in which they were not named and which did not exist. The only way to take advantage of the situation was to prevent the Hollywood Film Council, Flannery and other signers to the agreement from exercising their right of self protection under the thirty-day provision. On this score Brobeck could not contend that the agreement was no longer in effect on account of the showings, for it was in contemplation of such an eventuality that the agreement had been arrived at. By the act of sending the letter of May 18 Brobeck acknowledged that the agreement was still in effect. By preventing the agreement from operating as to Flannery and the Hollywood Film Council, the Corporation then found itself with no recourse but to sue for $2 million in damages.

The other aspect of the case that called for delicate handling was the issue of privilege under the Emde case. The rule here which Scully and Fransen tried in vain to invoke was the one of limited privilege to publicize the facts of a labor dispute. Had Plant designed his case consistently with Sanborn's press release, he would have had to roundly deny that there was any labor matter involved in the litigation, for that is what Sanborn had said. Plant chose an oblique response, allowing the issue to stand and giving the appellate court the opportunity to decide, in certain and precise language, that it was a labor question. The film was, as Plant himself had stated, part and parcel of a complete organizing campaign. In May 1960 Sanborn was already in the midst of a fray with the AWOC in Yuba and Marysville and the Corporation was spending funds to assure the farm workers their right to work in spite of Smith's pickets. Sanborn's disclaimer in the release was offered to the public with a straight face, but the facts gave the lawsuit and the release an inconsistent twist.

DiGiorgio's friends in agribusiness volunteered to explain the point even more clearly. The *News Letter* of the Council of California Growers said in its issue 17 November 1961: "If a judgment is awarded DiGiorgio Fruit Corporation in this case it could mean the final blow to AWOC's already tottering efforts to stay on its feet. It could also effectively prevent any attempted comeback of the AWOC organizing attempts by tieing up future assets the group might be able to come up with." On 8 July 1963 the Council reported: "So now DiGiorgio is awaiting receipt of a check for $60,000 plus interest of 7 per cent dating back from the time of the original judgment to the date the check is actually written."

The practical observations of the Council diverted attention from the contradictions and inconsistencies of the DiGiorgio strategy. The inconsistencies of Brobeck's line of attack passed unnoticed. Plant scorned Smith for failing to visit DiGiorgio Farms in 1960 to see for himself, while introducing as evidence the testimony of Morton who, back in 1949, failed to join the subcommittee whose report he was to sponsor with his name, or to visit the ranch about whose operation he was to publish such positive opinions.

With the judgment and appeal in hand, the Corporation received substantial advantages other than the $60,000 check, plus interest. *Poverty* was now doubly dead. Two organizing drives, ten years apart, had been demolished. A congressional report of obscure origin and modest literary merit had now been raised to the category of an official congressional subcommittee report. The reprint continued available in quantity ready for discreet distribution where it would embarrass union organizers. The Extension was well on the way to becoming an ancient document, defined in the law as "a writing more than thirty years old" by reason of the fact that "the same has since been generally acted on as genuine by persons having an interest in the question."[105]

Now the multiple uses of the Nixon-Morton-Steed report were more obvious. These were: judicial, in that it was a finding upon matters of fact and of law as to the guilt of notorious persons identified with the labor movement; evidential, in that it proved the fraudulence of their works; juridical, in that it ruled upon its own credibility and allowed its own admission as evidence; adversary, in that it pleaded the case for the Corporation and against the union; legislative, in that it clothed itself with all the prestige of a deliberative action of Congress; inquisitional, in that it was a sentence pronounced after a thorough investigation and study by a subcommittee of the House; publicitarian, in that it was always certain to gain widespread attention in the press; constitutional, in that it uncovered a perversion of the processes of the Congress; and prophetic, in that it intimated that Congress would never abandon the agricultural industry to the rapacity of farm workers by granting them the protection of Federal law.

Such was the Corporation's workable web at the termination of the Stockton lawsuit in July 1963. It must now be considered in the wider context of libel direct through the medium of a motion picture film with synchronized sound.

NOTES

86. Complaint for libel. *DiGiorgio Fruit Corporation v. American Federation of Labor et al.* Number 72635, par. VII.
87. Declaration in opposition to demurrer. Complaint for libel Number 72635. Stockton, Calif. 22 November 1960.
88. Partial transcript of proceedings. Stockton, Calif. Complaint number 72635. Testimony of Emmet Lucey, p. 19. Hereafter cited as Partial transcript of proceedings, Complaint number 72635.
89. Partial transcript of proceedings. Complaint number 72635, p. 208.
90. *Bakersfield Californian.* 16 December 1947.
91. Partial transcript of proceedings. Complaint number 72635, p. 77.
92. *Advance California Appellate Reports.* 14 May 1963, p. 636.
93. *Lyon v. Fairweather.* 63 CA 194; *Houston v. Interstate Circuit.* 132 SW 2d, 906; 53 CJS 50.
94. *Advance California Appellate Reports.* Cited above, p. 641.

95. *Words and Phrases.* West Publishing Company. 1940 edition. Vol. 4, p. 268: Miller v. State. 99 SW 533.
96. *American Digest System.* 1956–1966. Seventh Decennial Digest, Number 21, p. 684.
97. *Advance California Appellate Reports,* cited above, pp. 641–642.
98. *Emde v. San Joaquin County Central Labor Council.* 23 Cal. 2d., 146.
99. *Advance California Appellate Reports,* cited above, p. 632.
100. Nixon. *Six Crises,* p. 43.
101. Hinds's *Precedents of the House.* Vol. VI, section 635; *Congressional Record.* 2 July 1968, p. 636: *U.S. Code* annotated. Title 44, section 82-a.
102. *Prosser on Torts.* 1941 edition, p. 828.
103. Nelson. *Libel in the News,* p. 69.
104. *Jefferson's Manual and Rules of the House of Representatives.* 81st Congress, section 582.
105. 18 Cal Jur 2d., section 214.

7

LIBEL THROUGH
THE CAMERA'S EYE

By the time the appellate decision was handed down on 30 April 1963, closing the case of *DiGiorgio Fruit Corporation v. American Federation of Labor, et al.,* the long-standing Union-Corporation conflict had shifted its center. It was now a contest in the courts renewed periodically in lawsuits for libel. But these were not lawsuits to be decided on the basis of traditional rules of defamation by word of mouth or printed words. To the nebulous legal concepts of that tradition there were now added the unprecedented subtleties of libel by motion pictures with a sound track of words. Rules of law on this novel type of defamation were few, and these were still evolving, when *DiGiorgio v. Norman Smith, et al.,* was first filed.

There appear to be four classes of human speech: cognitive, the language of identification, which names the world in which mankind lives; pragmatic, the language of control and manipulation of that world; esthetic, which adds the passionate dimensions of fancy and longing; and therapeutic, the words that relieve the inner turmoils of the ego that must justify itself to itself or disintegrate.[106]

Defamation belongs in the last of these classifications and has probably characterized the behavior of men since they progressed from grunts to syntax. To feel and then to think thence to say and eventually to write nasty things about another marked a psychological evolution apparently as necessary to the human species as the discovery and use of tools and weapons. Prosser, writing on libel, sounded these ancestral depths in his observation that libel is "in the same class with the use of explosives and the keeping of dangerous animals"; for man is a dangerous animal as prone to explode in words as in bombs.

In the tradition of the Hebrews and Christians of the Western world the religious moral codes catalogued the loose tongue among the standing evils in society. The migrant Jews of Exodus received the law that "Thou shalt not raise a false report." They found it even in the latter days of the prophets a hard rule to follow. Job, in his apocalyptic debate with God, in spite of great provocation, still "did not sin with his lips." But he was hardly into the first verse of the third chapter when he "opened his mouth." He then prophesied obliquely the centuries of scandalous writings to come with his cry "Oh, that mine adversary had written a book."

It only remained for the western tradition to cross the English channel and after the fifteenth century to go through the refinements of the common law that drew the distinctions between slander and libel. The Christian dogma and the ecclesiastical courts lost jurisdiction over defamation as a sin to the King's judges who held it a tort. The book that Job had longed for became the libel, from *libellus,* a small writing, *libelo.* By the time of the Grand Abridgment of 1675, as reported by Potter in the *Historical Introduction to the Common Law,* libel had legally become "a scandalous writing or act."[107] Thereafter men who loosed their tongues in scandalmongering did not have them torn out, as had been the custom among the Anglo-Saxons and Germans. Punishment was tempered but the vice did not abate. At regular intervals trials like that of the Seven Bishops, Peter Zenger and Thomas Cooper turned words into spears. And the very air in the time of Alexander Pope must have been polluted by something more poisonous than smog; of eighteenth-century London he said, "At every breath a reputation dies."

It was into this never-ending cold war that jurisprudence moved. Its efforts, Pollock observed, were fertile in litigation and perplexed with minute and barren distinctions. Out of them nonetheless emerged the statutes, approved rules and accepted wisdom that govern libel law today.

Law of Libel. / The laws, cases and the dicta of the courts reflect the time, place, circumstances and mores of incessant social change. There was a time when to call a man a communist was not libelous, but around the time of Joseph McCarthy it became an actionable offense in some jurisdictions. There will eventually come a time when it will be such no longer. In the United States some two hundred expressions have been listed as grievously defamatory, such as saying that a man attempted suicide or that a preacher is a drunkard. To say that a woman is a cocotte is not actionable for it may mean that she is either a prostitute or a poached egg, and a technique for telling the difference to a certainty has not been found. The basic question is: What is the effect upon any respectable, substantial part of the community to which the statement was addressed?[108] If a noticeable part of those who read a statement think less of the person alluded to, it is defamation.[109]

Slander, the minor form of defamation, is defined as a false and unprivileged publication, orally uttered.[110] To establish the basis for a suit, the aggrieved party must prove that the precise words were said, and said publicly.

Gutenberg extended enormously the range of malevolent writings and therewith the seriousness of libel, but it lost ground with the invention and use of radio broadcasting. In *Griegorieff v. Winchell* (1943) it was held that words spoken over the air were libel and not slander even if they were read from a written script which the audience did not see.[111] Later, some of the lost ground was recovered with the amendment of Section 46 of the California Civil Code to read that an oral utterance, when communicated by radio is, after all, only slander.

While slander was held to be what is maliciously, untruthfully and damagingly conveyed by the sense of hearing, libel was received by the sense of sight. The reason, according to Justice Cardozo, was that "the spoken word dissolves, but the written one abides and perpetuates the scandal."[112] The written word becomes fixed, as in the language of Section 45 of the Civil Code of California: "Libel is a false and unprivileged publication by writing, printing, effigy or other fixed representation to the eye." The "writing" may be in the form of words, signs, hieroglyphs, caricatures, cartoons or pictures. The effect must be to expose any person to hatred, contempt, ridicule or other manifestations of social downgrading.

Just as defamation branches into slander and libel, so libel divides into libel *per se,* expressions which are bald, obvious and self-proclaiming, necessarily apparent, and offensive at first sight, in short, libel direct; and libel *per quod,* meaning expressions of

opprobrium which require props, explanations, extrinsic circumstances, refreshers, illustration from other sources, amplifications
and dressings of meaning to make them recognizable; in short, libel
indirect.

Libel indirect must bring its own witnesses into court. These are
inducement, innuendo and colloquium which, like three layers of
circumstance surrounding a scurrilous statement, must be peeled
off one by one until the sting or gist of the libel is bared. Inducement is the proof of the facts which in the first place gave rise to
the litigation. Innuendo is the evidence that the words spoken in
relation to those facts were understood to mean something oppro-
brious, malignant, scandalous and socially harmful. Colloquium is
the evidence that the words were spoken of and about the plaintiff
in the suit.[113] Two instances, one imaginary and one factual, will
illustrate the offices of inducement, innuendo and colloquium.

In a fictitious lawsuit it is proved by inducement that Citizen
Doe owns a house in an otherwise respectable neighborhood. The
house is allegedly not a home, and it is established by innuendo that
the reputed assignations which take place on the premises are
viewed with great revulsion by the respectable community. It is
further proved by colloquium that words said about a supposed
sleeping partner of the Madame in charge of the house refer to
Citizen Doe. The case for libel indirect is made.

Again, in an actual case, a corporation whose identity was
established by inducement was also known to be controlled by
Citizen Roe. By innuendo it was shown that certain alleged activities of the corporation and its owner were such as to constitute
reprehensible practices in business. By colloquium the owner of the
corporation was identified as Citizen Roe. This is a case of libel
indirect.[114]

Certain related rules must be noted.

In a libelous publication which contains both direct and indirect
defamation, the two must be clearly distinguished and separated.[115]

If libel indirect is pleaded by reason of the surrounding circumstances, the expression, the precise words, must be distinctly
alleged and proved.[116]

A libelous writing is liberally defined to include words, short-
hand notes, signs or pictures, provided that "what is so written is
intelligible to the reader."[117]

The media by which writings are conveyed include everything

upon which man may, and does,,leave his mark: newspaper stories, articles, letters, reports, signs, notices, headlines, captions, scrawls, graffiti, drawings and cartoons.

These are all fixed representations with which libel is concerned. With them the law has had little difficulty as physical evidence. If the basis of the complaint is a drawing or a picture accompanied by visible words, the two must be interpreted together.[118]

Libel law, being a part of the common law, evolved by the classical system of common law pleading. Preceding cases and their rules, which arose out of social conditions, customs and values that no longer prevail intact, are carefully selected by opposing lawyers to show that theirs is the contention endorsed by tradition and precedent. There is always a new order, however, working to displace the old, and as Gutenberg's invention had replaced the monastic scribes, radio broadcasters made the town crier obsolete, and Edison made still pictures move upon a screen simulating continuous motion.

There is a flaw in this progress which accounts for the pains and perplexities of the common law. As Justice Cardozo wrote, "When we get down to a sufficiently minute scale, everything really proceeds by jumps, like the cinema, which produces a misleading appearance of continuous motion by means of a succession of separate pictures." New cases, because they arise out of new conditions inexorably coming on, never correspond exactly to preceding ones. While opposing counsel must pretend that they do, judges are set up to dispel this illusion. There are gaps of analogy and reasoning, and it is in these gaps that judges must decide. Their instrument is reason, with which they take the old standards and mold them to new combinations of events and of values. Whether their reasoning is truly reasonable is a question that has troubled keen legal minds. What many lay litigants refer to as hair-splitting is to lawyers and judges the process of organizing and interpreting the law to give society a flexible but orderly legal structure. "Peculiar in method, and sometimes of almost barbarous logic, or casuistry, the judges have hammered out a system designed to meet their day and hour." Tort law is well named; it is from the Latin *tortus*, "tortuous, crooked." Defamation is part of tort law, and its path was made neither easier nor straighter when there appeared cases concerning

Libel by Motion Pictures with Sound. / In 1848 Charles Darwin, while pondering the evidence of biologic gradation, linked the thoughts of Peter Mark Roget in 1824, on the persistence of vision with regard to moving objects, with the 1861 invention of the kinematoscope. Darwin observed in the *Origin of Species* that "differences blend into each other by an insensible series, and a series impresses the mind with the idea of an actual passage." In 1872 Leland Stanford set his technicians to a crude experiment with fixed cameras that produced the idea of actual passage by racing horses. Edison toyed seriously with his peep shows and finally in 1903 *The Great Train Robbery* opened the era of the "flickers." These rapidly became the "movies" of the 1910s, which passed thousands of still pictures on celluloid before the human eye at the rate of 24 frames per second. In 1926 *Don Juan* was screened with a sound track synchronized to the continuous motion and was the first commercial "sound movie" of the age.

The revolution in communications thus completed now presented the law of libel with one of those gaps of which Justice Cardozo had spoken. It was not a small one. The rules and precedents on libel direct, libel indirect, inducement, innuendo and colloquium were firmly based on the simple fact that the libelous message was received by sight. Now libel became an instantaneous blend of visual images and word sounds, the images being not a fixed representation to the eye but an illusion based upon the fact that the camera is faster than the optic nerve.

During the first half century of motion pictures there were fewer than a dozen cases that dealt with libel in its new technical context.

Merle v. Sociological Research Film Corporation was the first of them. In 1915 a documentary film was published which dealt with certain commercial aspects of prostitution. One of the scenes showed a factory building such as those in which procurers operated. Over the building there was a sign that prominently displayed the owner's name, August G. Merle. Ruling upon the "somewhat novel proceeding" the New York State courts held that defamatory motion pictures identified by words which were also projected visually were actionable.[119]

It was not until 1934 that the two leading cases on libel by motion pictures with words in sound were decided. By that time judges were striving to adapt the ancient rules of defamation in print to speaking pictures in motion. Justice Cardozo's observation that spoken words dissolve was no longer true. They were as permanent as the film and by projection could be repeated as often as the pictures themselves. Judge Learned Hand recognized this. After a visit to Hollywood he concluded that motion pictures were apt to be "tawdry beyond endurance, trite, dreary and childish." To this esthetic judgment he added a legal one, that "light and sound were instantaneously . . . made permanent upon a tiny celluloid strip," by what he called a magic process that converted them "into some other essence."[120]

In *Brown v. Paramount Publix Corporation,* decided in New York in 1934, the Merle rule that libel may be committed by sound motion pictures was reaffirmed. The majority of the appellate court also dealt with the old rule that required the exact setting forth of the libelous matter complained of. Focusing on the pictures rather than the words, the court said, "The mechanics of the production is cited merely to show the futility of asking that plaintiff in such action as this actually set forth in his complaint a detailed description of all the scenes projected on the screen and the mechanical sounds accompanying them, be they words or otherwise."[121]

By this decision two important principles made their way into the law of libel: one, that in an action based on a sound motion picture words as the spoken medium of slander were assimilated to pictures as the visual medium of libel; two, that because of the manifest impossibility of setting forth visual scenes in a typewritten complaint, the words projected from the sound track need not be alleged verbatim.

In *Brown v. Paramount* Justice McNamara submitted an interesting dissent. Possibly with the Merle case in mind, he pointed out that no language had been shown on the film, that is to say, no words flashed on the screen to be seen and not heard by the audience. The entire charge was based on libelous matter in images which portrayed, depicted or gave appearance to the subject. "If language is made the basis of libel it must be pleaded," he argued. This was a plea to dissolve into precise components the "essence" that lurked, according to Judge Hand, in the melding of sound and image. While it was impossible to set forth in pleadings hundreds of pictured scenes, it was not impossible to set forth the precise words accompanying those scenes.

At the time that *Brown v. Paramount* was being decided, in England a special tribunal for libel cases was hearing *Youssoupoff v. Metro-Goldwyn-Mayer*.[122] Princess Youssoupoff sued the studios on the basis of certain scenes in a production on the death of the Russian monk Rasputin. Lord Justice Slesser held for the court that the photographic part of the film was indeed a permanent matter to be seen by the eye and actionable for libel if defamatory. The defamation in this case rested on the spoken and not the pictured matter. The court was perplexed; "This action," wrote the Lord Justice, "is one of libel and raises at the outset an interesting and difficult problem which, I believe, to be a novel problem, whether the product of the combined photographic and talking instrument which produces these modern films does, if it throws upon the screen and impresses upon the ear defamatory matter, produce that which may be complained of as libel or slander." The decision was for libel and the reasoning as follows: "I regard the speech which is synchronized with the photographic reproduction and forms part of one complex, common exhibition as an ancillary circumstance, part of the surroundings explaining that which is to be seen . . . and therefor properly a part of the libel."

A number of important elements are to be noted in the decision and the logic supporting it. The court did not say but very strongly inferred, by placing the defamation in the spoken words, that the pictures by themselves if screened without sound, would not have been defamatory. Further, if no distinction was made between libel direct and libel indirect, *per se* or *per quod,* the Lord Justice appeared to be saying that it was a case of libel indirect, since the pictures required surroundings and ancillary circumstances to give them meaning. Inducement, innuendo and colloquium were involved in the implications of the decision. There is no record that the court called for a written text of the narration, the words on the sound track, to verify by reading what it had heard when it saw the film.

Between the Brown and Youssoupoff decisions of 1934 and the DiGiorgio decision of 1963, legal contests over alleged libel by sound motion pictures were rare. *Warner Brothers v. Stanley* (1937) involved the publication in book form of the script of a film where the original publication was held to have occurred in the book and not in the film. Out of Warner came a significant application to a motion picture of the old rule of libel by writings. This rule held that the plaintiff must show "what impression it made on those who saw and heard it."[123]

In *Blake v. Hearst Publications* (1946) the meaning of the pictures was plainly derived from the accompanying text, suggesting again the doubtfulness of libel by pictures alone. Again, in *Kelly v. Loew's, Inc.* (1948) the central issue was the publication of a book based on a film, the exhibition being in the nature of a re-publication. Nothing significant was added in this field of defamation by *Stillman v. Paramount Pictures Corporation* (1959) or by *Felix Youssoupoff v. Columbia Broadcasting System, Inc.* (1965). The prince sued for invasion of privacy after the film *If I Should Die,* based on the Rasputin theme, was televised. Scholars who combed the legal inventories of libel actions between the *Great Train Robbery* of 1903 and the Youssoupoff of 1965 reported fewer than a dozen cases worthy of comment.[124]

It was upon these lean precedents that Prosser was able to base his conclusion that the courts "have found no difficulty in holding that the sound in a talking picture is libel, since it accompanies and is identified with the film itself." If the courts in more than half a century of litigation had not resolved this and other difficulties, it was not because they had not been pointed out. Chief Justice Slesser suggested one—that the locus of defamation could be in the words used and not in the pictures. Sir William Jowitt, defense counsel in the first Youssoupoff case, argued for assimilating the pictures to the words, which would have made it a case of slander and not of libel. Justice McNamara's dissent turned upon the interesting dilemma: the complaint was based upon the photographic portion of the film but the defamation was attributed to the spoken words. *Kelly v. Loew's Inc.* produced a printed text of the narrative, adding a third element to the mix of pictured scenes and spoken words.

This was, in sum, the situation when *DiGiorgio v. Norman Smith et al.* came to trial in 1961 and to appeal in 1963. There were questions to which the old precedents of libel by writings and the few of libel by sound motion pictures were to be applied; these questions were as follows:

1. May an action for libel be grounded on a silent film from which no words, legends, signs or other verbal writings are pro-

jected on the screen that describe, explain and identify places and persons?

2. If, in a case of libel by sound motion pictures, the defamation is declared to be in the sounds of the words and not in the pictures, can there be any defamation in the pictures themselves, considered as a fixed representation to the eye and not the ear?

3. If, in a case of libel by sound motion picture, the sounds of the words carry the defamation and the silent pictures do not, may a judgment be based upon the innocent rather than upon the culpable portion of the exhibition?

4. If, in a case of libel by sound motion picture, the printed text of the narrative appears in evidence, is such a text also an integral part of the exhibition, or is it auxiliary and explanatory matter, extrinsic to the film itself?

5. If, in a suit for libel by sound motion picture, there is no defamatory matter found in the silent pictures, and no direct libel in the text of the narrative, may a judgment of libel direct be based upon a combination of two elements neither of which sets forth libel directly?

6. If, in a suit for libel by sound motion picture, plaintiff alleges the obvious impossibility of setting forth in the complaint the scenes depicted in the film, may his plea be allowed also with respect to the spoken words which can just as obviously be set forth in exact form from the script of the narration?

7. In a suit for libel by sound motion picture, is the film similar or identical to a literary article, within the legal definition of this term?

When DiGiorgio and the AWOC faced each other in Judge Buck's courtroom these questions hovered in the background of the case. To have brought them to the fore would have posed difficulties. The complexities of defamation by sound motion pictures would have put judicial logic to the test of the questions raised above.

Neither the Stockton trial nor the subsequent appeal threw any light on these questions. Brobeck cited to the courts none of the theories of Merle, Youssoupoff and the other cases of record and the courts did not put their judicial logic to these theories. Between Merle (1915) and DiGiorgio (1963) was a large gap that would have stretched even Cardozo's mind to its remarkable limits, but in *DiGiorgio v. Norman Smith, et al.,* it was filled with an "article."

Nevertheless the proceedings, trial and appellate, in *DiGiorgio v. Norman Smith* did permit a closer look at

The Failing Web. / DiGiorgio's complaint against Norman Smith, the AWOC and other parties was based on the alleged violation of Section 45 of the California Civil Code. The libel was thereby attributed to a "fixed representation to the eye," a "writing" which in this case was a sequence of thousands of still pictures projected from a celluloid film. The cause of the defamation, in keeping with the ancient rule, was in the visual images of these pictures, received through the sense of sight.

It was, moreover, an action in libel *per se,* libel not requiring auxiliary explanations, in short, libel direct. It was charged that the film imputed certain crimes to the Corporation, this being sufficient grounds under the statute to classify the offense as libel direct.

On these legal premises Attorney Marion Plant based his list of some fifteen charges of defamation, beginning with the denial by the Corporation to its employees of certain rights enjoyed by other American workers, and ending with the smuggling of Mexicans across the border in collusion with headhunters.

Plant's case was remarkable in two respects. It did not cite a single case of libel by motion pictures with sound track; and as to all the charges listed, a settled rule was invoked for only one of them, the rule that an untruthful charge against a corporation of not providing habitable housing was actionable. By the first omission Plant avoided the perplexities that had troubled Lord Justice Slesser and Justice McNamara. He was also using the simpler guidelines of libel by means of articles, newspaper stories, letters and the like.

The choice of the attorney was the dilemma of the Bench. Judge Schottky and his two colleagues, though repeatedly stating in the appellate decision that they were dealing with a case of libel by sound motion pictures, reverted to the precedent of "an article libelous on its face."[125] They had before them no precedent of a "fixed representation to the eye" in the form of motion pictures having been held libel direct.

By the second omission Plant proposed to extend the catalogue of words punishable by the courts when said of a corporation. He offered over a dozen of these amendments and they were ap-

proved by the trial and the appellate courts. Henceforth, for
example, it would be defamatory to say that a corporation did not
provide medical services or that it provided no compensation for
injury or loss of limb.

Paragraph VII of DiGiorgio's complaint filed in Stockton in
May 1960 read:

> Because the words, sounds and pictures are contained on a
> motion picture film and sound track, and are inextricably con-
> nected and interdependent for their meaning and effect, it is
> impossible to set them out in this complaint.

This, it will be recalled, was the exact wording of the 1949 complaint by which Brobeck had succeeded in avoiding the require-
ment of setting forth specifically defamatory language. What Judge
Hand had adumbrated as a new and undefinable and magic essence Plant had reduced to a mix of words, sounds and pictures
that could not be unscrambled. Once the mix was accepted by the
courts as the central theory of the complaint it became a central
point from which all the other elements of the case evolved. The
appellate court noted that it "saw and heard" the film; the evidence
it found was indissolubly combined "in said film and sound track,"
and "everything said and depicted" in the "representations."

The legal locus of the defamation was in the "fixed representation to the eye," in the pictures themselves, since they were libelous directly. But by the theory of paragraph VII it was now
impossible to set them forth, first because they were visual images
untransferable to type, and second, because they were inextricably
mixed with the sounds of words.

The components of the mix were not as inseparable as Brobeck
had held them to be. The film could have been screened without
sound and stopped at any frame for close examination. It could
then have been judged whether the pictures alone, still or moving,
showed the unmistakable marks of libel direct. Plant did not suggest this method and neither did the court. This would have
stopped the way Plant was steering the argument. His legal logic
was moving from precision toward diffusion: The direct libel could
be in the pictures as well as in the words; it could be in the words
only but explained and supported by the pictures; it could be in the
pictures only, but explained and supported by the words; or it

could be in neither words nor pictures taken singly but in both taken together.

Once Plant had the mind of the court firmly in control, he proceeded to do the impossible. He set forth, in quite specific language, that part of his mix which was contained in the sound track. It was now possible to proceed to the vital objective of the complaint. This was to establish that the only and exclusive target of the film was the DiGiorgio Fruit Corporation.

Plant aimed straight at it. "The sound film *Poverty in the Valley of Plenty*," he told the appellate court, was a defamation "purporting to depict the strike at DiGiorgio Farms" and "was leveled at respondent in particular." The court agreed. "The film," it said, "which purported to depict conditions at DiGiorgio Farms" held up respondent "as the specific target" of its accusations. The objections made by Scully and Fransen were in vain.

This left no room whatever in the judicial awareness for the contrary contention that the film—especially those portions of the film singled out by Plant—was an accusation against an industry and not against an employer. Mitchell and Hasiwar had so testified in Washington and Bakersfield. The film was entitled *Poverty in the Valley* and not *Poverty on DiGiorgio Farms*. This was the theme of two-thirds of the documentary. Plant himself told the court that "The Union had searched the countryside for the most squalid, dilapidated shanties that could be found" and, as the film proved, found them in the heart of agribusinessland. The people who lived in them were not industrial but agricultural workers. Both courts found explicitly that these conditions did not exist at DiGiorgio and by inference that they did not exist anywhere. Since agribusiness was not a party to the suit it probably was deemed irrelevant to observe, as the evidence showed, that the conditions shown were true as to the agricultural industry.

What was missing in the findings of Judge Buck and the appellate decision was supplied by the spokesmen of agribusiness. In their minds there was no doubt as to the identity of the target. The *News Letter* of the Council of California Growers said on 8 July 1963: "The DiGiorgio Fruit Corporation fought and won a battle recently which might very well be of interest to all farmers in the State. . . . For their battle was fought not only to protect DiGiorgio's name and reputation . . . but that of every farmer

in California." There was no mistaking these views; they held
that the charges contained in the film were levelled straight at
the industry. And they had a respectable endorsement; Robert
DiGiorgio had told the subcommittee in Bakersfield that what he
called the film's gross, misleading, false and defamatory representations "discredit DiGiorgio Fruit Corporation and all the
farmers of Kern County. . . ."

It is to the credit of Plant's argument that conclusions so diamet-
rically opposed could be drawn from the same facts. Plant held in
his brief that Flannery "asserts" that DiGiorgio hired wetbacks
from headhunters. In the Werdel Extension appearing as Exhibit
20 at the trial there was this phrase: "In its motion picture *Poverty
in the Valley of Plenty* the union said. . . ." Plant's complaint
claimed false and defamatory "charges." The appellate decision
was guided by everything "said" and as well as depicted. It used
terms such as "statements," "remarks," "references" and "asserted." Now, these are functions of human speech and not of
fixed representations to the eye. What was said, asserted, stated or
remarked in *Poverty* could be verified in one of two ways—by
listening again to the spoken narrative or by examining the written
transcript of the words on the sound track.

Plant apparently intended to reinforce the first with the second.
He not only arranged to have the film screened in Stockton and
Sacramento; he also produced a printed text of Flannery's narration which was offered and received in evidence. Plant said to the
court: "I am going to offer in evidence . . . a transcript of the commentary in the film . . . correlated with the scenes . . . to identify
them . . . so when it comes to the court, the court will find it convenient to refresh his recollection of the film."[126] Plant knew that
what the eye racing after 24 pictures per second could not identify
as libel, the eye resting on typed words of the narration could.

This exhibit did more than refresh the recollection of the court.
It permitted a comparison of what Flannery had said, asserted,
stated and remarked with Plant's long list of libels. It now became
obvious that Flannery had not used the specific language with
which he was charged; nor had he made accusations against the
Corporation that agribusinessmen took as implicating themselves.
Put to this unexpected test, it became clear that in the sound track
Flannery did not say that the miserable hovels were on DiGiorgio

Farms, or that the DiGiorgio Fruit Corporation had smuggled and hired Wetbacks, or that it was the Corporation that collected $26 a month for shanties, or that the Corporation crowded nine or ten people into them.

This was not the whole of Plant's surprising exhibit, which had reposed in DiGiorgio's files since 1949, and which had not been produced for the benefit of the subcommittee in Bakersfield. The issue was now raised as to the legal effect of the printed narrative in the record. Plant had not offered it as an integral part of the film, but as a new and separate element of his case. He characterized it as a refresher but he entered it as evidence. Here he was maneuvering dangerously. Was the refresher also a qualifier, an explanation and a clarification as well? If so, inducement, innuendo and colloquium were coming into the case, bringing with them into Plant's perfect argument of libel direct the characteristics of libel indirect.

It had been stated long before in *Youssoupoff v. Metro-Goldwyn-Mayer* (1934) that the sounds accompanying the pictures were an ancillary circumstance and a part of the surroundings that helped to explain the meaning of the pictures themselves. The English court had gone further and placed the defamation in the sound track.

This was serious. If the libel was in the pictures themselves the defamation was in a fixed representation to the eye and the libel was direct, *per se*. If it could be located only with the assistance of inducement, innuendo and colloquium, then the case was one for the rules of libel indirect, *per quod*. In the latter event Plant's case was ruined and he would be out of court.

But ruin did not overtake him; the courts did not attach importance to the vigorous arguments that Scully and Fransen made along these lines.

Plant had overcome with confidence other hazards in this connection. Nixon, Morton and Steed in their report had drawn the meaning and intention of the film from "unmistakable innuendos." They added, "The film insinuated that the corporation had engaged" in smuggling aliens. At the Bakersfield hearings Nixon had collected not specific words but implications from *Poverty*.[127] Plant, with unusual dash, even quoted from the report the passage about "innuendos." Werdel had gone further. In his prefatory remarks he asserted the libelous nature of the film, and declared it a fraudulent falsehood. His testimony, too, was before the court as part of Exhibit 20.

Innuendo had come and colloquium followed closely behind, bringing the question: Who is it talking about? The Nixon, Morton and Steed report gave colloquium a hand when it stated "No one can doubt that these charges are levelled straight at the corporation." These words, too, as part of the Extension, were before the court as evidence among Plant's exhibits.

The way in which Nixon, Morton and Steed testified to these matters and others was also worth noting. Their testimony appeared in the text of Exhibit 20. Plant offered it with the explanation that it was to be taken as evidence, not of the truth of what was said in it but merely for the fact that the subcommittee had held hearings and that these had been printed in the *Congressional Record*. The exhibit soon broke through this limitation. It was quoted by Plant and by the court for the truth of what Nixon, Morton and Steed had reported. They became witnesses as to facts by way of a printed paper, beyond the reach of cross-examination.

This was a distinct advantage to the plaintiff. As has been shown, there were numerous untruths as to facts in the text of their report.* Since Morton was not in Bakersfield his confident testimony was pure hearsay. Nixon weakened his charge that the accusations relating to poor housing were levelled straight at the

---

*Some of the more glaring misstatements contained in the Nixon-Morton-Steed report excerpted from the text were: "That the Union had "no grievances"; that "the Union film was also shown to the committee in Washington on March 16, 1949"; that it was "the committee's belief in truth (of the film)" that induced it "to authorize and instruct this Subcommittee to investigate the facts"; that "the education director and western representative of the union insist that the film is a true picture of the DiGiorgio Farms"; that "wages are not a grievance or a strike issue"; that on the first day of the strike "a majority of the employees . . . continued to work"; that "the hearings and investigation were held at the request of the National Farm Labor Union"; that there were "no pickets"; and that "the evidence shows that a strike of any serious proportions in agriculture would choke off interstate commerce." There was no support for any of these misrepresentations in the official record of the evidence.

Corporation by admitting that "it did not say so." Fransen and Scully were confronted by three paper witnesses who could not be questioned.

In sum, the mix upon which Plant had staked his case remained inextricably and impossibly confounded. On close examination the web was beginning to come loose, but it still had a strong hold. As long as it held it provided a striking illustration of an idea propounded by the late Thomas Reed Powell: "If you think you can think about a thing inextricably attached to something else without thinking of the thing which it is attached to, you have a legal mind."

The outcome of the Stockton case surely proved that this is a useful skill in winning damages for libel. DiGiorgio's pursuit of the AWOC had come through by virtue of it. As a defense it was not to be so fortunate again. With four lawsuits behind him and five still to come, Plaintiff DiGiorgio was about to become Defendant DiGiorgio.

NOTES

106. Adapted from Henry S. Leonard, *Principles of Reasoning*, p. 116.
107. Fourth edition. London. 1962, p. 436.
108. *Kelly v. Loew's Inc.*, 76 Fed. Sup., 486.
109. 53 CJS 58.
110. Ibid.
111. *California Civil Code*. 1961. Section 46.
112. *Ostrowe v. Lee*, opinion by Justice Benjamin N. Cardozo, 175 NE 505.
113. *Prosser on Torts*. 1941 edition, p. 790.
114. *Brayton v. Crowell-Collier Publishing Company*. 205 Fed. 2d., 644.
115. *Fleming v. Albeck*, 67 Cal 226.
116. *Kingsbury v. Bradstreet*. 116 NY 211.
117. 53 CJS 33.
118. *Blake v. Hearst Publications*. 75 CA 2d., 6: Ostrowe v. Lee, cited above.

119. *Merle v. Sociological Research Film Corporation.* 152 NYS 831.
120. Hand. *The Spirit of Liberty,* p. 113.
121. *Brown v. Paramount Publix Corporation.* 270 NY Sup. 547.
122. *Youssoupoff v. Metro-Goldwyn-Mayer.* 99 ALR 865.
123. *Warner Brothers v. Stanley.* 192 SE 1311.
124. Information provided by Law Library, University of California at Los Angeles. 30 July 1968; Hartman. *Motion Picture Law Digest;* Lindley. *Entertainment, publishing and the Arts,* p. 314.
125. *Advance California Appellate Reports,* cited above, p. 641.
126. Trial transcript. Civil 10522. Third Appellate District, p. 79.
127. *Hearings.* Bakersfield 12–13 November 1949, p. 656.

PART THREE

8

THE PERILS
OF A PRESS RELEASE

The courts in which libel litigation is heard do not carve, as they undoubetdly should, an interrogatory over their portals: "Is this lawsuit necessary?" It would invite plaintiffs seething with indignation or wounded pride and little else to pause momentarily for ego identification. They might then consider that in the little purgatories they were about to enter the object is justice and not therapy. For those who could understand and accept the difference in time and draw back, a grateful and compassionate society would provide free and commodious treatment in a defamatorium. In such a place the trauma of defamation could be eased if not cured. The treatment might consist of complete freedom to shout the vilest obscenities against the putative libeler and to scrawl cartoons, outrageous symbols and other fixed representations to the eye on blank walls. Whatever was said and done within these walls would be, as in the chamber of the House of Representatives, absolutely privileged. The administration of justice would be speedier and less costly, leaving citizens at peace, not only with one another, but what is more important with their own minds.

This touch of fantasy is suggested by the emotional background of the Corporation's press release of 18 May 1960 and the events that were to pursue it during the next eight years. When word reached the executives of the DiGiorgio Fruit Corporation of Norman Smith's showings of *Poverty,* they were, to put it mildly, aroused. Dungan, the Corporation's chief complaint writer, testified that "the people were deeply shocked and deeply indignant and deeply wounded that anybody would say things about their company which were as false and vicious as the statements in this

film are."[128] Corporate wounds and shock are not a legal cause
of action; damage to business reputation is and, if proved, gives
grounds for punishment. But the wounds and the shock and the
indignation, as the testimony showed, remained the passionate
drive of the next contest in the courts. That it was a drive
accounts for the Corporation's lack of heed to the advice given
Mr. Peter Wright when he was sued by the Gladstone brothers:
"When one writes with indignation one should take care to write
the exact truth."

The Corporation was in a hurry. It knew that the AWOC was
conducting an ambitious and well-financed organizing drive on its
home grounds. Smith was adding insult to injury calling agribusinessmen "robber barons," DiGiorgio included. The company, Sanborn felt, must be protected from further damage to its feelings and
its business "as expeditiously as possible." On May 10 DiGiorgio
read of the showing of the film. On May 13 its investigator, Callan,
verified that the film was *Poverty*. On or about May 15 the decision
to sue was made. On or about May 16 a complaint for libel was
ready. On May 17 a press release was prepared; and on May 18 the
complaint was filed.

When the case was re-filed in September, two different chains of
events were set in motion. In Stockton and Sacramento Smith and
his associates were declared guilty and punished, the consequence
of the complaint. In San Francisco attorney James Murray and
Ernesto Galarza had reread with astonishment the contents of the
May 18 press release. The scissors-and-paste quality of the text
impressed them as they continued to study it from May to September. DeWitt Tannehill was not, as the release stated, assistant director of the AWOC. There was no court order prohibiting the reissue
of the film. Quotations from Werdel's prefatory remarks were
included as if taken from the Nixon-Morton-Steed report. There
was never a report that had been submitted in November 1949.
Neither Mitchell nor Galarza had ever shown the film again after
1950. The 1950 agreement was mentioned but not the obligation of
the Corporation to give a thirty-day notice before suing third parties.

On the face of it the release indicated the need for swift action
rather than for careful research and deliberation. The AWOC had
already threatened the cherry crop and was moving on peaches,
pears, grapes and tomatoes, all of them multimillion dollar "deals."

A sharp counterthrust was needed and that without delay. In 1950 a $2 million lawsuit had helped importantly to bring an end to a labor organizing campaign, banish the pickets, humiliate the California labor movement, and discredit the farm labor union leadership. The Stockton case proved that, for the second time, the Corporation's estimate of the situation was correct. In 1960, however, there was a vital difference. The application of the thirty-day notice provision had to be avoided, for it was in effect an alternative to a lawsuit. However, time was of the essence and the Corporation's strategy reduced it to one week during which it got Callan to Woodlake, drafted a complaint, issued a press release and started a lawsuit.

There was another advantage to be gained by these quick moves. They enabled the Corporation to join Galarza in a legal action which could find him guilty of contempt of court, bad faith and being a recidivist in libel. It was a promising opportunity to conclusively discredit the NAWU.

In the hurry there was little time to weigh other considerations, among them how Galarza might react to the charges in the complaint and particularly those in the press release. This defendant was in some respects in a worse position than Smith and his associates. He, and not the others, was accused of failure to perform the terms of an agreement and of deliberately flouting (the press release said "flaunting") a court order. Against him and Mitchell in particular were again arrayed the indictments published by Werdel, Nixon, Morton and Steed. Among these was the charge of perversion of the constitutional processes of Congress, not precisely an accusation of treason but faintly suggesting it. Since 1950 a reprint containing these indictments had been kept in circulation by DiGiorgio through the years among important government officials and others. The charges stood to be approved by the courts as admissible evidence and judged by them to be true testimony. As Galarza gave thought to these matters Murray proceeded to instruct the Corporation and its attorneys on the unfortunate misstatements and contradictions in the press release. The short educational course was tendered at no cost to DiGiorgio on the supposition that upon discovering the truth, the Corporation would publicly disavow those portions of the release and dismiss Galarza from the suit.

On September 13 DiGiorgio dismissed its complaint against
Galarza and Mitchell, thus avoiding the chance that Murray's
motion for summary judgment would be granted and a judicial
declaration entered against the Corporation. A rebuff by the Court
would have been damaging on the record and possibly newsworthy.
The Corporation did not retract, apologize or explain. Its attorneys
issued a perfunctory statement to the press that Galarza had not,
after all, participated in the showings of the film. On September 15
Murray initiated the fifth in the series of actions:

Complaint for Libel—the Fifth /   No. 503735
    In the Superior Court of the State of California
    in and for the County of San Francisco
    Ernesto Galarza, Plaintiff,
    v.
    DiGiorgio Fruit Corporation, a Corporation
    Robert DiGiorgio, Bruce W. Sanborn, et al.
    Filed 15 September 1960.

The matters complained of were two. The Corporation had
published "to news agencies and divers other persons" false,
defamatory and unprivileged statements in the form of a fixed
representation to the eye. This was pleaded as libel direct. The
Corporation had also instituted a lawsuit against Galarza without
sufficient grounds. This was pleaded as malicious prosecution.

As to the libel, it was alleged that "the press release did intend
to mean that plaintiff was untruthfully and maliciously charged with
dishonoring a ten-year-old agreement, flouting a court order, breaking a promise not to show the film again, compounding bad faith
and violating the Corporation's right to a good reputation. The
prayer was for $1 million general and $1 million punitive damages.

To a client a case sinks out of sight immediately after the filing
of the complaint. The pleadings that follow are hidden from his
view, not deliberately but because they move through labyrinths of
procedure familiar only to the initiated in the law. They are precisely laid down in the statutes and more inaccessible to a layman's
ignorance than the law upon which he bases his claims. Pleadings
move tortuously and slowly to the despair of every client. Milton's
line about those who only stand and wait is an exact description of
a litigant.

In their pleadings Brobeck, Phleger and Harrison shaped their defense. They invoked privilege in that the press release was a fair and true report of official proceedings in a court of law and in Congress. Plaintiff Galarza was blamed for the embarrassing turn of events on the grounds that he had concealed his resignation from the AWOC early in 1960. The defense affirmed that the agreement of 1950 and the confession of judgment had to be construed together making a violation of one a violation of both. The DiGiorgio Corporation also had acted only after consultation with its attorneys and not out of shock or indignation. Finally the defense said that the Corporation was entitled to the privilege of free speech in the release under the doctrine of limited protection for such speech in the course of a labor dispute.

Murray had no difficulty with these arguments. Whether or not something printed in the Appendix of the *Congressional Record* was a true report of House proceedings was not here a central issue. From Brobeck's own arguments Murray obtained the answer to the charge of concealment, for Brobeck had also pleaded that Galarza's affiliation with the AWOC as of May 18 was "a matter of common knowledge." The joint construction of the agreement and judgment was even less impressive, for there was no injunction that the film could not be shown again. As to the limited privilege of free speech in the course of a labor dispute, Sanborn himself had said in the press release that "there is no labor question involved." In Stockton Smith invoked this rule with no success whatever; in San Francisco DiGiorgio raised it as a shield, with equally poor luck.

Brobeck then took another tack. On behalf of DiGiorgio, a request was made for change of venue which if granted would move the trial to Bakersfield. Among the reasons advanced for this were the usual ones of the convenience of the witnesses the Corporation expected to call and the proximity of the scenes of 1948. Brobeck expected to exhibit *Poverty* in court on the ground that "the film is critical to the present litigation." With a jury of Special Citizens in Kern County the odds for the defendant were bound to rise. There was a touch of morbidity in this attempt to bring *Poverty* for the second time in a lawsuit. This was prevented by Murray's vigorous resistance to the motion, and it was denied.

On 10 June 1963, when the case was deep in thirty-three months of pleadings, DiGiorgio substituted attorneys. This did not neces-

sarily mean that Brobeck, Phleger and Harrison's 29 partners and
28 associates had been outmatched by Murray, a single attorney
in general practice. The Corporation had discovered that it had
an insurance policy against libel liability. It was sensible to allow
the insuror to pay the costs of the suit. Attorney W. E. Sedgwick,
senior partner of Sedgwick, Detert, Moran and Arnold, became
counsel of record for DiGiorgio. By this time one matter had been
settled, namely, that the center of the legal storm was no longer
Poverty. Other issues were moving to the front, the most command-
ing of them being the authenticity of the Nixon-Morton-Steed
report and DiGiorgio's connection with it, if any. This was now the
beginning of

Discovery, Little by Little. / Time was when surprise was a
weapon of resourceful pleaders-at-law. Not only was surprise dramatic; it could also be fatal to a case. But the law was moving in a
different direction. The object was to discover the truth and not to
brain an opponent in open court. The more facts that could be
known in advance of the trial, the fewer the contentions and the
clearer the view from the Bench of the substantive issues between
the parties.

During the pleadings Murray, like his adversaries, made use of
subpoenas, interrogatories, depositions and requests for admissions. By interrogatories and requests for admission Murray established certain interesting facts. One was the difference, reluctantly
acknowledged by DiGiorgio, between Werdel's prefatory remarks
and the report which followed them in the text of his Extension.
Another was a newspaper clipping from the *Los Angeles Times* in
which it was reported that the supposed Nixon-Morton-Steed
report as of 11 March 1950 had not been formally presented. As
of June 1963 DiGiorgio could produce no later evidence that such
presentation had ever been made officially.

To these items there were added the discoveries by way of the
depositions, thirteen in number, of which eleven were taken by
Murray.

As befitted his rank, Robert DiGiorgio was the first deponent
called by Murray. The former director of labor affairs and public
relations of the Corporation was now its executive vice-president.
DiGiorgio made some defensive points. He declared that the first

time he knew about the Nixon-Morton-Steed report was when he read it in the San Francisco morning papers.[129] This would have been on 11 March 1950. He based his conclusion that Galarza had violated the 1950 agreement on having seen the name listed among the officers of the AWOC "on some sort of sheet of paper." Very emphatically DiGiorgio declared that he had nothing to do with the Tenney committee investigation of the strike in 1948. His testimony also brought out that he had met with Werdel in the latter's office in Bakersfield on the eve of the 1949 congressional hearings to give the Congressman, at his request, a briefing on the issues.

Murray then examined Sanborn, who recalled his testimony before another House subcommittee in Fresno in November 1957. Sanborn stated at that time that the Werdel reprint he submitted had been "introduced in the House of Representatives." It was, Sanborn told Murray, "to the best of my knowledge an official report." As to the press release, Sanborn identified the same sort of piece of paper that Robert DiGiorgio had relied on as the basis for the charges against Galarza. He had approved the release but had not read it carefully. When Murray suggested that portions of Werdel's prefatory remarks should not have been presented as quotations from the report, Sanborn replied that "informing the public of anything in this document . . . would be helpful in understanding the situation." Questioned as to his connection with the attack on *Strangers in Our Fields,* Sanborn denied that he had cooperated with Edward F. Hayes, research director of that attack.

Murray's first two deponents were lawyers, and so was the third. Malcolm T. Dungan, now a partner of Brobeck, Phleger and Harrison, was steeped in the case. He, too, had briefed Werdel. He investigated the locations shown in *Poverty,* prepared the 1949 complaint and participated in the settlement of 1950. His deposition, in Murray's hands, showed what legal discovery could be at its best. In his small, crowded office, Murray not only practiced law but taught it to his clients. A rare combination of lawyer, newspaper reporter, teacher and actor, Murray explained and dramatized for his client's instruction the significance of a pleading, the pros and cons of a tactical move, the strategy of the opposition and the unpredictable ways of the judicial process. Now he had before him one of the architects of the perfect web.

Dungan declared that he knew of the Werdel Extension of

Remarks before it was printed in the *Congressional Record* "when
it was first signed by three members of the subcommittee." Murray
drove his next questions into the breach:

> MURRAY: Have you seen a signed copy?
> DUNGAN: I don't know whether I have or not. I kind of think
>   I have, yes . . .
> MURRAY: Do you have that in your file?
> DUNGAN: I suppose so.
> MURRAY: Could I have a copy of it, please?
> DUNGAN: Certainly.
> MURRAY: Would you send that in the mail to me?
> DUNGAN: Sure.[130]

What came to Murray by mail was a thirteen-page photocopy
of a mimeographed document entitled "Agricultural Labor at
DiGiorgio Farms, California," identical with the title of the Nixon-
Morton-Steed report. In the upper right hand corner of the first
page was handwritten Brobeck's file code number, 612–53. The
photocopy was made from an original mimeographing process that
had rested in Brobeck's files for ten years. It was not signed. The
names of the three rapporteurs appeared in typewriting slightly
larger than that of the text. Since 9 March 1950 the Corporation
had staked the authenticity of the report on the contention that
it had actually been signed, with the holographs of Richard M.
Nixon, Thruston B. Morton and Tom Steed to evidence the fact.
Now the Corporation admitted, in a sworn interrogatory, that none
of its officials or attorneys had ever seen such a signed copy.

Next Murray pressed Dungan to justify the inclusion of Galarza
as a defendant in the Stockton suit. This, Dungan explained, was
based upon the evidence the Corporation possessed in the form of
a press release issued by the AWOC on 26 April 1960, which had
been obtained by Callan on his quick trip through the Central
Valley. The release appeared on a printed letterhead with Norman
Smith's name as director. Immediately after it were the words
"Ernesto Galarza, Assistant Director," in neat, compressed handwriting. The release that Callan handed to Dungan in San Francisco made no mention of Galarza. Callan assured Dungan that the
investigation had established Galarza's official connection with the
AWOC. Thereupon Dungan added the handwritten words "as a

memorandum to myself." It was this memorandum that he produced when Murray asked him for documentary proof of Galarza's connection.

Other evidence was offered by Dungan. It was a clipping from the Communist newspaper, *The People's World,* which on 6 June 1959 had described the AWOC campaign. Galarza's name was mentioned but not as assistant director. Dungan's deposition also established that the preparation of the Stockton complaint was under way on May 14. That is to say, by midweek of DiGiorgio's hot pursuit and before Callan completed his investigation the decision had been made to proceed with the lawsuit. "It was an easy job, you see," Dungan explained to Murray, "because we knew all the facts except where the film was shown and who were the persons responsible."

Murray next questioned Albert O'Dea, publicity agent for the Corporation, who identified Sanborn as his principal source for the preparation of the release. Contradicting Dungan's memo to himself, O'Dea named DeWitt Tannehill as assistant director to Smith. Sanborn, in his hasty reading of O'Dea's copy, failed to note this, as he failed to edit out O'Dea's confusion of the Werdel preface with the text of the report.

It was now necessary for Murray to examine William Callan, who did not prove eager to give his deposition. He confirmed Dungan's explanation of the manner in which he had named Galarza assistant director of the AWOC. He was not certain whether it was he or the Corporation that produced the *People's World* clipping, but in any event he did not suspect a source so often and so devastatingly denounced by the Associated Farmers. Since it served the purpose in hand, the Communist connection might even be an advantage. Callan was fuzzy as to the identity of his informers— "the lady in Strathmore," and "the Farm Bureau couple. I don't know who they were." He could not recall seeing Galarza at any showing of the film and he wobbled between assumptions and direct evidence as to who was the real assistant director. Of the eleven documents he brought to Dungan—all AWOC publications —one was in Spanish which neither he nor Dungan could read. Considering the rough ground over which Murray was taking him, Callan's mind rattled a bit, and at one point Attorney Connors had to come to the rescue.

MURRAY: I don't object to Mr. Connors refreshing your recollection of that.
CALLAN: Somebody had better.

Now there dropped into the deposition one of those seemingly
trivial semantic blocks around which attorneys do battle. Murray
asked Callan if he had ever been asked to conduct an investigation
of the AWOC. Sedgwick objected. "Excuse me, just a minute, Mr.
Callan, I object to the word 'investigation.' I think inquiry or something of that kind would be more appropriate." Murray reframed
this question and Callan took the cue by saying that it was "nothing more than a field assignment." The word "investigation," he
added, "was never mentioned to my knowledge." There was beneath this brief exchange a dangerous legal shoal. The complaint
prepared by Murray charged the Corporation not only with libel
but also with malicious prosecution. The defense against such a
charge was that DiGiorgio had not proceeded with the Stockton
suit until it had caused to be made an independent investigation
of the facts, only then proceeding to sue on the advice of counsel.
The holes that Murray was already punching into Callan's performance could discredit it. DiGiorgio's attorney's had to hedge
against Callan's mistake; it was not an easy hurdle. DiGiorgio had
instructed Dungan to make an investigation and Dungan had testified: "I asked Mr. Callan to investigate, yes." The allegations that
Dungan set forth in the Stockton complaint were based on what he
again called "his investigation." "Thereafter" and only thereafter,
did the attorneys advise that the Corporation had a valid cause of
action. The defense against the charge of malicious prosecution was
leaning on a feeble reed, Callan.
Murray's next call was on former Congressman Werdel, who
after two terms in the House was now practicing law in Bakersfield.
While in Washington he had sponsored legislation to curb those
"labor cossacks" seeking to organize farm workers in Kern County
by force. Had his legislation passed, he said, the Union "would
have had a new set of officers at the end of about ninety days."[131]
In his deposition he insisted that his primary concern was for the
farm laborers living on the ranch. It was on their behalf and that
of the Democracy at large that he crusaded in the House against

secrecy in government.* As the political representative of DiGiorgio and other Special Citizens of Kern County, his Washington office was the center of pressures for the termination of the strike. During the interval between the hearings and the publication of his Extension of Remarks, "there were certain things that I wanted the subcommittee to have which I supplied to them." His orientation came from DiGiorgio and Dungan, with whom he had met shortly before the November 1949 Bakersfield hearing.

At the deposition Werdel promptly reminded Murray of his constitutional privilege not to be questioned about the events related to his Extension of March 9. He did not invoke Section 6 of Article 1 of the Constitution as vigorously as Connors, the defending attorney, who was present; but he was plainly uneasy as to his own possible involvement in the suit. Werdel also failed to produce any of the documents that Murray had subpoenaed "including correspondence between yourself and the law firm of Brobeck, Phleger and Harrison and the DiGiorgio Corporation and its officers." To make certain on this score, Werdel had burned a letter he had received from a fellow congressman that threw some light on the matters that Murray was pursuing.

Coming to the report, Werdel reconstructed the position in which he found himself in the early weeks of 1950. Public opinion in his constituency, meaning the Special Citizens, was demanding immediate correction of the propaganda effects of *Poverty*. Bailey, acting in the grand tradition of members of the majority party in control of House committees, was ignoring the slow burn of his Republican colleagues over his inaction in the DiGiorgio matter. He kept closed the files of the subcommittee, to which Werdel had no access, the rules of the House forbidding it. Relying on the Democratic majority and the support of chairman Lesinski, Bailey in effect shut off

*With respect to military affairs Werdel was a militant critic of secrecy; on one occasion he inserted in the *Congressional Record* confidential military documents covering 18 pages of close print. Such information, Werder declared, "should be a public record available to the press and to the public . . . What we need is more information going to our free people." *Congressional Record*. House proceedings. 82nd Congress, first session. 3 April 1951, p. 3225; Appendix. 17 October 1951.

all hope of official committee action on the hearings. Had he prepared a report it would probably have been sympathetic if not
favorable to the Union, for this was the same Bailey who had spoken against the threatened monopoly of the agricultural corporations. Such a report would have provided Bailey's opponents with
an opportunity to go on the record, by filing with it over their own
signatures the customary minority dissenting views. This solace,
too, was denied them by the adamant Bailey. He could not be
forced to act by a petition, for it was highly doubtful that enough
names could be gathered for such a step. Werdel did not try it.

Instead he attacked where Bailey could not thwart him. "So that
the truth of the matter would be available to the press as set out
in the report, I would have to do it by extending my remarks in the
Record." Nixon, Morton and Steed were informed of his intention.
They agreed, and no other Member of the House objected, as
Werdel carefully pointed out, after the Extension appeared in
the Appendix.

Werdel's account of the event follows:

". . . After the hearings were printed and after they were available, at least to the members of the subcommittee, the majority
report was drafted. Now, I assume that—and I have to assume
this—it was done by the minority representatives because I am sure
that both Mr. Irving and Mr. Bailey were opposed to the report
and it was drafted in accordance with the desires of Morton, Nixon
and Steed. Now, when the report was drafted and I was advised
that it was signed I obtained a copy of the report from the minority
administrative officer whose name I believe was Graham . . . Then
I asked them if they had signed it. Then I approached Mr. Steed
and asked him if he had signed it and he said he had. Then I told
them about my intention to put it into the *Record* as an Extension
of Remarks and I gave them my reasons for doing so which were
substantially these: That if such a report were filed with or given
to the chairman of the subcommittee, Mr. Bailey, it would probably
not be filed with the chairman of the main Committee, Mr. Lesinski, and it would probably not even be sent to the printers. . . ."[132]

Werdel further declared that he did no editing on the text that
he said he received from Graham and that had been signed. He
told Murray vigorously that the signed report was eventually made
a part of the main committee's file, signatures and all, but he did

not say when this was done. He instructed his staff to immediately send copies of the printed Appendix "to people who I knew would be interested." Werdel knew that DiGiorgio was interested. Out of his own pocket he paid for the reprints that Joseph DiGiorgio was so impatiently demanding.

Werdel, now a sick man, had performed creditably again. There was enough candor in his recital of events of long ago to give all the details the stamp of truth. He had admitted only the obvious. He had refused to yield documents that would have shed light on the case. Murray would have to piece the truth together from other sources.

Most important among these sources was a colleague of Werdel's in the March 9 enterprise, Tom Steed. On behalf of the Corporation, Brobeck arranged with Steed to take his deposition in Washington, D.C.

The congressman was examined by Attorney Donald Connors for the defendant and by James Murray for the plaintiff. The deposition was taken in Steed's office "on the hill," the slight bulge in the heart of the city on which the capitol stands. Atop the dome stands the plumed statue of Freedom, its seven-and-a-half tons of bronze looking down on a magnificent panorama nearly three hundred feet below. The capitol, the Supreme Court, the Library of Congress and the Senate and House office buildings enclose a park of broad lawns, American elms, tulip trees and laurel. Like a rampart the capitol halts the sweep of the Mall, spiked midway by the Washington Monument and sealed at the edge of the Potomac by the marble perystile of the Lincoln Memorial. In Capitol Park the squirrels sometimes cling upside down to the trunks of the elms, seemingly to establish a more sensible angle from which to view national affairs.

The south wing of the capitol belongs to the United States House of Representatives. In the chamber the Republican conservatives sit to the left of the Speaker of the House, the liberal Democrats to the right. In front of the Speaker's dais is the well of the House, an opening of unknown depth through which the bulk of the legislative business falls out of sight. It is also from the well that the Members speak—often, as in a well, to themselves, before a listless, nearly empty Chamber. Off the floor are the cloak rooms, the private lobby of the Members, and beyond them the architectural elegance of what Allan Nevins called "a place of resounding deeds." As they commute between the Chamber and the House offices the Members pass the grand stairway of white marble, the gold-green serpentine columns, Brumidi's frescoes, the purple and silver drapery, the storied urns and consecrated busts of the past. The members walk from their offices to answer the roll call bells through a tunnel, itself a symbol of the unseen underground where much of the business of the House is transacted. The smooth show of legislative operations that the visitor sees from the galleries is merely the final tailoring of work roughed out, log-rolled, lobbied and compromised out of sight. The subterranean life of the House is a partisan cold war of a thousand battles in every session, expressing the often bitter and near-mortal conflict of interests of American society. The battles end in votes in committee or on the floor. The winner must show a certificate of legitimacy—a resolution, an Act, a recorded vote, or a report, all in accordance with the Rules of the House.

There was something of this aura about Steed's deposition, taken on 30 April 1963 in his House office building suite. He sat comfortably behind his desk, a piece of polished architecture. The walls of his private office were overlaid with countless photographs of his public career—Steed in the company of famous men or Steed the participant in events worth memorializing. He sat plump, placid. and pleasant, ordinariness in the round, a man trying hard to be fair.

Attorney Donald Connors, representing DiGiorgio, handed Steed a copy of the Werdel print to refresh the witness's memory. Steed recalled his state of mind thirteen years past. He could not remember the title of the film, but he was strongly repelled by the fact that the miserable shacks shown in it were not on DiGiorgio Farms and that the film said they were. His interest in farm labor conditions in California was casual, and he realized keenly that Bailey's sympathy for migrants "was just the wrong view for me, and certainly wasn't the sort of thing I could go along with and still expect to survive politically in my district."

To protect himself, Steed drafted a statement of his own summarizing his impressions and reactions to the Bakersfield hearings. He intended this draft to be an expression of minority or dissenting views, to be attached to the majority report that he anticipated Bailey, in the normal procedures of the subcommittee, would issue.

"Then I circulated it to the members of the subcommittee as a matter of courtesy . . . Mr. Nixon, Mr. Norton and Mr. Werdel called me and expressed a very similar view about the matter."[133] Discussions among the four followed. These took place "in my office, . . . in Mr. Werdel's office . . . in Mr. Nixon's office . . . in the Cloak Room or the Committee Room, sometimes on the floor." Out of these discussions, Steed testified, came a new, much fortified version of his original draft.

About one detail Steed had a clear recollection. No member of the committee staff was assigned to prepare the final draft. "It was done by the Members." Werdel was "very active in the preparation of this report which we finally signed . . . I have in mind that he did most of the work on it." Thoughtfully Steed added: "He didn't have much choice not to be."

Asked by Murray if he had ever consulted the reporter's transcript of the hearings, Steed replied: "No, I have no record of it. It was a long time ago." He readily admitted that he had seen no evidence of corruption or fraud in the Union. Confronted with his contradiction in the report about picketing, where Steed and his colleagues had said there was none, yet the evidence showed there was, Steed explained: ". . . no pickets in the sense of what we would normally consider legitimate, legal pickets in a labor dispute." Steed was not able to produce, nor had he ever seen a copy of, the report with handwritten signatures. He made it clear that Bailey never submitted a report on the DiGiorgio matter to the whole Committee, nor did he know who exactly had handed the subcommittee chairman a copy of the document signed by himself, Nixon and Morton. To Murray's question, "But outside of the report that appeared in the Appendix . . . you haven't been able to find any documentary evidence of any kind bearing upon that report?" Steed answered: "That is right."

Connors closed with the vital question: "To the best of your knowledge, Mr. Congressman, did any officer or employee of the DiGiorgio Fruit Corporation have anything to do with the preparing of the report that you signed in 1950?" Steed replied: "Not to my knowledge."

When Murray and Connors left Washington they had in addition to Steed's, the depositions of Ralph R. Roberts, Clerk of the House, and Russell Derrickson, staff director of the Committee on Educa-

tion and Labor. Roberts had ordered a search of the records of
the House by his own staff. The search produced no original of
the report, and no evidence that the document had ever been turned
over to the Clerk for retention in the files of the House.[134] An official report, Roberts pointed out, would have been noted in the
minutes of the Committee and in the entries of reports processed
in the office of the Tally Clerk. During his forty years of service in
the House the Clerk could not recall any other committee or subcommittee report ever having been inserted in full in the Appendix
of the *Congressional Record*. The Nixon-Morton-Steed document
had appeared in print only in the Appendix. Subcommittee reports
attain official status "when they are reported by the full committee
and delivered to the House." To Murray's question of whether
Werdel's Extension had reached that status, Roberts answered:
"It is not a report. It is not an official report." In reply to a question
by Connors, Roberts explained that there was nothing illegal or
contrary to House rules in Werdel's Extension, only that it was
unusual.

Derrickson conducted his own search in the Committee files and
in the records at National Archives. He found no original report,
or any reference to one in the minutes of the Committee, or any
evidence that anyone had ever filed such a document with Bailey.
The only reward for his trouble was the now familiar text in the
Appendix. Nor could Derrickson find any other instance of a subcommittee report being submitted to the House by way of an
Extension of Remarks. Connors, striving to budge Derrickson with
some simple arithmetic, asked: "And these three would make a
majority of the subcommittee, wouldn't it?" Derrickson answered:
"Three would make a majority . . . but it doesn't necessarily make
a committee report. The subcommittee report can only be officially
submitted by the chairman of the subcommittee."

Derrickson played some important sidelights on the contest
between Murray and Connors. He declared that the minutes of the
Committee were complete and that there was no evidence of anything missing from the files. As staff director of the Committee he
did not rate the Nixon-Morton-Steed statement as a majority report. In the Committee on Education and Labor majority reports
are never signed, he said. The proper attachment to a subcommittee report is a letter of submittal (Werdel's Extension reproduced

the letter of authorization). The reporter's typewritten transcript of hearings is sent to the Government Printing Office where it is cut up and eventually destroyed in preparing the printed volume.[135]

The search for the truth now moved back to California. Murray subpoenaed Edward F. Hayes, former chief of the State Farm Placement Service, and Hon. Charles S. Gubser, congressman for the 10th district of California, lying mainly in Santa Clara County.

Hayes, by now deposed from his control of the farm placement machinery, proved an erascible witness. Murray elicited from him the fact that he had been a DiGiorgio stockholder for many years. His interest in DiGiorgio dividends went hand in hand with his public duties of certifying Mexican *braceros* to the Corporation and declaring that labor shortages existed to justify certification. He was also something of a spokesman for DiGiorgio Corporation characterizing Union charges of abuses in connection with the program as falsehoods and harassment. Hayes was the public servant appointed by a joint committee of agribusiness and government officials to research and discredit *Strangers in Our Fields*. For that purpose Bruce Sanborn, vice-president of DiGiorgio, provided Hayes with several copies of the Werdel reprint.[136]

Gubser, the next deponent, put Murray to some ingenuity to serve the subpoena. He came into the case in a roundabout way. In 1963 he was the political neighbor of Hon. Burt Talcott, congressman from Salinas, both being well established and well-thought-of spokesmen for the corporate farming enterprises of the area. In Congress Gubser had supported the stabilization of the price of sugar at its higher limits on behalf of the American housewife by means of a duty guarded by the Louisiana Sugar Cane League and the American Beet Growers Association. He perseveringly and successfully championed the construction of a tunnel that would bring water from the Central Valley to Santa Clara's prosperous farmers and to his own modest ranch. He was in favor of a shorter school year to release children for prune picking. Not an intellectual beacon in the House but a steady man in Republican harness, he nevertheless made important philosophical discoveries such as, in the matter of postal rates, that "diamonds are more expensive to handle than coal."

With these credentials, Gubser was the man for an important assignment on behalf of agribusiness, the immediate origin of which was the collision of a freight train and a farm labor bus on 17 September 1963 near Chualar, Monterey County.* In that accident 32 Mexican *braceros* were killed. Congressman Adam Clayton Powell, Chairman of the Committee on Education and Labor of the House, ordered an investigation of the accident and appointed Ernesto Galarza to make that investigation.

On October 16 Gubser spoke for an hour in the well of the House, attacking the investigation and demanding that the investigator be removed.* Gubser balked at the thought that the prestige of Congress should support a person whom Congress itself had already discredited. To prevent it he came heavily armed for his attack. He talked by telephone with Connors and Sanborn in San Francisco, obtaining from them the details of the 1950 events, complete with references to the Werdel Extension of Remarks. From these Remarks Gubser quoted copiously: "wholly false . . . in disregard of the truth . . . a shocking collection of falsehoods. . . ."

Immediately following this attack Congressman Don Edwards, also from Santa Clara County, challenged the authenticity of Gubser's documentation.[137] Edwards concluded by suggesting a House investigation of the now notorious report. In this Edwards was on solid ground. In 1876 a paper released as a committee report but not adopted by a committee aroused the ire of the House and an inquiry was ordered.[138]

On October 24 Gubser returned for the rebuttal. Through fur-

*By the end of September 1963 seven state, federal and Mexican consular investigations of the accident were under way. None, except that of the House Committee on Education and Labor, resulted in a public report. See the *Report on the Farm Transportation Accident at Chualar, California, on September 17, 1963.* Committee on Education and Labor. House of Representatives. 88th Congress, second session. Washington, D.C. April 1964.

*Gubser said, "First of all, regardless of Mr. Galarza and his qualifications, I question the propriety of such an investigation. This matter is involved at the present moment in the Courts of California. It is being adjudicated as a criminal case, and civil suits will certainly result. It is before the courts, and I question whether or not the Congress of the United States has the right to be investigating." *Congressional Record.* 16 Ocober 1963, p. 18638.

ther consultation with DiGiorgio and with Steed he had been
assured that "every word of that report is the truth." He sought
the cover of illustrious names, "a former Vice-President of the
United States . . . a United States Senator."

Pressed by Murray Gubser retreated from these dramatic peaks.
"The report was not officially filed by the Democratic majority as
an official House report." "Whether the report was officially filed,"
he observed, "is immaterial . . . it was signed." Murray rephrased a
question: "Would you characterize that as a House document?" To
which Gubser responded that the answer would be "no." Then
Murray asked: "What is its nature?" and Gubser replied: "It is a
piece of paper signed by a majority of a committee."[139] Nevertheless, it was a piece of paper of some worth "which would have
been lost for all time" had it not been for Werdel's timely Extension of Remarks.

Murray concluded his round of depositions by examining Richard M. Nixon. Like Callan, Gubser and Hayes, Nixon was not
enthusiastic about appearing as a deponent in *Galarza v. DiGiorgio
Fruit Corporation*. Beginning on May 10 and through the summer
of 1962 Murray tried and failed to reach him through his attorneys
in Los Angeles. He was at the time a candidate for governor of
California cross-hatching the state in his campaign travels. There
was also the coincidence that Werdel was his campaign consultant,
by which certain political dangers could be raised such as Werdel's
well-known connection with the ultra rightwing America First
Party. When Murray offered to guarantee that no information
would be given to the public about the deposition since its purpose
was not to embarrass Nixon politically but to enlist him in the
search for the truth, there was no response.

Murray had to resort to the expensive and frustrating service of
a subpoena upon Nixon. Attorneys know better than anyone else
the techniques of eluding a process server as well as how to counter them. As a former newspaper man Murray began to watch the
advance notices of Nixon's appearances. He was scheduled to
arrive at the Pomona county fair by helicopter before noon of
September 12 to open his campaign. As Nixon alighted and moved
forward into the crowd with his customary aggressive friendliness,
the process server fell into stride beside him, stretched out a wel-
coming hand and made the touch required by law for formal ser-

vice. Herbert Klein, Nixon's aide, tried to deflect the summons from contact with his chief but he was too late.[140] Murray was notified and the witness was cited to appear on September 24.

The election was two months away, and Nixon's aides moved for a postponement of the deposition. Represented by DiGiorgio's lawyers, a motion to extend time for taking of the deposition was filed in the Superior Court of San Francisco. It was declared on the candidate's behalf that he had numerous appearances already scheduled, including television sessions and staff meetings, for September 27, 28 and 29. The court was petitioned "to protect the witness from annoyance, embarrassment or oppression" by the untimely citation. The court reset the examination for December 18, with the stipulation that the witness would appear. At the request of Nixon's legal advisers Murray agreed to a further extension of time to 7 January 1963.

On the appointed day Murray and Nixon, with Donald Connors advising him, traded questions and answers in Nixon's Los Angeles office. It was a small one, appointed for confidential talk rather than for legal research. A tasteful selection of Nixon's political memorabilia decorated the walls. On the period desk there was an exquisite ivory carving of a ceremonial barge, given in admiration on some Asiatic mission. In the prim, cameo atmosphere of that collection no one but Galarza, present as a party to the suit, noticed the absence of a *memento mori* to the dead *Poverty*.

Nixon entered slightly behind time. His trim matched that of his office. He wore a bluish-gray suit of conservative cut, like a man who keeps his body toned as well as his clothes. The four-in-hand tie had a dash of stripes suggesting, just barely, an orderliness and discipline of mind. The face was as solidly tied as the knot of the cravat, but far more mobile. The forehead swept back a little more than it had in Bakersfield thirteen years before but the dark waves of the hair had not been streaked by time. He was freshly shaved down to the lightest hue of a tanned complexion, his eyes more persistent than piercing, the jaw, nose and ears better proportioned full front than in profile. There were in the face weariness and wariness at once, a mask of many talents in which there seemed to be, in the smoggy light of that morning, no trace of compassion.

Murray proceeded to assist Nixon to recollect the bits and pieces of the past that concerned the lawsuit. Nixon's administrative assistant had telephoned someone in the DiGiorgio organization to advise that the Werdel Extension of Remarks had appeared in print on March 9, and with it the subcommittee report. The assistant also sent a copy of the print. The witness picked up some of the threads directly.

MURRAY: And has your recollection been refreshed since? . . .

NIXON: It was my procedure in my office, where I was a member of the Committee, to read the reports before my approval was given to them. I was very careful in that respect, more careful than most congressmen. . . .

MURRAY: Did you ever see a document which purported to be a majority report of Subcommittee No. 1 of the Committee on Education and Labor? . . .

NIXON: My recollection was that a member of the Subcommittee brought it to my office . . . I know that this report was brought to my office. I read the report and approved it. That was the way it worked with me . . .

MURRAY: Can you tell us, did you assign to anyone on your staff the task of preparing this report? . . .

NIXON: No. I had nobody on my staff that was an expert in labor relations . . .

MURRAY: Was there any evidence, Mr. Vice-President, that the men who had something to do with the labor disturbance at DiGiorgio Farms were corrupt? . . .

NIXON: I recall no questioning with regard to that particular matter. You are speaking of corruption in the sense of the Hoffa-type payoffs and so forth?

MURRAY: Yes.

NIXON: This union did not involve that, as I recall.

Nixon was refuting Werdel's prefatory remarks as to corruption in the Union.

MURRAY: I am going to show you again the pages of the *Congressional Record* and ask you to look at the report itself in an effort to find a date on the report, if you please. . . .

NIXON: I don't think there is one.[141]

Beyond this point Nixon's memory, which was rated by Ralph K. Bennett of the *National Observer* as "fantastic, both for facts and for people," began to falter. He could not remember any specific meeting of the subcommittee "to discuss the report," nor any vote taken on the matter at such a meeting. He had "no independent recollection of affixing my name to the report," or whether he saw any other signatures. Likewise his recollection was uncertain as to the hearings or the visit to the DiGiorgio ranch.

By a slightly irrelevant turn Murray tested the witness's knowledge with regard to the rules of the House. He answered "yes" to Murray's question whether it is proper to make reference on the floor of the House to proceedings in a committee or subcommittee if those proceedings have not been formally reported. The correct answer was "no." Murray also wanted to be enlightened as to whether the papers and files of a subcommittee may be demanded by a Member of the full committee who is not a member of the subcommittee before it reports to the full committee. Nixon recalled that this was true, but again the answer was no. Werdel had been a member of the full committee in 1950 but not a member of Subcommittee Number 1.

On this quiz Nixon's memory proved to be consistent, if not accurate. Where it was still sharp it threw important light on the origins of the report. The lapses were understandable. Nixon had left the House in 1950. The Bakersfield event had not been one of his six crises. It was one of many incidental chores and required little more than one public appearance and the reading of a document he did not write and probably did not sign. A mountain of such chores all faithfully performed through the years had become the pedestal of his rise.

Nixon himself gave the clue as to why that event had left so slight a trace on his mind. The report had been printed in the Appendix and nowhere else. Nixon observed, without a question from Murray before him, that "while the general public impression is that some very earnest congressmen sit down and read the *Record* from cover to cover each day—I know some congressmen in running for re-election make a point of that—I would only suggest that anyone who does make that point should not be re-elected because it is a waste of time." The date was 7 January 1963. In the Third District Court of Appeals in Sacramento three judges were closely examining Plant's Exhibit 20 preparing to endorse a document that had been copied from the Appendix of the Record and that bore the name of Richard M. Nixon.

Closing the cycle of depositions, Murray could now add to his discoveries those that had come to light through other research since 18 May 1960.

By law all official reports and documents of the House are bound and indexed at the close of each session of Congress. The search for an official print of the DiGiorgio subcommittee report began there. More than four hundred subcommittee and committee reports to the 79th, 80th, 81st and 82nd congresses were checked. The government checklist for all House documents for those sessions was examined—over 13,500 entries by title and serial number. For the 81st Congress, second session, during which Werdel delivered his Extension of Remarks, seven reports of the Committee on Education and Labor were found, none relating to the Bakersfield hearings. Committee prints, which sometimes are issued without a number, were dug out in the Library of Congress, the New York City Library, the library of the University of Notre Dame, and the official repositories at the Universities of California, Southern California, Texas, Los Angeles and San Francisco. The *Congressional Record* Index from 1948 to 1952 was scrutinized under entries of the names of the four congressmen and Chairman Bailey, subject matter, bills offered, and remarks recorded. For the same period the *Journal,* in which all reports filed with the House are listed, was inspected, and the *Daily Digest,* another critical source, was studied. In the *Monthly Catalogue of Government Publications* all House reports must necessarily be entered on the month following official publication. Every available collection of such publications was checked—in the House library, the House Documents Room, the Government Printing Office, the National Archives, the offices of the Committee on Education and Labor and the Superintendent of Documents. To these searches were added those of the Committee staff, the Clerk of the House, personnel of the Library of Congress, the Legislative Reference Service, and of Brobeck, Phleger and Harrison. Congressman Edwards made inquiry before speaking on the floor of the House on 23 October 1963. Gubser was diligently preparing for his Chualar assignment. Both Morton and Nixon were asked for information on the missing official document and both had answered with nothing closer than the Appendix print. Bailey was asked by letter and answered on 24 August 1960; "There is no indication that an official report was submitted by the subcommittee, nor was there any formal report filed on behalf of the full committee." H. L. Mitchell and Congressman John F. Shelley had made a hasty check while Werdel's Extension was still in fresh printer's ink, but had found nothing.

From the dead-end trails, the blank clues, the false hunches and the dust of the archives the official report did not emerge, but some other useful information did.

Proceedings of hearings are printed for the information of the members of the Committee assigned to a matter as well as for that of other Members of the House and the public. It is upon this printed record that Committee members base their findings and reports. The *Monthly Catalogue of Government Publications* for May 1950 showed that the printed text of the Bakersfield proceedings had been published by the Superintendent of Documents in April 1950.[142] The file copy in the Superintendent's repository was stamped with the date "April 7, 1950." On the cover of the print was the customary notice "Printed for the use of the Committee on Education and Labor." By 1963 copies of the 1950 volume were scarce, but one was obtained, adding valuable items of information to Murray's file.

Another significant document that came to light was a printed copy of the *Report to the Stockholders,* by Joseph DiGiorgio, dated 1 June 1950. The four-page mailer was routinely deposited by the Corporation in the Social Science Reference Room of the library of the University of California at Berkeley. Attached to it was a photocopy of an editorial from the *San Francisco Chronicle* of 15 March 1950, which noted the release of the report in Washington on March 9 and quoted from its more purple language. The entire first page of the stockholder's document was given to the report and Joseph DiGiorgio's commentaries thereon. Introducing a paragraph about *Poverty in the Valley of Plenty,* he wrote: "The official report contains the following statement about the film." The document praised the report as a vindication of the Corporation's opposition to the Union and a confirmation of the libelous character of the film. Mr. Joseph also told his stockholders that he had instructed the attorneys "not to consent to any settlement unless the defendants agreed to a judgment" confirming the libel, "nor unless all other matters in issue were disposed of at the same time."[143]

This discovery indicated that other reports of the Corporation might be of interest to the plaintiff. One issued in 1960 was. It referred to DiGiorgio's attention to the AWOC campaign and obliquely mentioned what the company had done about it.[144]

The results of three years of research had not given Murray very much substantial information. The facts he had were few, but they shone exceedingly bright in comparison to the haunting failure to produce an authentic, official, legitimate and certified subcommittee report. They were the plaintiff's stake in the trial to which all this was a prelude.

NOTES

128. Malcolm T. Dungan. Deposition. 7 November 1961, p. 62.
129. Robert DiGiorgio. Deposition. 9 December 1960, p. 29.
130. Malcolm T. Dungan. Deposition. 7 November 1961, p. 58.
131. Thomas H. Werdel. Deposition. 31 July 1962, p. 59.
132. Ibid., p. 28.
133. Tom Steed. Deposition. 30 April 1963, p. 6.
134. Ralph R. Roberts. Deposition. 29 April 1963, p. 23.
135. Russell C. Derrickson. Deposition. 29 April 1963, p. 23.
136. Edward F. Hayes. Deposition. 22 January 1963, p. 20.
137. *Congressional Record.* 21 October 1963, p. 18980.
138. Hind's *Precedents* . . . Vol. III, section 2611, p. 1086. *Congressional Record.* House. 25 May 1876, p. 3339.
139. Charles S. Gubser. Deposition. 28 December 1964.
140. *Los Angeles Times.* 13 September 1962.
141. Richard M. Nixon. Deposition. 7 January 1963, p. 31.
142. *Monthly Catalogue of U.S. Government Publications.* May 1950, p. 30.
143. *Report to Stockholders.* DiGiorgio Fruit Corporation. 1 June 1950, p. 1.
144. *Annual Report.* DiGiorgio Fruit Corporation. 1960.

9

DiGIORGIO ON TRIAL

When the case of *Galarza v. DiGiorgio Fruit Corporation* was called by the clerk of the Superior Court of San Francisco, the Hon. H. A. Van der Zee presiding, on 26 February 1964, the fifth lawsuit and the second trial in the wake of *Poverty* was under way. The Corporation's press release had charged publicly that plaintiff had broken an agreement, exhibited a libelous film, damaged the company's reputation, scorned a court order and committed divers evils of which a responsible congressional subcommittee had found him guilty. To punish and recover, the Corporation filed an action for libel and now, with the roles reversed, it was charged with publishing malicious untruths and suing without reasonable cause.

The four previous prosecutions by DiGiorgio, technically separate and unrelated actions, had by now become the frame on which a complicated pattern was emerging. One by one the dominant motifs appeared in the pattern; the authors, declared or presumed, of Werdel's Extension of Remarks; the official status of the report, stated or insinuated; the private connections between the Corporation and Werdel before Bakersfield and after, if any; the probable or improbable knowledge by the Corporation of the report before its publication; the character of the Appendix considered as a record of official proceedings of the House; and the coincidence, deliberate or fortuitous, of the Corporation's lawsuits with farm labor union organizing campaigns.

Other questions, no less important and intriguing, were now arising. Was the Nixon-Morton-Steed writing a majority report? Did Bailey ever file his own minority report? Had the three congressmen ever actually signed their report? What sort of evidence

172

was before them when they prepared their draft? Was it indeed their draft or was it someone else's? Had the minutes of the Committee been purloined by persons unknown? Had one copy of the court reporter's typescript of the Bakersfield hearings survived, and if so, had it been put to uses vital to the issues of all this litigation? In due course witnesses became confused within this weave of disputed facts, stumbling more and more into inconsistencies and contradictions that began to raise doubts as to their credibility.

The date of the trial was itself an indication of this state of affairs. The Stockton suit had opened with the filing of the Corporation's complaint on 13 September 1960; the trial ended in November 1961. The San Francisco complaint had been filed on 15 September 1960 and was delayed more than forty months in coming to judgment. DiGiorgio's attorneys maneuvered for time, waiting for the appellate decision in Sacramento, which was not handed down until 30 April 1963. The theory and strategy of their case in San Francisco could well hinge on that decision.

While they waited, the usual legal facilities for delay were available to them. DiGiorgio changed attorneys; depositions were paced at long intervals; attorneys and principals on the defendant's side went on vacations or on business trips; interrogatories were rebuffed; a change of venue was demanded; the new lawyers asked for time to take over from Brobeck, Phleger and Harrison. After their victory in Sacramento they were in no hurry to face a new antagonist, James Murray.

Courtroom drama, when it is genuine, is the controlled explosion of passionate encounters screwed tighter by the uncertainties of a trial. The rule is that anything can happen, and frequently it does. It is like the heat of a small volcano creeping underground in search of fumaroles through which to belch. To open the right ones and plug the wrong ones is the professional task and the exciting reward of a trial attorney. His tools are motions, objections, argument and above all questions put to witnesses under oath. The pitch of the drama depends upon the nature of the case. Men appear to value property, life and reputation in that order. And while a criminal trial for murder offers the most in emotional excitement even to onlookers, a lawsuit for the theft of goods or reputation can be a wrenching experience for those involved in it.

Unlike Stockton, it was Brobeck's decision to make this a jury trial. Sedgwick and Murray proceeded to choose the jurors by the process of examination called *voir dire* in which, as usual, only the attorneys are allowed to ask questions. The jury box filled rapidly with twelve men and women, average citizens who, according to Justice Cardozo, "have their roots in the customary forms and methods of business, and of fellowship, the prevalent convictions of equity and justice, the complex of belief and practice which we style the mores of society."[145] Their charge was to decide whether there was libel in the tangle of facts to be laid before them.

Constantly before them were the bailiff in sharply pressed brown uniform, the armed bodyguard of Justice and the personal page of the Judge; the Clerk, custodian of the vital papers of the record, marking exhibits and handing documents to and from the Bench; the court reporter, staring into space and tapping out the short-hand of every word of the proceedings; and the Judge himself, in black gown, making notes on a yellow pad, caustic and benevolent by turns, the arbiter who is himself on trial for fairness, impartiality, legal knowledge and supra-legal intuition.

Sedgwick played his defense in a minor key. A specialist in insurance, he was now making good on a policy against libel liability which DiGiorgio belatedly discovered it was carrying. What Murray magnified he minified. What to his opponent was notorious to him was niggling. "Galarza," Sedgwick said, "has made a profession of this case," tingeing his words with a bored sneer.

His array of documents was not as formidable as Plant's had been in Stockton. There were two new items. One was a carbon copy of the typescript prepared by the court reporter in Bakersfield, a two-volume set of some six hundred pages. Sedgwick read from it but did not offer it in evidence. Another was a photocopy of pages 67 to 98 of that transcript, containing Galarza's testimony at the hearings. These were only a few items from an impressive file of documents loaned to him by Brobeck for the trial, including the printed volume of the hearings and numerous clippings, photocopies and reprints.

His prize resource however, was Congressman Steed, flown by the Corporation from Washington for a day to take the witness stand.

Steed's message to the jury was a brief and simple one. Referring to the draft of the report he testified: "We signed a copy for each one of us. . . The moment the report was signed it becomes an official report. . . It was an official act. We were members of a subcommittee to a committee to make a report, and we did that. . . . The only official report was the one that had our signatures on it. . . ." Prompted by Sedgwick, Steed retold how he had disagreed with Bailey's views about their assignment, prepared his own draft as a minority or dissenting view and developed that with Nixon and Morton into the final report. Sedgwick also elicited from Steed that there was nothing unusual in what Werdel had done.[146]

Since Sedgwick had no evidence that Galarza had been assistant director of the AWOC, or that he had shown the film in 1960, or that he had damaged the Corporation's reputation, or that he had violated an agreement, or that he had flouted a court order, his strategy was to draw the attention of the jury away from these defects. This he did by resting the burden of the Corporation's defense on the report. In that document the plaintiff came out very badly indeed. At best the jury could conclude that if he had not committed all those perverse acts, he was the kind of person who associates with persons who had. At worst, the jury could find for him on the facts but regard him as not deserving of money damages.

The immediate advantages were offset by difficulties that this line of defense would raise over the long term. The principal one was that it drew more attention than ever to questions regarding the authenticity, origin, genuineness, reliability, consistency and status of Brobeck's chief exhibit, the report.

Murray cross-examined Steed. The witness took pains to make it clear that he had not wanted the DiGiorgio assignment, was drafted into it and was anxious to get it over with. There had been no meeting with a quorum present to discuss the report. Steed did not himself file a copy with Bailey. He stated directly that Bailey had not filed it with Lesinski, chairman of the whole Committee.

As to the actual writing of the report, Steed said that "Mr. Werdel probably did most of that." To augment the draft that he, Steed, had started out with, the three congressmen "had to go out" to gather some of the factual details. "Some of the actual language was prepared by somebody else outside."

When Murray attempted to pin down the sources the three had relied on Steed floundered. He identified them, in addition to the

"somebody else outside," as the stenographic transcripts from Bakersfield. "That," he said, "I had." He was equally certain that they
did not have the printed volume of the hearings and then went on
to state "I have not reread the hearings since the day we took
the testimony."[147]

Steed concluded that Werdel's procedure had been unusual. He
answered Murray that "I cannot honestly say that I know" of any
instance of the insertion of a subcommittee report in the Appendix.
To Murray's question whether the report was an official act, Steed
answered unequivocally "No." "It didn't get the proper treatment
. . . the report was lost in the shuffle." His last remark on the
Appendix was: "I have a lot more important things to do than
read a lot of junk that gets into the *Record*."

Murray then called Robert DiGiorgio. On the witness stand,
DiGiorgio looked the part of president of one of America's largest
corporations, in food growing and distribution the largest. He
would not be hurried in his answers, which he gave in the trained
manner of one who knows how to make them swing, like doors,
in opposite directions. Where Joseph DiGiorgio, his predecessor in
the presidency, had been smallish, peppery and tightly wound,
Robert was deliberate, sat tall and stayed cool. He spoke the part
of an executive who had been deeply wounded, deeply shocked
and deeply hurt.

Murray drew from him the fact that he had knowledge of the
AWOC's activities in 1959 and 1960, the Corporation's relationship
to the Associated Farmers and its long-standing hostility to farm
labor union organization. The questions shifted to a crucial point
—the origins of Dungan's document filed as number 612-53.

> MURRAY: Now you testified that you got copies. . . .
> DI GIORGIO: I said I got a copy.
> MURRAY: A copy; was it printed?
> DI GIORGIO: Yes, it was printed. . . .
> MURRAY: And is it your testimony that from something that
>   was printed you had this [612-53] typed up?
> DI GIORGIO: I don't believe that I testified that I had it done,
>   but that it was done.

Sedgwick took over on cross-examination and led DiGiorgio

again over this dangerous ground in an effort to arrest Murray's
progress.

> SEDGWICK: And do you now have any recollection of where
> you got your copy of that subcommittee report?
>
> DI GIORGIO: I wouldn't recall.
>
> SEDGWICK: Do you recall whether or not you had some copies
> made or mimeographed of that report, wherever
> you got it?
>
> DI GIORGIO: Well, I believe we did . . . we had a very fine
> mimeograph. . . .
>
> SEDGWICK: And is it your recollection that these copies were
> made on your mimeographing machine in your
> office here in San Francisco?
>
> DI GIORGIO: Yes.[148]

Before he left the witness chair DiGiorgio again disavowed any
connection in the 1960 lawsuit between Norman Smith the alleged
libeler and Norman Smith the labor organizer: "This was the matter of a libel action. It was not a labor action. . . . It had nothing to
do with the labor question."

Vice-President Sanborn testified next. He said that there had
not been, after all, a congressional report issued in November
1949, as the release had said. He described Callan's assignment as
an "investigation." The letter which Brobeck had sent on May 18
to Gilbert and Nissen was not sent by the Corporation. "We left it
up to the attorneys."

> MURRAY: But you have more than once, as a corporation,
> referred to the existence of this congressional com-
> mittee document in reference to labor matters, isn't
> that true?
>
> SANBORN: That is true . . .
>
> MURRAY: You knew as a fact, didn't you, that the words
> deliberately fabricated falsehood were contained,
> not in the report, but in the prefatory remarks of
> Congressman Werdel?
>
> SANBORN: I don't recall those exact words in the report at
> all . . . I had never studied it as carefully as that . . .

MURRAY: Now did it come to your attention that Congressman Gubser made a very violent attack on the
floor of the House of Representatives against Mr.
Galarza?

SANBORN: Yes.

MURRAY: Weren't you providing him with information in
order that he might make such an attack?

SANBORN: No, sir . . . he had heard about the local lawsuits
between Mr. Galarza and the DiGiorgio Fruit
Corporation . . . and he wanted to know about
that Stockton lawsuit, where he could get information on it, and what part Mr. Galarza played in it,
because he was then, I think, being consulted, or
was advising on whether Mr. Galarza should be
appointed to this recent committee that he was on
. . . So I told him what I knew of it.[149]

Murray was approaching some decisive moments. For years he
had mulled over all that the record showed and the much more it
did not. In his small office overlooking downtown San Francisco
he had groped for the helve of the case, and had not found it.
A large Irishman with a proportionate temper he brooded and
exploded by turns, literally sweating out his perplexities even while
sitting at his desk. A persistent chaos in his papers bothered him,
but not much. He mislaid them but always found them, in alpha-
betical disarray, with the delight that discovery always brings. Murray took his defeats like his successes, with sweep and feeling,
keeping his client informed and justice in view. Between these
swings he moved deliberately, sensing the pitfalls prepared for him
and pondering his own. He was at his best in court, a courteous,
mirthful combatant with red hair and an appetite for the dangerous
clutches of a trial. At this point there were some

Intimations from an Old Typewriter. / Murray called Malcolm
T. Dungan, now promoted to partnership in Brobeck, Phleger and
Harrison. Somewhat nostalgically, as if sharing with his witness
some recollection of a past they both knew and cherished, Murray
asked:

MURRAY: You prepared that complaint [of 1949]?

DUNGAN: Yes, sir, I did. . . . This paper that you have handed me is a copy of the complaint in what I call the 1949 action against the labor union, in the form in which it was filed and served.

MURRAY: And it was prepared in the office of Brobeck, Phleger and Harrison?

DUNGAN: Well, the draft of it, yes. . . .

MURRAY: It looks to me like it is a mimeograph.

DUNGAN: That is exactly what it is.

MURRAY: Where was it done?

DUNGAN: It was in the office of the DiGiorgio Fruit Corporation.

Murray offered, and the court received, the old complaint in evidence.

Murray then skipped over thirteen years and picked up from his papers the copy of document 612-53.

MURRAY: . . . when your deposition was taken I asked you if you had an original signed copy of the report signed by Richard Nixon, Thruston B. Morton and Tom Steed?

DUNGAN: It is true you asked me if I had a copy in signature form.

MURRAY: And you found that you did not have it in signature form?

DUNGAN: No, sir. I had what I referred to in my deposition.

MURRAY: And you provided me with . . . this?

DUNGAN: I believe it is. . . .

MURRAY: The document I have handed you was the document you sent me from your files?

DUNGAN: . . . I am certain it is.

MURRAY: Do you know the source of where you got plantiff's exhibit 33[612–53]?

DUNGAN: No, sir.[150]

Number 612-53 went into the record close after the 1949 complaint.

Sedgwick, uneasy over this curious procession of Murray's documents, complained. "I might suggest," he said, "that if Mr. Murray would show me these things before he does this — I don't know what is coming."

Murray immediately called to the witness chair Lowell W. Bradford, consultant in physical evidence and director of the laboratory of the Sheriff's Department of Santa Clara County.

Murray and Galarza had made a close comparison of Dungan's 612-53 and the 1949 complaint. As they searched for clues as to language and construction, line by line, there appeared to be some similarities of type faces. Preliminary enlargements with a candid camera showed that in both documents the o's were dented in the lower left quarter. The s's and the e's leaned away from each other in the same manner when juxtaposed in the two texts. In all *and*'s the *a* was on a higher baseline than the *d*. In *aint* of *unpainted* the *t* had slipped to the right. In *Giorgio* the *o* tended to float upward like a slightly dented soap bubble. The baseline of other letters and combinations of them wavered up and down in identical manner in both documents as if they had been typed at the instant of a slight quake. They were the tremors of an aging typewriter.

There was enough, it seemed, to lay the matter before an expert. Bradford was provided with the two documents and retained to prepare a report on them.

In court his testimony, supported by charts and enlargements, was brief and conclusive. He traced to the same source the two exhibits that Dungan had identified, "the thirteen-page photocopy of a purported draft of a manuscript [612-53]" and the mimeographed copy of the complaint in Civil Action Number 566888 of 1949. Bradford's conclusion before the jury was that "the typewriter used to prepare the stencils of the Summons and Complaint for Libel . . . was also the machine used to type the manuscript draft of the *Congressional Record* article."

Sedgwick, if he was stunned or even mildly surprised, did not show it. He had no questions for Bradford. Louis Nizer's comment on the subject came to mind: "Even in the mechanical realm that which seems the same on the surface is entirely different when our senses are enlarged."

The rest was anticlimax. In the arguments Murray piled up his evidence and Sedgwick eluded it. The case went to the jury.

There is no time like the time parties wait for the jury to return a verdict. At opposite ends of the corridors the antagonists huddle, stealing glances, trying to make something of the juror who lifted an eyebrow or lowered his head, sorting out the possible good ones from the impossible bad ones, guessing and speculating in lowered voices because there is nothing else to do.

The jury returned. The verdict: Unanimously found that the press release of 18 May 1969 as it concerned the plaintiff was not true; defendant did not make a full and fair disclosure of all the facts known to him; defendant published the release with no actual malice; defendant did not commence the lawsuit of May 18 maliciously and without probable cause.

No money damages were awarded to plaintiff.

The parties go their ways, each with his attorney, to start the review on points lost and won. To the winners, the faces of the jurors pass again in review looking like good citizens who have served the ends of justice. To the losers, they look like bunglers who have brought an end to justice. The winners go home to celebrate a brief and happy acquaintance with twelve reasonable men and women. The losers depart convinced that Descartes was never more wrong than when he said that good sense, is, of all things, among men, the most equally distributed.

The jurors left the court with the thanks of the judge in their ears and the modest fees for service in their pockets. The sequel of their split verdict was of no further interest or moment to them.

Murray moved for a new trial on grounds that the jury had not followed its instructions from the Bench, and because of certain irregularities. His motion denied, he then prepared to appeal, but the loose ends of the case were tied up and on 6 August 1964 plaintiff moved for dismissal.

This was the end of a lawsuit but not the end of the contest. DiGiorgio was even then preparing for the sixth action in libel, arising out of circumstances created by the San Francisco trial. For the Corporation there was more comfort than disappointment in the verdict, enough at least for it to continue its pursuit. It did not appear to notice that since the Stockton victory the workable web had become

The Bending Web. / The connecting threads in the pattern now began to show through even more clearly: the authorship of the "report"; the sources of the information it contained; the question of its status as a document; its authenticity as proceedings of the House; the signatures of Nixon, Morton and Steed; the circumstances of filing as a report; its characterizations as a majority report; Bailey's minority report; the internal consistency and logic of Werdel's text; contacts between the subcommittee and DiGiorgio; advance knowledge of the report by the Corporation; implication of labor issues in the lawsuits; uses of the reprint; and inconsistencies in the evidence and testimony.

On some of these themes the pleadings, discovery and trial of the San Francisco lawsuit threw new light.

The three printed names that appeared at the end of Werdel's Extension of Remarks by no means established the authorship of the report. Steed testified that he knew it was prepared by the Members themselves[151] but Nixon said he had no labor expert on his staff and he was not one himself.[152] Morton was not in Bakersfield, and heard no testimony at any other time or place. Steed made it clear that no committee staff members had been assigned to prepare a draft, the usual procedure in the House. It was his opinion that "Mr. Werdel did most of the work" on the draft.[153] Clerk of the House Roberts called it "his report"[154] but Werdel was careful to declare that he received the copy he used for his Extension of Remarks on the same afternoon of the insertion.[155] The person from whom he said he received it was John O. Graham, the minority clerk, who had attended the hearings. Reached in August 1963 to comment on this attribution, Graham said he was not the author, did not edit or otherwise have anything to do with the draft. This explanation agreed with the slip in the text which said: ". . . the subcommittee came to Bakersfield and visited DiGiorgio Farms." The writer of these words was possibly in Bakersfield at that time, almost certainly in California. Graham was in Washington.

As to the sources that were available to the anonymous author or authors, it should first of all be noticed that the subcommittee did not screen *Poverty in the Valley of Plenty*, when it returned to Washington. The print deposited with the majority clerk disappeared. Dungan's number 612-53 could have served as the original text, except for the prefatory remarks. The 612-53 text showed over seventy faults of style, spelling, punctuation and technical terms, such as "North-Laguardia" for "Norris-LaGuardia," "special Committees" instead of "Special Subcommittee Number 1," and "Fair Labor Standards" for "Fair-labor standards." A proofreader with the *Style Manual* of the Government Printing Office in hand can be easily imagined to have edited the 612-53 text, if it was a draft. As a mimeographed paper 612-53 was hardly suitable for circulation to newspaper editors and others. It had no date, lacked the identification of the prefatory remarks and did not otherwise show the place and time of publication. Besides, Werdel had at his disposal sixty courtesy copies of the *Congressional Record* on March 10, which by his instructions to his staff were sent immediately to California to interested persons. By air these copies could have been in San Francisco on Saturday, the eleventh; by train not later than Tuesday the fourteenth which for the time being filled DiGiorgio's needs for copies. It is likely that Nixon's administrative assistant, who also sent a copy or copies, was no less prompt in getting the prints to California.

The garbled 612-53 clearly did not serve purposes of publicity and circulation. Yet it was not an ordinary piece of writing. Dungan preserved it carefully in his files, with duplicate copies, from 1949 until 1963. Murray proved that it had come to Dungan as a mimeograph process from the offices of the Corporation in San Francisco, a fact which Robert DiGiorgio acknowledged. Yet, under oath, the Corporation's officers, in answer to one of Murray's interrogatories had declared in January 1962: "The source of this copy is unknown." Brobeck, Phleger and Harrison's Dungan knew then and before where 612-53 had come from. Murray was pressing to discover its origins and thereby possibly its use as the model for Werdel's insertion. The evidence of this possibility remained, after the San Francisco trial, circumstantial.

It was not so difficult to eliminate other possible sources. The one that came to mind first was the printed volume of the Hearings. It is well established in committee proceedings in the House that the preparation of reports can begin only after its members have received the printed text of the testimony. Time and again the Nixon-Morton-Steed text referred to the "evidence" before it, there being no other official evidence upon which to base a report than the print of the hearings. Werdel knew this, for in his deposition he declared that what he inserted in the Appendix was prepared "after the hearings were printed." *The Monthly Catalogue of Government Publications* for May 1950, however, listed the Bakersfield volume as published in April, later than the Extension of Remarks by three weeks. Passages were quoted verbatim from it by Steed and his two colleagues but they had no text with those passages before them—a feat possible perhaps for Nixon, with his fantastic memory, but not for Steed, who could not even remember the title of the film, much less for Morton who had not even been there. All this was confirmed by Steed himself, who answered Murray's question—"you did not have printed hearings to work with?"—. . . thus: "no printed hearings, no, we had to work with stenographic copies. . . . There were several references we had to identify, and that is how we did it."[156]

By stenographic notes Steed meant the typescript prepared by the reporter after the hearings. All but one of the copies were delivered to the Committee Clerk, Mr. Boyer. In February they were already at the Government Printing Office, their pages dispersed and cut up in the process of printing.[157] If Bailey had ordered a carbon copy of this document in two thick volumes for each subcommittee member and if these copies had been the basis for discussion and drafting, it would have been another first in congressional history. Bailey had absolute control of these sources. Werdel, not being a member of Subcommittee Number 1, did not have access to them. Steed added to the confusion on this point by reversing himself. In his deposition he declared that he had no record of the transcript, and at the trial he testified that "I have not reread the hearings since the day we took the testimony." Other facts already brought out corroborated Steed's total lack of documentary material when he drafted his own preliminary impressions as a minority report, or when he talked with Nixon, Morton and Werdel in and about the House of Representatives. If in fact Steed had used the indispensable reporter's typescript in drafting the Werdel Extension of Remarks, Sedgwick did not avail himself of a brilliant opportunity to strengthen his case with the crucial document. He had in court a carbon copy of the two volumes of the reporter's typescript. How Sedgwick came to have this copy was no mystery. Immediately after the hearings DiGiorgio had ordered an extra set for the use of the Corporation and its attorneys. This was permissible under the rules. In San Francisco

Steed was not asked either to identify this extra copy as a duplicate of the one he had allegedly used in 1959 or to declare under
oath that this was in fact the documentary source of the draft.

Now Sedgwick made an odd move. He introduced into the
record a photocopy of a portion of the typescript, pages 67 to 98.
It contained Galarza's testimony at Bakersfield, portions of which
Sedgwick used at the trial. This document, identified only by the
page numbers, also had been prepared by Brobeck, Phleger and
Harrison. Why this section was cropped from the complete document is not difficult to explain. Sedgwick did not want Murray to
examine the entire record as it came from the reporter's typewriter.
Murray was keenly interested in comparing certain passages, expressions, spellings and phrases in Dungan's 612-53 with the manuscript the reporter prepared for the subcommittee. To avoid this
risk Sedgwick did not offer the complete document in evidence,
although it lay on counsel's table in the courtroom.

There was still another difficulty, of which Sedgwick was apparently unaware. The report stated that "the subcommittee interviewed DiGiorgio employees" on its tour of the ranch. "No one
of them signified," it declared, "a desire to become a member of
the Union or his acquaintance with any other employee who did."
The official reporter did not accompany the subcommittee on the
tour. The company's employees were interviewed at the ranch in
the course of the formal inquiry into the labor disturbance. They
were not sworn in. What they said was not set down in the record,
and therefore did not appear either in the reporter's typewriting or
in the printed volume. This much of the evidence at least could not
have been present in any record in Washington four months later.
These circumstances also raised the question of the propriety of
gathering testimony that was to influence the subcommittee's conclusions with such nonchalance. Nixon and Steed did not interview,
during those two days in Bakersfield, any Union members or
officials off the record.

Next, there was the question whether the report was or was
not "official." For the Corporation it was vital that it should be
accepted as a genuine, authentic and official report of the House.
Sanborn so stated to another House subcommittee in Fresno in
1957. "To the best of my knowledge," Sanborn again declared in
November 1960 in his deposition, "it was an official report." And

it had finally come to light that Joseph DiGiorgio called it "their official report" in 1950. This was not only the cachet of respectability; it was the seal of legislative power, dignity, decision and legitimacy. It was the thunder of the State.

The seal was now beginning to blister showing blemishes beneath. All official reports are dated, and this one was not. As of March 11 it had not been formally presented to the House.[158] In asking permission to extend his remarks, Werdel described his text as "the report of the subcommittee of which he is a member," but which he was not. An official report required a letter of transmittal and his had only a letter of authorization. Now Murray got from Clerk of the House Roberts that "it is not an official report." Steed testified that it was not an official act and Gubser finally characterized it as "a piece of paper signed by a majority of a committee."

Donald Connors, of Brobeck's, was beginning to notice the drift. The question of what makes a congressional report official "is not material to this lawsuit" he observed in one of the depositions.

A closely related problem was whether the Werdel Extension was or was not a record of the proceedings of the House. Attorney Plant, in the Stockton trial, had greatly emphasized in his arguments that it was. Now it was becoming clear that what DiGiorgio's lawyers insisted were proceedings were more like goings-on. Steed described his ambulations in the House with his three literary colleagues as "just friendly give and take discussions."[159] Some of them had taken place in the Cloak Room, described by Congressman Miller as "a very private place, a place of escape."[160] Nixon, Morton and Steed did indeed proceed, but to a hole-in-corner privacy that bore no resemblance to the proceedings of the House, as defined in its rules.

Moreover, the fact that the report appeared in the Appendix did little to raise its prestige, even in the eyes of those whose names it bore. Nixon was of the opinion that reading the Appendix was a waste of time and Steed described its contents as "a lot of junk."

Worse than this, the Extension itself was coming apart. The Corporation had distributed reprints of it under a headline that covered both Werdel's prefatory remarks and the report. Sanborn's press release skipped about choosing phrases from both indiscriminately. Plant submitted the document complete as Exhibit 20 in Stockton. Obviously at Brobeck's and DiGiorgio's nobody was paying close attention to Werdel, who was not confused on this point. He clearly indicated that the report proper and his prefatory remarks were separate. "The report," he said, ". . . follows."

After the end of the San Francisco lawsuit it was also abundantly clear that not one but many diligent searches had failed to turn up the original, official proceeding. Galarza had searched for it and failed to find it. So had the Clerk of the House, Derrickson, Edwards, Gubser, Steed and Plant's agent, Lucey. Murray was particularly careful to establish that Brobeck had tried and failed. In his interrogation of 12 December 1962 he asked: "Has any officer, employee or agent of your company ever attempted to locate the original of the alleged report?" The answer was: "Yes, an attempt was made by Brobeck, Phleger and Harrison . . . in the summer of 1962. The endeavor, in any event, failed to locate the original report."

These difficulties did not stand in the way of the key argument of the Corporation, which was that Nixon and Morton and Steed had in their own handwriting affixed their signatures to the draft which Werdel entered in the Appendix. Brobeck's tenacity in holding to this point through all the lawsuits made it clear that the attorneys rested their claim of authenticity, genuineness and official status on that one element. It was Dungan's eagerness to prove it that prompted him to produce his document 612-53 in the mistaken recollection that it showed three holographic signatures. The argument wasted away as Murray probed and questioned. Nixon could not remember signing. Morton never declared himself on the point one way or another. Steed swore that not only had he signed but that he had seen the signatures of the others, too. The draft that Werdel delivered for printing was not signed; he had to ask his three colleagues whether they had signed. And Steed never again saw a signed copy, even though he testified that several duplicates carried the signatures. No officer or employee or agent of the Corporation ever saw one.

As to the filing of the report DiGiorgio's case was not improving. To become official, a subcommittee report must be presented by the chairman of the subcommittee to the full committee. Nixon's testimony was explicit: "The subcommittee comes back, gets a report printed, and it is filed with the full committee and through that method becomes public." Werdel said in his prefatory remarks of March 9 that the report had not yet been printed. Steed declared that he did not hand a copy to Bailey himself and did not know who had.[161] Gubser knew and declared that "the report was not officially filed by the Democratic majority." There was no ambiguity in Steed's testimony in San Francisco: "For this one not to have been filed is a very usual situation."

The Corporation's assertion that its prize exhibit, though undated and unsigned, was a "majority report" of the subcommittee was becoming less and less tenable. There are no majority subcommittee reports in the House; there are only reports and minority or dissenting views appended to them. It is the minority views that by custom require the signatures of the dissenters. The reports themselves are never signed. They are accompanied by a letter of submittal which is signed, but only by the subcommittee chairman. As Derrickson pointed out, it was not the nose count of three-to-two that was decisive but whether Bailey himself had submitted the report to the full committee. In a game of tick-tack-toe DiGiorgio would no doubt have won. Against Derrickson's testimony, it could not.

Two closely related questions were now raised. Did the Corporation maintain continuing correspondence and communication with Werdel? Did it have advance knowledge of the report?

On the first question, it will be recalled that Robert DiGiorgio and Dungan met with Werdel immediately before the Bakersfield sessions. In the preceding months Governor Warren had forwarded to the Congressman certain information which would be useful "to correct such misinformation as may have been conveyed by the motion picture."[162] Whether he made this information available to the subcommittee Werdel could not recall when questioned about it, but he did remember that "there were certain things that I wanted the subcommittee to have which I supplied to them. . . ."[163] Werdel was in Bakersfield in December 1949 during the congressional holidays. The strike was continuing and the Special Citizens were up in arms. It is unlikely that the congressional representative of the district would not have been in touch with his most influential constituent while he was in the area.

Nor was it likely that the Corporation was deliberately kept in the dark by its congressman as to what was going on in Washington. Dungan supplied the answer to that:

MURRAY: You knew of the existence of that congressional printing before May 18, 1960?

DUNGAN: Oh, yes, I knew of it before Mr. Werdel put it in the record. I knew of it when it was first signed by the three members of the subcommittee.[164]

It was part of the Corporation's strategy when it filed the Stockton complaint in May 1960 to draw a sharp distinction between the lawsuit and the labor troubles it was having. There is "no labor question involved in the present action," Sanborn stated in his press release. This thread in the web, too, was beginning to wear thin. Sanborn and Hayes used the Werdel reprint in a labor matter in their attack on *Strangers in Our Fields*. Gubser brandished it when he tried unsuccessfully to stop an investigation of a farm worker's tragedy affecting the notorious labor issue of the *bracero* program.[165] Joseph DiGiorgio instructed Brobeck, Phleger and Harrison to reject any settlement which did not dispose of "all other matters in issue" including the strike. In respect to the AWOC organizing drive the Corporation made an attempt to support Sanborn's disavowal. On 12 December 1962 answering an interrogatory by Murray, "What steps did your corporation take to prevent that drive from being successful?" Robert DiGiorgio declared under oath: "None."[166]

In giving this answer, Robert was standing on a rug and his Corporation's own 1960 Report to the Stockholders pulled it from under him. It contained this paragraph: "Your company encountered this problem in its Dantoni and New England orchards. . . . Pickets were established. . . . Higher harvest costs resulted, . . . [the Company incurred] expenses necessary to maintain the rights of the farm workers to work. . . ."[167] Among these costs were contributions to the Tri-County Agricultural Committee created to stop the organizing drive, support for the Northern California Growers Association in its encounter with Smith and financial arrangements for the confidential exchange of information with other agribusinessmen. Robert's testimony to the contrary his corporation had indeed taken steps.

By August 1964, when the San Francisco suit was formally closed, the pattern of the web had not only become more complex but also less and less believable. Now the issue of the truthfulness of witnesses was coming to the fore. Sanborn denied that he cooperated in the attack on *Strangers in our Fields;* Hayes confirmed that he had. Robert DiGiorgio denied that he had anything to do with the Tenney committee investigation; one of the sessions of the committee was held at the ranch. Lawrence Webdell signed an anti-Union petition as a "worker"; he was the office manager at DiGiorgio Farms. Gubser listed some of his expert informants in his speeches on the floor of the House, he omitted Sanborn and Connors. Robert testified that the company had taken no steps to stop the AWOC; it laid out moneys to ensure farm workers their right to work. DiGiorgio Corporation swore that it did not know where 612-53 came from; Dungan admitted such knowledge and so did Robert.

Credibility, as Nizer pointed out, is of one piece and the lack of it at one node in a mesh of arguments will spread to the rest of the net. It was no longer possible to believe Sanborn's statement of May 18 that the Corporation had no alternative to legal action. The agreement of May 1950 offered such an alternative if the Corporation had merely complied with its obligation to notify the parties to it and give them thirty days to stop the showing of the film. Sanborn was straightforward about the matter. "I wasn't thinking in terms of any agreement," he testified.

The Corporation's complaint of 18 May 1960 was based upon the advice of Brobeck, Phleger and Harrison, and this advice was in turn grounded on what the law required, "a careful and prudent investigation of the supposed facts."[168] Brobeck hired William Callan, of Associated Farmers, to investigate, carefully and prudently. Both Sanborn and Dungan were positive that what Callan was asked to do was to make an *investigation*. Nevertheless, Sedgwick objected to the word, and insisted on another, such as *inquiry*. Here, then was a dilemma, with Dungan trying to comply with the legal rule by stressing *investigation,* and Sedgwick trying to evade it by substituting *inquiry*. Sedgwick may not have been aware that Callan's *investigation* was far from being careful and prudent, but the record was soon to make this clear. Murray's discovery showed that Callan had collected and delivered to Dungan several undated AWOC publications and one that was in Spanish. Callan turned up one assistant director to Norman Smith. Dungan produced another by writing in Galarza's name on a letterhead. In fact Smith had no assistant director.

If Callan was slack it was partly because he was not held to very high standards of investigation; Brobeck, Phleger and Harrison's own weaknesses in research were becoming noticeable. It alleged in one brief that the film was shown to the Committee on Education and Labor, which was not true. It referred to a subcommittee report "rendered" in February 1950 but without submitting proof as to the place where it had been delivered. To the appellate court Attorney Plant declared in his brief that upon viewing the film the House Committee on Education and Labor "forthwith appointed a subcommittee to investigate conditions at DiGiorgio Farms," the facts being (a) that the Committee never saw the film, (b) that there could not be a forthwith action to an event that never occurred and (c) that in response to Congressman Elliott's demand the subcommittee was appointed seven months after Plant's non-event.

Callan could be excused for not patching the tears in his investigation, since the Corporation did not seem to care about mending the gaps in its own evidence. Crompton, in his *Life of the Spider*, was not describing DiGiorgio but the common house spider, *Tegenaria domestica,* which "spins incessantly and soon fills up any rupture in its handiwork."[169]

The Nixon-Morton-Steed report was now looking less like an official House document and more like a collage of testimony, briefs, quotations, indictments and privileged libels. It was the product of a rump subcommittee with no chairman, no records and no rules.

It was, by the end of 1964, a straining web, but still serviceable. Some of its assets remained undiminished by discovery, depositions, subpoenas, and cross-examination.

Among these was the unfailing willingness of Hon. Tom Steed to testify that he signed the report and that he and his two colleagues were contributing authors of the report. Plant suceeded in accrediting before two courts of law the Appendix print as admissible evidence of an official report of a responsible committee of Congress. Bailey's statement to the newspapers on 11 March 1950 saying that he would issue a minority report, the Corporation continued to exploit in two ways: it argued that Bailey's statement admitted there was a majority report; and it pointed out persistently that the chairmen never delivered on his promise; or as Dungan phrased it "he never got off the dime."

Moreover, the Corporation persevered in casting suspicion upon

unnamed persons for supposedly removing and destroying the minutes of the subcommittee and possibly the original report. Bailey
had not been able to locate the minute book when he responded to
Galarza's letter in 1960. DiGiorgio read this letter and seized upon
it to suggest darkly that these vital documents had been purloined,
and certainly not by friends of the Corporation.

Bailey was also held to account for another circumstance that
favored the Corporation's case. As chairman of Subcommittee
Number 1 he was personally charged by Lesinski with the responsibility of presenting a report to the full committee. Such a report
was not known to have been made. This, together with Bailey's
failure to issue a minority report responsive to Nixon, Morton and
Steed, made him appear as lazy or irresponsible, if not conniving.

Furthermore, *Poverty in the Valley of Plenty* was now twice condemned. Of the hearings transcript only one copy survived and that
was in the possession of the Corporation. As Werdel took pains
to point out, no Member of the House objected when he asked for
permission to insert in the Appendix the irregular report. Nor did
the House take Congressman Edwards seriously when he questioned the misrepresentation of the Extension of Remarks as a
legitimate document.

There was enough here for DiGiorgio to believe that it was still
in possession of the field, on which it might yet be necessary to
wage future battles. *Poverty* was legally dead, and in any event
with the passage of the years its defenders were becoming fewer
and their memories more dim.

But there were still some who believed that the Corporation had
had something to do with the preparation of the Werdel text, that
the report was illegitimate and that it had served to combat unionization of farm workers.

DiGiorgio could no more abide that these things be said in print
than it had been able to tolerate the public showing of *Poverty*. And
when they appeared in a public journal the Corporation, still with
Brobeck at its side, sued again.

NOTES

145. Cardozo. *Growth of the Law,* p. 53.
146. Testimony of Tom Steed. Reporter's partial transcript. Complaint number 503735, pp. 4–11.
147. Ibid., p. 13 ff.
148. Testimony of Robert DiGiorgio. Reporter's partial transcript. Complaint number 503735, pp. 61 ff.
149. Testimony of Bruce W. Sanborn, Jr. Reporter's partial transcript. Complaint number 503735, pp. 3, 60.
150. Testimony of Malcolm T. Dungan. Reporter's partial transcript. Complaint number 503735, pp. 55–59.
151. Tom Steed. Deposition. 30 April 1963, p. 6.
152. Richard M. Nixon. Deposition. 7 January 1963, p. 27.
153. Testimony of Tom Steed. Reporter's partial transcript. Complaint number 503735, p. 26.
154. Ralph R. Roberts. Deposition. 29 April 1963, p. 35.
155. Thomas H. Werdel. Deposition. 31 July 1962, p. 29.
156. Testimony of Tom Steed. Reporter's partial transcript. Complaint number 503735, p. 31. "The reason—the main reason—for printing hearings is to create a record that members can use in their deliberations of any legislation that may be considered as a result of the problem on which the hearings have been held . . . sufficient copies are printed to supply members of the public as well as Congress."
     Russell C. Derrickson, Deposition. 29 April 1963, p. 19. "A catalogue of government publications shall be prepared by the Superintendent of Documents on the first day of each month, which shall show the documents printed during the preceding month, where obtainable and the price thereof." *U.S. Code,* annotated, Title 44, section 77. *Monthly Catalogue U.S. Government Publications.* May 1950. Entries 8483-10315. Issued by the Superintendent of Documents. Washington D.C. 1950. No. 9170. Education and Labor Committee, House. Investigation of labor-management relations before special investigating subcommittee, 91st Congress. L. C. Card 50-60517, p. 30.
157. Russell C. Derrickson, Deposition. 29 April 1963, p. 23.
158. *Los Angeles Times.* 11 March 1950.
159. Tom Steed. Deposition. 30 April 1963, p. 11.
160. Miller. *Member of the House,* p. 79.

161. Tom Steed. Deposition. 13 September 1965, p. 53.
162. *Hearings.* Bakersfield 12–13 November 1949, p. 663.
163. Thomas H. Werdel. Deposition. 31 July 1962, p. 16.
164. Malcolm T. Dungan. Deposition. 7 November 1961, p. 58.
165. *Congressional Record.* 16 October 1963, p. 18637 ff.
166. "60. Is it not true that officials of your corporation knew that a unionizing drive was being conducted so far as farm field workers were concerned in the year 1959–1960?

"61. What steps did your corporation take to prevent that drive from being successful?" Interrogatories to defendant DiGiorgio Fruit Corporation. 26 November 1962.

"60. Yes, it is true.

"61. None." Answers of defendant DiGiorgio Fruit Corporation to plaintiff's interrogatories, 12 December 1962.
167. *Report to the Stockholders.* DiGiorgio Fruit Corporation, 1960.
168. *Moore v. Northern Pacific Railway Company*, 33 NW 336.
169. Crompton. *Life of the Spider*, p. 42.

10

THE PRINCIPLE

OF THE THING

The trial in the matter of *Galarza v. DiGiorgio Fruit Corporation*
received no notice in the San Francisco press. To the litigants the
case had intensely newsworthy qualities. The defendant corporation
was in the midst of a widely publicized resistance to the efforts of
the Agricultural Workers Organizing Committee. Robert DiGiorgio
was an outstanding citizen in the city of the Golden Gate, as familiar as the Coit Tower or the Ferry Building, and far more eminent.
The Corporation moved at the very center of financial and political
power in California, the pacesetter in a three-billion-dollar industry
that advertised itself as the bedrock of the state's economy.

Competent newspaper reporters are quick to sense a controversy
that needles the nerves of those who hold social or political power
and those who contest it. Newspaper publishers are even more so,
the business of publishing being itself one of the forms of that
power. News coverage of a libel suit that might arouse the hunting
instincts of a working reporter must reckon with the allergy of
publishers to the whole subject of defamation. Freedom of the
press, about which publishers can become livid, in practice means
also the freedom not to inquire into the confidential workings of
established power. In 1950 the Nixon-Morton-Steed report had
commanded space in the news columns and editorial pages of the
San Francisco Examiner and *Chronicle*. In 1964, when the remains
of that report were brought by James Murray into open court, the
event was not noted in either of those important dailies.

None of these handicaps applied to Jeff Boehm, a veteran
reporter for a chain of labor newspapers published by Sheldon
Sackett, owner of the Olympic Press. Boehm had been one of

several editors of these newspapers since 1956, winning several awards by the International Labor Press for his stories on California labor. He wrote on several occasions about the struggles of farm labor in the Central Valley, including the DiGiorgio strike of 1947 to 1950.

To Boehm the revelations of the San Francisco trial gave fresh interest to a story that had been standing in type for over a decade. It was a story, moreover, that suited Sheldon Sackett's sense of the appropriate. There were no policy restrictions on Boehm in covering it. From depositions and sworn testimony he proceeded to give his labor constituents in plain, belligerent and sometimes harsh prose an updated account of the now notorious document.

"Twice within the past two years," Boehm's article began, "this newspaper has asked: Did a Congressman and the DiGiorgio Fruit Corporation, conniving to crush a farm worker's union, fake a congressional hearing report and have it placed in the *Congressional Record?* We can now report that there is overwhelming evidence that they did."

"That fraudulent document," Boehm continued, "was the major weapon used in breaking the strike and slandering union leadership back in 1950." Recalling that the Werdel Extension of Remarks was offered as evidence by the Corporation to win a $60,000 award against the AFL-CIO, Boehm said that in 1963 the document was used "in an effort to discredit and obstruct an investigation of the Chualar labor bus train collision in which 32 *braceros* were killed." Warming to his theme, Boehm concluded by rating the report as a "phony," a counterfeit.

Boehm's piece first appeared in the *Union Gazette* of Santa Clara County on 17 April 1964. It was reprinted in the *Monterey County Labor News* and other weeklies of the Sackett chain. A clipping of the story was sent by Galarza to George Ballis, editor of the *Fresno Valley Labor Citizen,* which published it on April 24.

These publications and republications were as challenging to the Corporation as Smith's exhibition of *Poverty in the Valley of Plenty.* They raised the issues that had haunted the Stockton and San Francisco trials, principally concerning the genuineness and validity of the Nixon-Morton-Steed document. Boehm's attack shifted the center of the controversy even further away from the film itself and toward the murky circumstances under which the slashing attack on the farm labor union had been produced in 1950. DiGiorgio was now on the defensive and was faced with

A Hard Choice. / During nearly fifteen years it had distributed and endorsed the Werdel reprints as an official House document, a notable congressional endorsement of Joseph DiGiorgio's anti-unionism, produced in the regular and legitimate course of congressional business. To be identified with such a document was honorable. DiGiorgio's signal victories in court underscored the pride the Corporation felt in the vindication bearing the distinguished names of Richard M. Nixon, Thruston B. Morton and Tom Steed. Now Boehm put together enough testimony, adding to it the sting of his own conclusions, to suggest that DiGiorgio's prize exhibit was illegitimate.

In defense against this accusation DiGiorgio could take the high road or the low one. The first would have been an unequivocal declaration of the genuineness of the alleged report, backed by documentary evidence of DiGiorgio's connections with it, whatever they may have been. The second would be a detour around Boehm's most damaging point, that the Corporation had in fact been a party to the preparation of the report.

The high road had certain moral considerations to commend it. It would stamp the prestige of the Corporation upon the report. It would confirm the good faith, the competence and the legislative integrity of the three signers. It would display publicly the enduring and finer qualities of loyalty and gratitude of the old partnership of DiGiorgio-Werdel-Nixon-Morton-Steed. It would offer a decisive opportunity to crush the libel-prone and mendacious labor critics.

This route, paved with good intentions, was nevertheless a dangerous one. It would subject to proof facts which the Corporation had been successful in eluding for fifteen years. It threatened to throw back upon the Corporation the damaging questions and innuendos which the alleged report had first hurled at the farm labor union. These questions, particularly those raised by Werdel in his prefatory remarks, might now be rephrased: Had three congressmen collaborated in the preparation and publication of a phony congressional report? Were there in the Werdel document certain deliberately fabricated falsehoods? Had the Corporation and its congressional friends done a disservice to the free enterprise

system? Had the authors and publishers of the Werdel Extension
of Remarks and the reprint tampered with the processes of the
United States Congress? Could not the farm workers now turn the
text to their account and ask responsible corporate leadership to
join them in decrying the attempt of the Corporation to win its case
by dishonest representation?

The detour which DiGiorgio chose indicated that the Corporation was not prepared to take these risks, nor was it willing to
assume the burden of proof which they implied. This burden was
now dropped on the shoulders of the four congressmen, and the
practical decision was made to deny flatly that the Corporation
had ever had anything to do with the preparation of the report;
that it had had any correspondence with Werdel or any other
member of the subcommittee between 13 November 1949 and 9
March 1950; or that it ever had advance knowledge of the preparation and contents of the report.

To the problem of strategy there was now added, from the point
of view of the Corporation, the question of tactics. Boehm's article
could have been answered by DiGiorgio in a press release. There
was an obvious advantage in this form of response. It would leave
the choice of credibility to the reader, with a strong chance that
Boehm, Ballis and the Sackett newspapers would print the rebuttal.
More importantly it would prevent the further use of subpoenas,
interrogatories, depositions and other lethal devices which Murray
had already used with such telling effect.

The alternative was to sue for libel once again and to take the
risks of adversary discovery proceedings. To be sure, in another
lawsuit the Corporation would itself have available subpoena
powers. Its attorneys could grill Boehm and Ballis and other defendants to the purpose of proving that they had been guilty of misrepresentations motivated by malice. The misrepresentations, however, could be proved only by a full and detailed disclosure of the
history of the Werdel document, and the uses to which the Corporation had put it. In another court battle this would become the
prime target area of the opposition.

A feeling of cool confidence must have induced DiGiorgio to
set in motion again the ponderous machinery of legal process. After
all, Brobeck, Phleger and Harrison had a nearly perfect record in
the courts *re Poverty* over a course of fifteen years and five law-

suits. Boehm's denunciation of the Werdel print as a "phony" rankled Robert DiGiorgio. "It imputes dishonesty to me," he said, "and we believe that our reputation is such that, and our actions are such that this was an unfair and untrue statement and that it hurt our reputation."[170]

Joseph DiGiorgio's bronze bust was watching, a reminder that the Corporation had been vindicated of the *canard* that it forced its peons to live in miserable huts. Robert was now about to sue for vindication against the charge that he and his agents and associates had been in any way connected with the preparation of the document that Joseph DiGiorgio hailed so proudly in 1950.

This was the principle behind what Nixon, Morton and Steed had done, and which now became the drive behind the sixth

Complaint for Libel—the Sixth /   No. 122891
   In the Superior Court of the State of California
   in and for the County of Fresno
   DiGiorgio Fruit Corporation,
   a Corporation, Plaintiff,
   v.
   Valley Labor Citizen, Jeff Boehm, George Ballis, et al.
   Filed 9 June 1964.

The complaint charged the defendants with four scurrilous and defamatory allegations: (1) that the Corporation had connived to crush a farm worker's union; (2) that it had faked a congressional report; (3) that it had slandered union leadership, and (4) that it had used the faked report to win two lawsuits brought against the unions. Special damages of $100,000 were asked and additional damages of $250,000 by way of punishment for "wanton and reckless heedlessness of plaintiff's rights."[171]

Since Boehm's article appeared in a public journal the Corporation demanded a public retraction. Notice to this effect was served on defendants on 6 May 1964, before the San Francisco lawsuit had ended. The officers of the Fresno Central Labor Council, publishers of the *Valley Labor Citizen*, together with Ballis, discussed the demand. They decided that if Sackett disavowed the Boehm piece they would also. Sackett was not penitent and the Council voted to let the Ballis republication stand.

In the course of pleadings DiGiorgio made it known that it

intended to present a witness from Washington, D.C., at the trial. It also introduced a copy of Werdel's Extension of Remarks from the Appendix of 9 March 1950, which extract set forth "a report of a congressional committee investigation, which is signed by Richard Nixon, Thruston B. Morton and Tom Steed." This exhibit carefully differentiated, for the first time, between Werdel's prefatory remarks and the report proper.

DiGiorgio also offered as a preliminary exhibit a clipping from the *Bakersfield Press* containing the following sentence: "The committee report, which has not yet been filed officially, has been read into the *Congressional Record*." This quotation was attributed to Werdel.[172]

A significant piece of legal strategy in the complaint was the omission of Galarza as a defendant. Brobeck argued in a memorandum that "every person who directly or indirectly publishes or assists in the publication . . . is liable for the resultant injury." Boehm's direct testimony was cited to the effect that "the basis for the article" in the *Valley Labor Citizen* "was furnished by Galarza, and thus it cannot be denied that the article was the joint product of Galarza and Boehm, and it matters not which one of them sent it to Ballis."

Since Brobeck was later to argue that the Ballis's republication was in the nature of a conspiracy, there must have been weighty reasons why the vital link in the conspiracy between Boehm and Ballis was avoided. Furthermore, in arguing that Boehm's article was a joint work product of Boehm and Galarza, Brobeck was stepping squarely into Boehm's defense. This was that he had relied implicitly on Galarza as his source, together with certain depositions and other documentary evidence which he read before writing the piece.

In hastening its attack on the *Valley Labor Citizen,* the Corporation set the stage for

The Progress of Discovery. / It is one of the peculiarities of the common law: a witness is sworn before the court to tell the truth, the whole truth and nothing but the truth, so help him God. But against the Divine Assistance there is immediately pitted the forensic ingenuity of lawyers intent on excluding those bits and portons of the truth that damage their argument. Their weapon is the

Objection, a sharp instrument with which a skilled practitioner can adroitly hack away at the Whole Truth. When opposing counsel have rested their cases what is before the court and the jury is not the Whole Truth but only those portions of it which have survived the fine mincing process of objections.

Legal discovery, a latter day reform of the common law, is a device to give divinity a helping hand. It now came into play during the two years that preceded the trial of *DiGiorgio v. Valley Labor Citizen.*

Attorney Donald Connors, who now assumed the burden of the case for DiGiorgio, had little difficulty in establishing from Boehm's deposition the sequence of events—the preparation of his article, the sources he relied on, his conversations with Galarza, his total disconnection with Ballis. In addition to the plain straightforwardness of his story, Boehm stated the clutch of the case: "The material that I have read indicates that it was prepared in a co-operative activity of DiGiorgio Farms, or some of the officers or lawyers of DiGiorgio Farms, and . . . Congressman Werdel."

Had Connors believed in signs or premonitions something in Boehm's answers would have put him on guard:

CONNORS: Where did you work before 1956?
BOEHM: In the Olivet Cemetery.
CONNORS: What did you do there?
BOEHM: I was a grave digger, a gardener.

With a touch of legal elegance, Connors then asked why Boehm had abandoned his work at Olivet:

CONNORS: What were your mental processes?
BOEHM: Mental processes? These were rather economic processes. . . . I had a family to support.

Ballis was the next deponent. He, too, showed Connors a disconcerting candor as to the facts that led to his republication of the Boehm piece. He had not personally researched the facts reported by Boehm, had made no inquiries about it, had not personally checked the accuracy of the details. He had never met Boehm before the publication in the *Valley Labor Citizen.* The witness was a newspaperman of long experience who held a degree from the University of Minnesota. It appeared that Connors was scoring.

Ballis's lack of concern for painstaking research seemed to back
him into a corner. But it was a corner which Ballis himself had
selected. He declared to Connors that over many years he had been
familiar with the background of the DiGiorgio controversies, and
had accumulated papers and documents on the subject. Above all it
was the source of the clipping which had prompted him to publish
it. Like Boehm, Ballis accepted it unequivocally on the authority
of Galarza. During some eleven years the exchange of information between them continued. When Connors tried to separate what
Ballis had learned through his own reading from the information
given him by Galarza, Ballis answered that he had not classified his
facts by sources over so long a period since he had not planned on
being cross-examined about them. On the question whether he had
kept a diary or any other record that would date his sources, Ballis
volunteered the comment that "only generals keep diaries." He
chronicled his career for Connor's information with a disconcerting grandiloquence: "The day Eisenhower entered the White
House I entered Fresno." Connors' pursuit of conspiracy ran
abruptly into blind alleys:

> CONNORS: Well, give us your best recollection of what you
> said and what Mr. Boehm said.
> BALLIS: I told him who I was; and I told him that we had
> published this article; and I told him that we had
> been served with a demand for a retraction.
> CONNORS: And what did he say in response to that?
> BALLIS: I remember his first words were "Oh."

In the course of his preparations, Connors had taken a second
deposition of Congressman Tom Steed. The Corporation had paid
Steed's expenses to San Francisco from Washington for the purpose. Including his direct testimony in the San Francisco trial, this
was Steed's third appearance for DiGiorgio in the evolution of the
Werdel affair.

Steed once more emphasized that his own original draft of
opinions and views after Bakersfield was in the nature of dissenting
views. When he wrote it he anticipated that Bailey's report would
be politically unacceptable to him, and he prepared his minority
statement only on the basis of private conversations with Bailey.
When he circulated his draft to the subcommittee members and

found to his delight that Nixon and Morton concurred enthusi-
astically, the three then decided "that we would make a complete
statement as though we were covering the whole issue and not just
dissenting views from something that had been prepared by somebody else."[173] In other words with three of the five subcommittee
members in agreement, it was now possible to prepare what would
appear to be a majority report.

This raised certain problems, psychological and technical. Steed
was bored with the assignment and did not have sufficient interest
in it to take part in the preparation of a more elaborate draft.[174]
Morton was even less concerned. Nixon was intent on his pursuit
of Hiss and a seat in the Senate. The three were fully aware that it
was Bailey's prerogative to assign the preparation of the report to
a staff member, and that the resulting document would reflect
Bailey's and not Steed's views. Bailey did not make such an assignment, Steed pointed out, and the three dissenters had no staff of
their own. Steed deposed that in this predicament they turned to
Werdel "who furnished the people to do the actual typing."

More serious than the problem of stenographic service was that
of obtaining the documentary sources for the draft. Steed declared
that the subcommittee possessed no files, and he agreed that consideration of a report required that the committee members have
before them the printed transcript of the Hearings. "It is my impression," Steed said in response to a question, "[that] Mr. Werdel
probably supplied most of the material." Drawing on him, Steed
said, "We beefed it up" until the dissenting views took on the heft
and bulk of a majority report.

With Werdel supplying the typists and the sources, the three
congressmen used a procedure for preparing an official committee
report not heretofore known to the House. There were no executive
sessions of the subcommittee, Steed testified, no called meetings,
no minutes of proceedings. The three discussed the matter "walking
back and forth to the chamber" in what was "just a give and take
friendly discussion."

Connors again led Steed to the subject of the signing of the
report. The witness reaffirmed that he had put his own signature
to the document and that he had seen the handwritten signatures
of Nixon and Morton preceding his. There were, Steed said, not
one but six copies so signed. Steed insisted that this made the docu-

ment an official House report "at least in an embryonic stage."

Cross-examined by Murray, Steed had no recollection that either he or any one else handed Bailey a copy of the "beefed-up" draft. His assumption was that Nixon had taken care of so important a detail. Murray also elicited from Steed that there was no evidence in Bakersfield that Union officials had been guilty of fraud or bribery. Even so, Steed remained convinced that the Union was a racket, "a scheme to get something for nothing." He testified that the Union attempted to change his mind about the report through Walter Mason, legislative representative of the A.F. of L. in Washington:

> STEED: Mr. Mason approached me at the suggestion of Mr. Bailey to try to change my mind about this report.
> MURRAY: Did Mr. Mason know about this report?
> STEED: Oh, yes.
> MURRAY: Before it was signed?
> STEED: While it was under discussion.

Steed finished his deposition in a repentant mood. The due process of the House, he suggested, had indeed been violated concerning the report. "It did not complete the full course that was required of it. Somebody was derelict in the fact that it didn't. . . . It still isn't right not to have the matter done according to the rules of the House. . . . I think that there has been a dereliction here on the part of the Congress . . . It is unfair to leave something hanging in the air . . . if you were this careless all the time, there is no telling what harm you could do to a labor union or a business institution or something of that sort." Even back in 1950 Steed had not rated his role in the affair very highly. When Werdel's Extension appeared in the Appendix on March 9, he did not bother to read it. He was not "particularly interested in that stuff."

Murray now called as his deponent Robert DiGiorgio. He followed the story line that had been laid down in previous lawsuits.

> MURRAY: You wanted whoever read it to think that it was an official report. . . ?
> DI GIORGIO: That's what it was and that's what I still believe it to be. . . . Mr. Steed's testimony is that he signed it . . . and Mr. Nixon and Mr. Morton . . . and this

> is three of the five members of the subcommittee.
> It seems to me that's official enough. . . .

MURRAY: Well, did you have any evidence that it was ever considered by a committee of Congress?

DI GIORGIO: No, I don't. . . .

MURRAY: You circulated Werdel's prefatory remarks?

DI GIORGIO: Certainly . . . We circulated it to vindicate the corporation's position in the strike. This is what we thought this congressional report did. . . . This is a public document of an action of a portion of the legislature of the United States. . . .

Murray attempted again to elicit from DiGiorgio a more coherent account of the origin of the Dungan document, the cryptic number 612–53.

MURRAY: That was typed up in the DiGiorgio Fruit Corporation office. Isn't that true?

DI GIORGIO: I don't know that, no.

MURRAY: So this mimeographed document of thirteen pages you don't know anything about?

DI GIORGIO: No.

MURRAY: Have you learned anything about its origin?

DI GIORGIO: No.

MURRAY: Made an inquiry?

DI GIORGIO: No.

MURRAY: Been told anything?

DI GIORGIO: No.

Murray drew another blank with respect to the carbon copy of the reporter's transcript that the Corporation had obtained in 1950. Connors intervened vigorously to help DiGiorgio deal with this dangerous subject.

CONNORS: Just a moment, I'll object to that. We have a copy Brobeck, Phleger and Harrison acquired. We got a copy . . . I think we still have a copy . . .

MURRAY: Would you be kind enough to enter into a stipulation that Brobeck, Phleger and Harrison did acquire a copy of the reporter's transcript. . . ?

CONNORS: Yes, with the proviso that I don't know if it's complete. . . . I simply don't know. But it appears to be.

Again DiGiorgio declared that "the first knowledge we had that
it was in the *Congressional Record* was when I read it in the newspapers that morning." Forgetting or ignoring Lucey's testimony in
Stockton, he denied that any of the Corporation's agents had ever
looked for an original of the report. He further denied any knowledge of the February 1948 petition of DiGiorgio's employees
rejecting the Union, declaring "I don't know who was instrumental
in it." The Tenney Committee held one investigative session on
DiGiorgio Farms, but DiGiorgio testified "I don't know that they
did or didn't." As to the Special Citizens Committee pamphlet
A Community Aroused, he could not recall having anything to do
with its publication.

Murray's efforts at discovery were now running in circles of dim
recollection and baffling contradictions. They became even dimmer
and less consistent when he called up his next deponent, Attorney
Malcolm Dungan.

Murray pressed Dungan on three crucial aspects of the case—the
Corporation's correspondence between the closing of the Bakersfield hearings and 9 March 1950; Brobeck's carbon copy of the
reporter's transcript; and the origins of document 612–53.

On the first of these, Dungan was explicit and helpful:

> MURRAY: Did you yourself write to anyone of the three Con-
> gressmen . . . before 9 March 1950 . . . in relation
> to the investigation . . . in Bakersfield in 1949?
> DUNGAN: I believe that I did. . . . It was either Mr. Bailey or
> it was the subcommittee counsel or one of the staff
> members, the subcommittee chief clerk, or some-
> body of that sort.
> MURRAY: And that was before 9 March 1950?
> DUNGAN: That was after 12 November, 1940, and before 9
> March 1950; yes, sir.[175]

In due course Dungan would disclose the purpose of this correspondence, though it would require three more lawsuits for libel
to reach that point of discovery.

Dungan was intimately familiar with the matter of the reporter's
transcript, but as of 7 February 1966, the date of his deposition,
he simply did not know where it was. "It is not a question of
recalling; I have not looked," he said. "Four things could have

happened. . . . It may still be in the file, or Mr. Sedgwick may have it or we may have sent it back to the company, or it may have been discarded. I do not know." Dungan was referring to two bound volumes of carbon typescript totalling some six hundred pages of double spaced pages.

As to the elusive thirteen-page number 612-53 Dungan told Murray that Brobeck had received a copy "on or shortly after 9 March 1950." This was a stencil impression of a mimeographed text that had been run off in the Corporation's office in San Francisco.[176] What Dungan had sent Murray was a photocopy of this impression, which remained in Brobeck's files as one of the originals from DiGiorgio's mimeograph.

Murray had learned how 612-53 had got to Brobeck.

On two other important matters Murray made little progress. How and from what source, Murray wanted to know, did the text of 612-53 come into DiGiorgio's possession? Connors interposed a suggestion that gave Dungan a helpful lead:

> CONNORS: Excuse me, Mr. Murray. I may be able to help you here. It is my impression that there is a TWX connection between DiGiorgio's Baltimore office and their San Francisco office. Mr. Dungan, does that help your recollection any?

It did.

> DUNGAN: . . . That brings another recollection to my mind, that they had a teletype. I may have seen it first in teletype form on long yellow sheets of paper.
> MURRAY: Like the AP has or the UP?
> DUNGAN: No. Private TWX. . . . It was by one of those means that the full text of the report was made available in San Francisco on the day it was made public.

That day was 10 March 1950, the publication date of the previous day's *Congressional Record*. The matter on the long yellow sheets, Dungan surmised, had been transcribed by a DiGiorgio stenographer.

The explanation, not likely to impress Murray, appeared to leave Dungan uneasy. If it should later collapse, some way of retreating with dignity was needed. Dungan prepared it:

MURRAY: Do you know whether . . . [612–53] was copied
from something else?

DUNGAN: Well, I think it was copied from a telephone call . . .
that on the day the report was made public it was
telephoned from Mr. Nixon's office in Washington
to the office of DiGiorgio in San Francisco . . . the
call was made on March 9 or March 10 . . . Mr.
Harrison told me . . . it was . . . or that a similar
document was taken down in shorthand by a stenographer, someone reading at the other end of the
line and a stenographer taking it down in short-
hand here.

One additional point was raised by Murray. The number 612-
53, Dungan explained, "is our firm's file number for one of these
libel suits that was filed in 1949 or 1950." Murray asked, "Is there
anything else on file presently, today, in file number 612-53?"
Dungan answered: "I have no idea whether there is or not."

An important and bulky part of this file was the two-volume
carbon copy of the reporter's transcript that Sedgwick read from
at the San Francisco trial. Murray now asked Brobeck to allow
him to make a copy of this document. Connors delayed producing
it and Murray obtained a court order to that effect. On 16 March
1966 Connors, in a sworn declaration, said: "I caused an intensive
search to be made throughout the office but the transcript was not
located." The search team included Sedgwick, Vincent DiGiorgio,
employees of the Corporation and two clerks of the law firm.

DiGiorgio's alleged losses of vital documents reduced further
discovery to whatever surprises a trial might produce.

NOTES

170. Reporter's transcript on appeal. Case number 122891. Fifth
     Appellate District, Vol. I, p. 49. Hereafter cited as Reporter's
     transcript. Case number 122891.
171. Second amended complaint. Case number 122891.
172. Tom Steed. Deposition. 13 September 1965, pp. 9–10.
173. Ibid.
174. Ibid., p. 47.
175. Malcolm T. Dungan. Deposition. 7 February 1966, p. 21.
176. Ibid., p. 28.

II

THE TRIAL OF
AN UNREPORTED REPORT

In the Superior Court sitting in the city of Fresno, capital of agribusiness, the trial opened on 21 March 1964, the Hon. Milo Popovich presiding. Connors chose to try the case before a jury. Without much contention the twelve were impaneled, ordinary citizens called from housekeeping and shop and commerce to sit for a week in puzzled judgment on a narrative of lost documents, absent witnesses, congressional nonproceedings and the ghost of a dead motion picture. They were to hear two intense attorneys dropping famous names that had somehow attached themselves to a strike fought, lost and forgotten long ago. They would have to guess at a hundred nuances of testimony, forced to sit dumb in the jury box while a stream of words passed by them. Out of the fabric of the whole truth swatches would be scissored by opposing counsel and arranged in clashing patterns—the jurors would have to decide which one they liked best.

In opening the proceedings the Court sounded a note of modesty. "We have a new panel that's only tried one case, and that was a criminal case. This will be their first experience with a civil case." For Judge Popovich also it would be in some respects a new experience. He said: "Unfortunately, this case was given to me late Friday afternoon, and I am not current on the present law of libel in the strict sense."

Robert DiGiorgio, the first witness called by the plaintiff, sat well before the inexperienced jury. His pitch, unlike Norman Smith's, was low and restrained, getting over the impression of an upright and important executive whose personal and corporate reputation had been traduced. His indignation was subdued but his wounds

were showing. Trained in the law he modulated his answers skillfully. He spoke for one of the world's most powerful corporations
in the role of a supplicant before the decency and fairness of the
ordinary Americans in the jury box.

His recital, in response to questions from both Connors and
Murray, covered the familiar ground. He disclaimed any knowledge of Werdel's views on the strike or any awareness that the
congressman representing the DiGiorgio district was sympathetic
to the Corporation. There were no dealings, he testified, between
DiGiorgio and Werdel to correct the unfavorable publicity stirred
by *Poverty in the Valley of Plenty*. To Connor's question whether
the Corporation had any correspondence or conversation with
Werdel the answer was cool, precise: "No, sir." Connors broad-
ened the question: "Now, after the hearings closed . . . did you
yourself . . . did anybody employed by DiGiorgio Fruit Corporation have any correspondence with or communication with any of
those congressmen?" This meant any member of the subcommittee
and the answer was still: "No, sir."[177]

A dangerous reef was next successfully skirted by DiGiorgio.

> CONNORS: Did you yourself . . . have any hand in preparing
> the report . . . ?
> DI GIORGIO: No, sir.
> CONNORS: To your knowledge, did anybody in the employ of
> DiGiorgio Fruit Corporation have any hand in
> preparing that report?
> DI GIORGIO: No, sir.
> CONNORS: To the best of your knowledge who did prepare
> that report?
> DI GIORGIO: Three congressmen that signed it.

DiGiorgio again stressed that the report was "an official report
of the Subcommittee of Congress and that it was filed." In distrib-
uting the reprint the witness stated that the document needed no
explanation: "It speaks for itself what it is."

Going back to the exciting news of 10 March 1950 DiGiorgio
recalled that it had been a great delight to Mr. Joseph and his
kinsmen. "I thought it very fully expressed the point I wanted to
make and it still does." Mr. Joseph's order had been to obtain
immediately a quantity of the prints for distribution "to people

who were interested and who followed this very closely and with whom he discussed it." And, again to stress a most important point, DiGiorgio declared that the newspaper stories of March 11 were "the first time he knew about it . . . first any of us knew about it."

DiGiorgio's own evaluation, sixteen years after the event, coincided exactly with the Union's reaction when Werdel's Extension was first publicized: "I think the effect of the report was a severe blow to the cause of the Union." Connors added for emphasis: "The congressional investigative process is absolutely vital to this country, and if anybody is accused of tampering with the Senate or House of Representatives, then he is dealt a mortal blow." Connors, of course, was referring to Boehm's piece about DiGiorgio, not to the reference in the report to Mitchell and his associates. The Nixon-Morton-Steed report said: "The processes of the Congress of the United States have been perverted and misused by the National Farm Labor Union in order to furnish a sounding board for its claims." Nevertheless, Connors had unwittingly driven the point home: The Union had been dealt a mortal blow.

Murray tried to lead DiGiorgio back to the persistent mystery of document 612-53. In his opening argument, Connors had promised new light on the subject. "Robert DiGiorgio will testify . . . that he got a copy of the *Congressional Record* containing this report from our law offices and that it was typed up in his office and mimeographed."

The testimony did not come through so neatly.

> CONNORS: Did you at any time see a mimeographed copy of the report?
>
> DI GIORGIO: I believe I did; yes, sir.
>
> CONNORS: Do you recall whether that was the first copy you ever saw?
>
> DI GIORGIO: I believe it was. I believe that was prepared before we could get copies of the actual printed Congressional [*sic*] or excerpts from the *Congressional Record*.
>
> CONNORS: Do you recall where that was mimeographed?
>
> DI GIORGIO: I believe in our office.
>
> CONNORS: And do you recall where you got the copy from which it was mimeographed?

DI GIORGIO: I don't recall, but I assume that your office furnished it to us, but I don't recall.[178]

Answering Murray's questions, DiGiorgio admitted that he had
seen the Dungan document before the printed version, then reversed his testimony:

MURRAY: Have you since discovered that [612–53] was typed
           in the offices of DiGiorgio Fruit Corporation?
DI GIORGIO: I have not discovered it, no.
MURRAY: You don't know who typed up this [612–53]. . . .
DI GIORGIO: No.
MURRAY: Or when it was typed up?
DI GIORGIO: No, I do not.
MURRAY: Or from what?
DI GIORGIO: No, I do not.

Murray was wringing inconsistencies from DiGiorgio, but no
admissions. Nor did he have better luck on another tack:

MURRAY: You don't remember the booklet *A Community
           Aroused?*
DI GIORGIO: I do remember a booklet. We had nothing to do
           with it. I had nothing to do with it, and as far as
           I know, no one in our company did.

Connors then called for the reading of Steed's deposition, since
the Corporation had decided not to have him testify in person.
The readers, Connors and Murray, droned through the text for
the benefit of the jury and the judge. From the 76 pages of testimony in the deposition Connors would glean those portions essential to his case—that the three congressmen had personally affixed
their signatures to the report, that they had taken part in the drafting, that the report had been filed, that it had appeared in the
Appendix of the *Congressional Record*. Steed's deposition was
worth Connors's trouble and DiGiorgio's expense. It was the only
direct testimony on how the Werdel text came to be, and in it
there was no trace of any connection with the Corporation.

As Murray sorted out the flaws in Steed's story he kept probing
for such a connection. It seemed unreasonable that communication between DiGiorgio and Werdel had been completely severed
during four critical months. While Connors was vehemently assert-

ing this to protect the Corporation from the taint of authorship, the Court was inclining to agree with him, but for a different reason, namely, the legitimacy of ghostwriting. The Court observed:

> It's quite common for people who have those responsibilities, such as these congressmen, to have others mechanically prepare their text, such as the speeches that people publicly make are written by ghostwriters. I wrote a decision for a certain judge who was assigned to the appellate court protem because he didn't know anything about the subject matter, and asked if I would be kind enough to write him an opinion. I wrote it out. All he had to do was sign it. . . . So it doesn't mean that there is any subterfuge or ulterior purpose. It merely established [that] these people who were probably less forensic used someone else's office in writing their text for them.

It was established, in the judgment of the Court, that the congressmen—Werdel, Nixon, Morton and Steed—because of forensic handicaps, "had used someone else's office in writing their text." The Court went on to accept Steed's testimony that they had in fact affixed their signatures and that this "gives it the stamp of dignity whether you like it or not."

The Court clearly was addressing Murray. The undercurrent was running against him. His Honor had come to the brink of the case—that someone else had done the writing for the congressmen —pulled Connors back from the chasm opening at his feet, and led the plaintiff back to safe ground with a homily on the social utility of ghostwriting. No proper trial is complete without at least one of these psychological wrenches. What Murray was hearing was language to this effect: "There is a ghost writer in this case but there is no subterfuge, for I was once a ghost writer myself."

Ballis now came forward. A smallish man, he looked even smaller surrounded by the shining upholstery of the witness chair. A former United States Marine, his manner was as leathery as his face, on which there was no make believe. Had Ballis affected any importance of personality, his deeply grooved features might have been described as craggy. The seam between his lips, however, when he spoke, parted into a grin that heightened an innocent wonder in the blue eyes of a reporter disposed to have fun in looking for facts.

Connors, broad and hefty in proportion to his six-foot height, got his answers from the witness crisp and to the point. Had he ever heard of Boehm? Never. Had he ever spoken to Boehm about the article before April 24? Never. Had he read the report itself? Never. Had he talked with Bailey? No. With any of the three signers? No. Or talked with anyone of the staff of the House committee? No. The picture of a negligent, nonchalant newspaper-man that Connors was beginning to outline was never completed. Ballis broke into the cross-examination to testify that his familiarity with the subject was of long standing, and that he had published "on the basis of the fact that the story came to me recommended by Galarza." In the approved manner of journalists Ballis was put-ting his "reliable source" on the line, and obliquely challenging Connors to call that source to the stand and impeach him. The source was sitting in the courtroom ten feet from Connors's chair at counsel's table. From his sources, Ballis told Connors, he had concluded that the subcommittee had never met; that the text of the alleged report was entered by Werdel, who was not a member of the subcommittee; and that if the three signatures had in fact been affixed, it did not make the "piece of paper" a committee document. Ballis refused to be budged either by Connors's arith-metic or his heraldry:

> CONNORS: What's a majority of five?
> BALLIS: . . . three members of Congress . . .
> CONNORS: Do you see the seal there? What's that a seal of?
> BALLIS: The United States of America.

They were back to Ballis's contention: "We never actually said that a person actually put words on paper, but that there was co-operation between the parties, that DiGiorgio in co-operation with Werdel had great influence in the tenor and final writing of that fraudulent report."

It was not Ballis's answers so much as Connors's questions that provided the novelty in this cross-examination: "Did this raise any question in your mind . . . to the effect that in two previous law-suits, this congressional report was accepted as authentic? Did you know that after the hearings were concluded . . . that DiGiorgio through its counsel . . . sent a brief to the subcommittee? . . . that both DiGiorgio and the Union were seeking to influence the tone of what might come out of that committee?" Upon these questions

Connors was using the familiar technique of "loading" messages intended for the jury, but in this case with unfortunate possibilities for his case. They weighted the record to the effect that (a) the Werdel document had been used in two previous lawsuits in successful actions by DiGiorgio against the unions, (b) that someone in the employ of DiGiorgio had indeed been in communication with some of the congressmen after the Bakersfield Hearings, and (c) that the Corporation had attempted to influence the tenor of the report in the critical period between 12 November 1949 and 9 March 1950.

These were three of the four contentions in Boehm's article that now brought him as a defendant within the range of Connors's interrogation, with which he now proceeded.

As with Ballis, Connors had no difficulty in fixing the facts that led from Boehm's writing to its appearance in the *Valley Labor Citizen*. Grey-haired, stocky, somewhat stooped from years spent over a typewriter, Boehm was soon reciting the grounds for his conclusions. He had noted the inconsistencies of the report, which, for example, said both that there was no picket line at DiGiorgio Farms and that the picket line had been a peaceful one. Lowell Bradford, the expert on evidence, had traced document 612-53, produced by Dungan, to a typewriter in the office of the Corporation. Werdel had not read his prefatory remarks in the House, yet they had been presented as an integral part of the report in the Corporation's reprint and had been quoted in that light in Sanborn's press release. It was Bailey and not Werdel, Boehm observed, who had been instructed to prepare and present a report to the chairman of the Committee on Education and Labor. He corrected both DiGiorgio and Connors by noting that the Union had not called for the investigation of 1949. The Clerk of the House, Roberts, had not in forty years experience known of a subcommittee report to appear in the Appendix of the *Congressional Record*. Whatever connections in his knowledge were not supplied by his own reading of depositions and other sources, Galarza had provided over the years in several conversations. As to the signatures Boehm testified that "it didn't matter very much. I was convinced that the operation through which it appeared in the Appendix of the *Congressional Record* was completely irregular."

Boehm, like Ballis, was carefully preparing his major defense as

a reporter, the reliability of his sources. The Court did not receive
his testimony in that light. Judge Popovich detected something
slightly sinister in Boehm's respect, as a reporter, for Galarza's
knowledge of the subject The Court said: "Here the tenor is more
befriending of Mr. Galarza and furthering Mr. Galarza's efforts in
a more personal way than you would expect of an experienced
editor. . . . A good question to then ask is, 'Is there some alle-
giance by reason of some affiliation in membership in an organization?', whether it be a lodge, a fraternity. . . ." Connors had asked
Galarza, Ballis and Boehm in depositions whether they had ever
been members of the Communist Party. His foundation for the
question was appropriate; he had been an investigator for the FBI
and was well read in the literature of the House Un-American
Activities Committee. In the courtroom such a question would
have caused an explosion. Connors limited himself to raising it in
chambers with the judge and Murray. He withdrew it, a chivalrous
concession which nevertheless left a suspicion tugging in the judge's
mind. It is one of the quaint conventions of trials that loaded questions by attorneys can be erased without trace from the recollection of judges and jurors by a sustained objection or a withdrawal.

At this point Murray sought to introduce expert testimony on
the Rules of the House of Representatives. Judge Popovich would
not allow it. Instead, he suggested that Congressman B. F. Sisk,
then campaigning in Fresno, be asked to testify. As a member of
the Rules Committee of the House, he was singularly equipped to
explain these arcane matters.

There was a tug-of-war between Connors and Murray over his
testimony. Murray was testing the legitimacy of the report, the
Corporation's claim that it was official, by checking its course from
Bakersfield to the Appendix against the precise rules laid down by
the House. Connors resisted these efforts. Each now sought from
Sisk what comfort he could.

Responding to Connors, the witness agreed that the appearance
of the purported report in the Appendix did not necessarily make
it a fake or a phony. If Bailey had failed to transmit the subcommittee's report, Sisk agreed, it could be regarded as "a species of
failure to do his duty." And since Bailey had said publicly that he
would file a minority report this necessarily implied that Werdel's
text was indeed a majority report. And, Connors continued, had

not the 1950 Appendix been preserved in a bound volume, thus becoming a part of the permanent record "of the doings of Congress?" Sisk agreed that was right.

Now Murray canted the testimony in his favor. Sisk explained that it is the chairman of the subcommittee who makes the report, thereby ruling out the legitimacy of a report presented by any other member. Subcommittees, he stated, have no status under the rules of the House, and neither would any report of a subcommittee until it had been acted upon by the full committee. Without formal filing in the prescribed manner no report could become a House document. Nothing could be a House document that was the work or the creation of a subcommittee, and insertion in the Appendix did not confer any status on it. The material in the Appendix was not held in high regard by Members of the House; matter appearing therein was merely the expression of individual opinions. The informal chats Steed had described, from which the Nixon-Morton-Steed document emerged, Sisk considered as something apart from the formal actions of committee meetings held on call at a set time and place. The circumstances of the case in hand were, Sisk said, "a handling that I have never known to occur in the House of Representatives."

Sisk had not helped Connors's case greatly. In closing his exchange with Sisk, Connors dropped one more inexplicable nugget into the record: "Well, I guess that's where I don't understand you, because this is not a committee action. This is action only by three members of the committee in preparing the report." Boehm, sitting in the audience, scratched his grey crew-cut. Ballis' face uncragged into an unmalicious smile. The remark by counsel for the plaintiff reminded them vaguely of something they, too, had said.

Connors's offhand concession seemed like that of a strong but weary man carrying dutifully a small and mean burden that shrivelled bit by bit with each succeeding lawsuit. As the Corporation's attacks slipped a cog here and there, Brobeck had passed the assignment to junior partners in descending order. Connors was now obliged to maneuver his way out of difficulties in which his predecessors had left him entangled.

One of these was in the remarks with which Werdel had prefaced his Extension. Joseph DiGiorgio had circulated hundreds of reprints under a headline that bracketed the remarks with the text of the report itself. Sanborn's release quoted indiscriminately from both. Plant offered them *in toto* as evidence in the Stockton trial. After these repeated exposures in court, Werdel's portion of the document lost all its glamour. Both Steed and Nixon testified that it had no basis in the evidence. Judge Popovich held that "Werdel had no proper place in this case." Connors retreated. He was "happy to stipulate" that the opening remarks "of Mr. Werdel are not part of the report as such."

Connors was also tethered to evidence his associates had made much of, including the newspaper clippings of 11 and 14 March 1950. These clippings quoted Bailey to the effect that he intended to file a minority report in answer to Werdel, thus making Bailey himself the authority for the argument the Nixon-Morton-Steed text was indeed a majority report. Unfortunately, the clippings also said that the report had not been officially filed. In sixteen years DiGiorgio found no evidence that there had been an official filing, except for Steed's zig-zag testimony. From this it resulted that Connors's own clippings denied what his associates had so persistently argued—that the report had been officially filed.

Connors was now in a weakened position. He conceded that the congressmen could not have prepared the report without copies of the transcript before them. With Steed's testimony in the record that neither he nor his two colleagues had contributed most of the text, Connors added even more to the puzzle by absolving Werdel from authorship. The Rules of the House were in evidence and with them Sisk had pruned the report to the status of a recipe for Irish stew.

Connors made another statement which, unnoticed, contradicted some important testimony of Robert DiGiorgio. Connors's statement was: "Whether it's official, unofficial, semi-official, quasi-official, nobody in DiGiorgio has taken a position on it."[179]

In his closing argument Connors puttied these cracks with disparagement. Bradford, who had tied number 612-53 to a typewriter in DiGiorgio's office, was a "so-called handwriting expert." Galarza's detailed research was not "worth much." Bailey had been at fault for stopping the report in midcourse. As reporters Boehm and Ballis had been careless, wanton, irresponsible, superficial and malicious.

On the pattern of the once-perfect web the outline of DiGiorgio's dilemma was becoming clearer. In 1950 Werdel's Extension had been a major but secondary weapon in convicting *Poverty* and demolishing the strike. Mr. Joseph's delight with the vindication turned into a fervent and public attachment to the document. "DiGiorgio," Connors said, "if he wanted anything, wanted that report to attain the fullest possible status."

Other uses for the document were found and hundreds of reprints were distributed to serve them. In the course of many years and several successful lawsuits the Corporation's commitment to the document deepened. It became a decisive legal weapon in the litigation, a testimonial of formidable prestige and the keystone of evidence that impressed judges and juries. To be identified with it was to have been associated with famous men in the performance of a noteworthy public service.

Things that are loved must be cared for. DiGiorgio's affection for Werdel's print through the years was not matched by a tender attention to the innumerable details of the record that were beginning to corrode it. When Boehm examined in one article the rusting seams of the artifact, both the authenticity of the document and the integrity of the Corporation were challenged. If it renewed its vows to Werdel, Nixon, Morton and Steed, the Corporation risked the humiliation of eventual proof that Boehm was right. If it disowned what it had once acclaimed with so much pride, Boehm was already half justified. This was the dilemma, and DiGiorgio had sued again to avoid it. Of Ballis, Boehm and all their associates Connors said to the Court and jury in Fresno: "We want to still them all."

The only way to do this was to continue suing. The issues were narrowing to one overriding question: Did the Corporation or its attorneys or agents have anything whatever to do with the preparation of the report?

The circumstantial evidence, which Connors told the jury "isn't worth a darn," was beginning to point to a connection between the Extension of Remarks, Mr. Joseph's kinsmen and their attorneys. Only they had in their possession a copy of the reporter's typescript of the Bakersfield Hearings. Document 612-53 had appeared in Brobeck's possession from a source not yet identified not later than 10 March 1950. Steed identified six copies of the draft, but the only paper that had the appearance of one was number

612-53. And now, at a most critical moment, DiGiorgio's carbon transcript, six hundred pages of it, had been lost. Judge Popovich suggested a chilling possibility: "He says he doesn't have it. Presumably they destroyed it." During the trial Werdel was a hundred miles away in Bakersfield, well within the jurisdiction of the Court, but Connors did not call him. Galarza was named as an active conspirator with Boehm and Ballis and was present throughout the trial, but Connors studiously ignored him.

The significance of these circumstances seemed obvious to Murray and the defendants, but there was still the uncertainty of how it would impress the Court and the jury, for the truth and how people see it are not always the same thing. How the jury saw it and whether Connors had taken the risk successfully was now to be declared.

With the arguments closed the Court proceeded to instruct the jury. Instructions are offered by the opposing attorneys to which the Court may add its own. They set forth, in numbered paragraphs, the rules and principles of law by which the jury is to be guided in weighing the evidence before it. Reading them from the Bench, the judge addresses the jury, who must in one brief cram session master the rules on admission of evidence, the burden of proof on a preponderance of testimony, credibility, actual malice, circumstantial evidence, damages compensatory and general and punitive, fraud, privilege, libel *per quod* and *prima facie,* persons, corporations and fair comment. Connors wanted a jury well educated in the law of libel. Of the 65 instructions, 52 were proposed by him.

Behind the solemnity of this ritual of instructions, there was a disquieting psychological problem of communication of which the Court was aware. Judge Popovich somewhat ruefully told the attorneys in chambers that he was having a hard time following passages such as "The publication of defamatory matter is no more than its intentional or careless or negligent communication to at least one person other than the corporation defamed." "The jury," said the Judge, "for sure is going to ask me to explain." The attorneys continued to ply him with more instructions until the Court was moved to comment: "The thing that concerns me now is this business of passing this junk to [the jury]." And to make communication even more difficult between the learned Bench and the lay jury, the Court confessed to a touch of paralalia, saying, "I have poor pronunciation anyway."

Finally the case went to the jury, the last words from the Bench, at least, coming through clearly: "In your deliberations there can be no triumph excepting the ascertainment and declaration of the truth."

The jury returned with a verdict for DiGiorgio—general damages of $5,000 and $25,000 in punitive damages. Counsel moved the Court to reduce the punishment to $20,000. So far as could be told the jury had no difficulty with the intricacies or enigmas of the trial. It set the price of a fractured reputation as easily as if it had been charged with fixing compensation for a broken leg.

Judge Popovich dismissed the jury and proceeded to a lecture from the Bench improvised for the redemption of the losers:

> I agree with what the jury did. From a factual point of view this was a gross libel . . . these writers, they are way out in another world. . . . And they should not be permitted to be spokesmen for labor. . . . Why should somebody that's got a kooky idea come in and contaminate their paper with an article like this? . . . They ought to be stopped in their tracks . . . so they won't do it again . . . any guy that gets a crackpot idea that wants to put it in writing can send it to somebody, and if they can get it published, why they have got everybody at their mercy. I think it's time they be put to a stop . . . Boehm and Galarza . . . need to learn there is a place of reality they must get in tune with. . . . Don't crusade for a lost cause. You are on the wrong end of the ledger and accept it and be reasonable about it.

From this account the price of honor between Stockton and Fresno had fallen from $60,000 to $30,000 by the verdict and to $25,000 by grace of the Corporation. It was to fall even lower. When Murray made a motion for a new trial, Judge Popovich ruled that the motion would be denied if the plaintiff agreed to forgive $12,000 of the last bid. The Corporation agreed and defendants were given the option of paying $13,000 and submitting to the verdict. For DiGiorgio the offer, though greatly reduced from the $350,000 they prayed for in the complaint, was still on the right side of the ledger.

Defendants, unimpressed with the Court's sermon, were no more ready to submit to the verdict than they had been to retract the article. During the trial motions by Murray for non-suit and a directed verdict had been denied. He now moved for a new trial on the grounds of abuse of discretion, errors in law, excessive damages and irregularity in the proceedings. He further argued that Boehm had not been proved to be the agent of any of the other defendants and that Judge Popovich had erroneously instructed the jury on this point. He filed notice of appeal and requested that the transcript of the trial be prepared.

Connors, still in a deprecating mood, regarded all this as a legal lark. "Your Honor," he said, "if this case is tried ten times, the only difference is in the amount of money." With a tinge of self-satisfaction he requested that the trial transcript be augmented by adding "the remarks of Judge Popovich on 9 May 1966, after defendant's counsel argued his motion for a new trial." Thus the sermon from the Bench would be perpetuated in the record, another vindication in memory of Mr. Joseph.

By these proceedings the ground was laid for

The Appeal. / At every sitting of a court of law in the United States, except those of the Supreme Court in Washington, D.C. there is an unseen presence, the recourse of appeal. A trial judge is master of his courtroom. He has the power to order the arrest of citizens, send lawyers to jail, punish for contempt, grant or deny motions, admonish witnesses, put jurors under close custody, accept or reject evidence and command the appearance of persons and papers before him. Yet the seeming rigor of his rule within a small but awesome domain is an accountable one. Reversible error committed by the lower Bench can be appealed for review before a higher one, where the contested judgment will have to stand on the bare record, the target of attacks the lower court will not even have the opportunity to answer. This is the pure theory, tempered by the fact that appeals are expensive; but it is a workable check within the balances of the judicial system. The appellate protection, once carried to its peak in the Supreme Court, may still fall short of justice, whereafter the Democracy (again according to pure theory) may vote itself a legislature that will amend the laws and put even justices in their place.

Murray filed notice of appeal on 25 May 1966 and presented his briefs to the Fifth District Court of Appeal in Fresno. The Corporation, Murray argued, had failed to prove malice. It had made a fatal mistake in not joining Sackett, Galarza and the Olympic Press in the action. The appearance of the article in the *Valley Labor Citizen* was, Murray contended, a case not of publication but of republication, and there was no evidence that Boehm could have foreseen it. The judgment should have been rendered separately and if Boehm were now let out there would be no way to apportion the damages. No effort had been made by the plaintiff to show that Boehm's reliance on his sources had been misplaced, even though Connors had argued that the article was a joint product of Boehm and Galarza.

Connors responded. He contended that the Werdel document had official status from the testimony by Steed that it had been signed, as well as from the fact that it had been printed in a permanent bound volume of the Appendix "maintained in numerous libraries which act as depository for the Federal Government." Congressman Fisk, Connors said, had given the report some kind of official status as well. Quoting authorities, he asserted that Boehm and Galarza had been partners in a conspiracy. Republication of his article had indeed been foreseeable by Boem, for he knew "that DiGiorgio had ranches in the Central Valley." Total reversal of a judgment was not in accord with California law when one defendant was found blameless.[180] In his brief, Connors referred to the "mass of data" upon which Boehm had based his article, obliquely conceding that he was well documented. Contradicting Robert and Plant, Connors asserted that other than the hearings in Bakersfield there had been no legislative proceedings in the course of the preparation of the Werdel Extension of Remarks.

The three justices sitting *en banc* allowed Murray and Connors each fifteen minutes for oral argument before them. The presiding justice, white-haired, plumpish and with an utterly kindly face, beamed on the two attorneys as if they both would receive their hearts' desire. He was flanked by a lean and silent associate who interrupted once or twice. His colleague at the other end of the Bench plied the pleaders with searching questions. The attorneys were dismissed and the matter was "under advisement."

On 21 March 1968 the Court unanimously reversed the libel

judgment below. It was held that there was no evidence that Boehm had authorized, consented to or participated in the republication; that there had been no proof that Boehm had been a party to a conspiracy; that Boehm was not responsible for the decision not to retract, demand for which should have been served on Sackett; that actual malice had not been proved; and that the judgment for separate punitive damages, once Boehm was out, could not reasonably be distributed among the remaining defendants.

As to the necessity of serving a demand for retraction upon the publisher of the newspaper where the offending article originally appeared, the appellate decision said: "A contrary holding . . . would subject the publisher of a newspaper (who had no control over retractions by other newspapers) and all others who participated in the original publication of defamatory matter to multiple suits for general damages."

The appellate court also took notice of the confusion in the giving of instructions. Judge Popovich had instructed the jury that it was to make "a separate determination as to the liability of the defendants, both as to the question of punitive damages and the compensatory damages separately. The court compounded the confusion by allowing the jury to return a verdict holding all defendants jointly and severally liable for both general and punitive damages contrary to its instructions."[181]

The case was remanded to the Superior Court for retrial nearly four years after the Corporation had filed its complaint against the *Valley Labor Citizen*. The Corporation paid the costs of the appeal and kept the option of pressing its complaint. Once more it was DiGiorgio's choice, but now one to be considered against the damaged condition of

The Straining Web. / The trial and the appeal in Fresno sharpended the Corporation's dilemma in pursuing its course. The record of the Werdel affair, in and out of court, was in 1966 voluminous and unwieldy. The warp and woof by now were a tangle of issues in which witnesses were beginning to tie themselves into knots. As Brobeck passed the successive lawsuits from one partner to another inconsistencies were lost sight of, evidence was weighed differently. The significance of a newspaper clipping or a mimeographed paper was blurred or missed in the shifting context of sixteen years of controversy. Local attorneys who were retained by Brobeck as associate counsel appeared to see before them only a wedge of the cake that the Corporation wanted, sugared with damages and frosted with vindication. They did not seem able to visualize the cake itself, which had been baking since 1948. Connors was now reckoning with the difference between a legal firm and a legal mind.

Murray's defense and successful appeal not only thwarted Brobeck; they left a growing deposit of contradictions, back-trackings and shifts in the record.

With respect to authorship Steed was now on that record to the effect that no member of the House committee staff had been assigned to prepare a draft. Connors himself energetically denied that Werdel's staff prepared the report. Robert DiGiorgio testified that no one in the employ of the Corporation had a hand in the writing of what once had been, to Mr. Joseph and himself, a beautifully cut literary diamond. He credited this to "the three congressmen that signed it" but they had declined the honor. In turn three congressmen—Nixon, Morton and Steed—were left in search of an author.

The reason for this was now becoming obvious. The author would have to prove his sources and the Werdel team had none. Connors himself pointed out that without a transcript before them, the members would have had to rely on recollection. Steed confirmed this. He realized that in his friendly, give-and-take chats with Nixon, Morton and Werdel they used yellow foolscap writing pads, not a reporter's typescript or a print of the hearings. And he told Murray that after Bakersfield he had not read the record.

In his probing for authors and sources Murray kept rounding up the circumstantial evidence relating to Dungan's document 612–53. It had now been located in Brobeck's office no later than 10 March 1950. Nothing closer to a draft than these thirteen pages ever turned up. The Corporation could by no means admit that the document had originated in California. Dungan and Connors insisted that it was transmitted by private teletype, TWX, from DiGiorgio's Baltimore sales office to San Francisco. "It's as simple as that," Connors observed. Nevertheless it was not that simple. In March 1950 DiGiorgio's fruit auction in Baltimore did not have TWX equipment. The Corporation's only direct connections by private wire were between New York, San Francisco, Chicago, Delano, and

DiGiorgio Farms in Arvin.[182] Then there were the technical difficulties. In 1950 TWX was equipped with only 26 keyboard code combinations in two shifts. Only capital letters could be used. It was therefore not possible to transmit characters like those that appeared in the Werdel text such as "8(b)" or "10(j)". Neither was there a code signal for underlining, which was used in the headings of 612–53. In 1950 some teletype transmitters had no signals for parentheses or semicolons. There was no device for spacing or centering paragraphs.[183] At the rate of transmission then usual, 60 words per minute, it would have taken some 70 minues to send the 4400 words of Werdel's Extension. Added to all this it would have to be imagined that on the morning of March 10 a courier sped from Werdel's office in Washington to DiGiorgio's Baltimore Fruit Exchange, where business was suspended for more than an hour while an operator peered at nine columns of close six-and-half point type as he tapped out signals that were missing on a machine that was not there.

All this, it is to be remembered, took place because Mr. Joseph was demanding instant copies of the text. This would indicate that a request was made by someone in San Francisco for urgent transmission by TWX. But no record of such instructions was ever put in evidence, and in any case no one there knew anything about the report until March 11. In addition, Robert DiGiorgio was emphatic on one thing: there had been no communication with any congressman after 13 November 1949 and before 9 March 1950. Yet intricate arrangements would have been necessary to have the words of the report on the wires of the Corporation's private network the morning of March 10. In a few days Brobeck received numerous copies of the daily edition of the *Congressional Record,* complete with the Appendix. The mimeographed 612–53 was never circulated, so the purposes it actually served still remained unexplained.

Evidently neither Connors nor Dungan expected their TWX story to remain glued. They therefore offered Murray an alternative: the text had probably been telephoned to San Francisco from Washington by Nixon's office. Robert DiGiorgio declined to endorse this version. As to the carbon copy of the transcript, it was now lost.

The appearance of officialness, which the Corporation argued incessantly on behalf of the Werdel print, continued to peel away like strips of weathered bark from a eucalyptus tree. Steed again declared that it never got to an executive session of the full committee. Connors withdrew from his exchange with Sisk with the comment that "this is not a committee action." He was now drawing a difference between Werdel's prefatory remarks and the report proper, and offered no objection when Judge Popovich threw the latter out. Nor did Connors notice that the text of the report he submitted in evidence was a photocopy from a bound volume of the Appendix published a year after the daily edition had been printed. The rules of evidence being what they are, this oversight of a vital link in the chronology of the document was curious.

The falling off of official prestige was completed by the introduction of the House rules. Drawing his authority from the Constitution itself, Thomas Jefferson had written the first guide for orderly and responsible House procedure in his Manual. Through the years this congressional bible increased greatly in subject matter, but its purpose remained unchanged. "The committees are creatures of the House and exercise no authority or jurisdiction beyond that specifically conferred by the rules or by the special authorization of the House itself."[184] Around Jefferson's Manual there accumulated interpretation and exegesis of his text. Hinds and Cannon cross indexed and annotated over 11,000 parliamentary rulings printed for the convenience of Members in eight thick volumes. Cannon's *Procedures in the House of Representatives* summarized these and was adopted as an official guide. The purposes of the law of the House had been stated long ago by Jefferson himself and by James Madison: "that order, decency and regularity be preserved in a dignified public body" and that the probity of Congress be protected "amidst the frailties of man."

It was Connor's task to resist the application of these rigorous tests to the Werdel Extension. Murray broke that resistance in Fresno through the testimony given by Sisk. Had he needed other authority, it was available. In *Christoffel v. United States,* the Supreme Court decided that the written rules of the House must be applied to determine what is official action by a committee: "The question is what rules the House has established and whether they have been followed."[185]

By these rules the contention that the Nixon-Morton-Steed report was an official document was demolished.

Reports of subcommittees are made to the whole committee; Werdel had addressed himself to the House by way of the Appendix. Reports are read to the committee and agreed to as read; Nixon, Morton, Steed and Werdel read their document only to themselves. Committees agree to a report only when acting together at a duly authorized meeting:[186] Bailey called no meetings of the committee in the DiGiorgio matter. A committee may authorize a report but only when an actual quorum is present; there was no testimony respecting a quorum except Connor's observation that three is a majority of five. Committees may not meet except by special authority during sessions of the House. Steed and his companions were holding peripatetic discussions on their report during such sessions. Committees are required to keep records of all actions taken; the Werdel team had no files of its own, none of the testimony or evidence taken in Bakersfield. Reports are filed by chairmen of committees exclusively; the only presentation related to the Bakersfield matter was Werdel's in the Appendix. Signatures are not customary on majority reports, being required only for dissenting views; the Corporation insisted that three signatures made the document a majority report. Reports must be submitted to the Clerk of the House and must be printed by order of the chairman of the whole committee; Werdel declared that the report he was inserting in the Appendix had not been printed. The proceedings of the House are those matters which are taken down by the official reporters of the House, all other matters not connected therewith being rigidly excluded; nothing said or prepared by Werdel, Nixon, Morton or Steed was taken down in the regular course of business of the House. The only record of proceedings that may be introduced in evidence in the courts is a certified copy of the *Journal;* Brobeck repeatedly introduced photocopies from the Appendix and even these were not certified by the Clerk of the House. The filing of a report is its presentation to the Clerk of the House; Brobeck's evidence showed that no official filing had occurred between 9 March 1950 and 21 March 1966.[187]

One of Connor's major feats in the Fresno trial was his persuading the jury that no one connected with the Corporation had had any communication with any of the congressmen between 12 November 1949 and 9 March 1950. But credibility was reaching the breaking point. Even when Werdel was in Bakersfield for the

Christmas holidays in December 1949 he was not in touch with DiGiorgio. DiGiorgio testified that he did not know Werdel's attitude on the "labor disturbance" until they talked in Bakersfield on the eve of the hearings. This was contradicted by Werdel's own document which was before the jury; it declared that he was in active communication with the Special Citizens of Kern County, who knew the contents of the report and were anxious to have it published to discredit *Poverty in the Valley of Plenty*. Robert DiGiorgio, the director of labor relations of the Corporation, was completely in the dark as to these developments until he read about them in the San Francisco newspapers. In the same news reports there appeared quotations from Corporation officials who were already familiar with the report, but Robert did not identify himself as one of them.

Boehm's story was coming through the multiplying holes of the Werdel tale. Of the four charges complained of by the Corporation —that the Werdel document had been used to crush a strike, that it had been propagated to slander union leadership, that it had been used to win two lawsuits and that the Corporation had participated in faking the alleged report—the first three had received unexpected support from the plaintiff. Werdel's remarks, which contained the most violent slanders, were repudiated and thrown out of court. Connors acknowledged the usefulness of the document in two successful lawsuits. DiGiorgio characterized the publication of the Extension of Remarks as a serious blow to the Union. The circle of attention was contracting around the fourth of Boehm's charges. To prevent Murray from hitting this final mark the Corporation would have to persist in trying to silence its critics by legal action. It did.

NOTES

177. Reporter's transcript. Case number 122891. Vol. I, p. 43.
178. Ibid., Vol. I, p. 46.
179. Ibid., Vol. I, p. 26.
180. Plaintiff and respondent's brief. 5 Civil 740.

181. *West's California Reporter.* 22 April 1968, pp. 87–90.
182. *Teletypewriter Directory.* American Telephone and Telegraph. 1949–1950 edition.
183. *Science Encyclopedia.* 1964 edition, p. 454.
184. *Cannon's Procedures in the House of Representatives.* 81st Congress, p. 81.
185. *Christoffel v. U.S.* 338 U.S. 87.
186. "A report must be authorized by a committee acting together, and a paper signed by a majority of a committee acting separately was ruled out." *Jefferson's Manual and Rules of the House of Representatives.* 81st Congress, sections 407 and 408.
187. *Cannon's Procedures* . . . 81st Congress, pp. 84–90; *Jefferson's Manual and Rules of the House of Representatives,* 81st Congress. Sections 408, 582, 743, 821, 924, 821 and 943; *Hinds's Precedents.* Vol. IV, section 4668, p. 974; Vol. V, sections 5080 and 6962; Vol. VIII, section 2491; Extracts from the Journals of the Senate and the House of Representatives, and from the Executive Journal of the Senate when the injunction of secrecy is removed, certified by the Secretary of the Senate or the Clerk of the House of Representatives, shall be received in evidence with the same effect as the originals would have." *U.S. Code,* annotated. Title 28, section 1736. 62 Statutes 947. 25 June 1948.

12

AFTER TWENTY YEARS

Arguing the Corporation's case before the Fresno jury, Connors conceded as gracefully and offhandedly as possible that there was some substance to three of Boehm's contentions. On the fourth the Corporation chose to make its last stand. "We are here," Connors said, "to show that whatever the state of the report may be Di-Giorgio had nothing to do with it."[188]

This was not a forced choice. The plaintiff had two other options.

The first was that lobbying of committees is as much a part of the congressional process as the lobbying of the House itself. Both are in a sense an exercise of the right of petition and neither is regarded as irregular or reprehensible. Congressmen have come to lean heavily on the selfserving statements of parties interested in legislative matters pending before committees. What they accept or reject from such material is a matter of sensitive political judgment. In the process the Members of the House receive not only opinions colored by interest but also a good deal of information which neither they nor their staffs have time to research. Investigative hearings are in fact formal opportunities for open lobbying by contesting parties. Committees remain accessible to extensions of the record of hearings as well as to written arguments, memorials, petitions, briefs and documents that may prove persuasive. If the Corporation had acknowledged that it tried to influence the nature of the report before Werdel put it in the Appendix, and the means by which it had done so, it would have been in keeping with the accepted practice of open lobbying. Not as matter of truth but as one of strategy the Corporation chose not to do so.

The second option was to have followed Judge Popovich's hint that ghostwriting is a commendable art and a praiseworthy way of serving mankind. The Werdel Extension, by all of DiGiorgio's testimony, was no mean piece of literary hacking. To have had a hand in its preparation would have brought honor rather than discredit to its real authors. It was a credit that the Corporation declined.

Rather DiGiorgio again made an issue of its reputation, "the right of receiving respectful consideration from the world," as the Court said in the Youssoupoff case. It stood no risk, like Othello, of losing "the immortal part of myself," at least not as long as its Delaware charter remained unrevoked; but it could lose standing and prestige in the business world. It staked the issue on a vigorous denial that it had in any way cooperated in the creation of the Nixon-Morton-Steed report.

DiGiorgio's determination to defend this line was understandable. The vindication of 1950 with its fringe benefits rested upon the acceptance by the public of a purported report presumed to have been issued independently by the House and written on the basis of objective evidence by three unbiased Members. This presumption carried weight with Judge Buck in Stockton and the appellate court in Sacramento, which declared it a finding by a responsible committee of Congress.

These were practical considerations. There was also a legal difficulty. It had been held by the Supreme Court in 1952 that it would be unfair to admit as evidence in litigation a publication prepared by one of the parties to a lawsuit and entered in the *Congressional Record* as a speech read on the floor of the Senate.[189] The case was particularly appropriate because it, too, was an action for libel. If a speech made in the Senate and printed in its official proceedings under those circumstances was inadmissible, an Extension of Remarks from the Appendix would hardly rate a second look in a court of law. Belatedly discovered, this case was now in Murray's files.

Boehm was republished not only by the *Valley Labor Citizen* but also by Sackett's newspapers in Monterey, Santa Clara and Shasta Counties. To "silence them all" the Corporation had filed further

Complaints for Libel—the Seventh, Eighth and Ninth. /

Complaint for Libel—the Seventh /   No. 57404
   In the Superior Court of the State of California

in and for the County of Monterey
DiGiorgio Fruit Corporation, a Corporation, Plaintiff,
v.
Monterey Bay Labor News, et al., Defendants
Filed 16 June 1964

Complaint for Libel—the Eighth /   No. 544–554
In the Supreme Court of the State of California
in and for the County of San Francisco
DiGiorgio Fruit Corporation, a Corporation, Plaintiff,
v.
Union Gazette, et al., Defendants
Filed 22 June 1964

Complaint for Libel—the Ninth /   No. 326363
In the Superior Court of the State of California
in and for the County of Shasta
DiGiorgio Fruit Corporation, a Corporation, Plaintiff,
v.
Cascade Labor News, Sheldon F. Sackett, et al., Defendants
Filed 22 April 1965

In its sweep the Corporation named several central labor councils in Northern California with a total claim for damages against them of $1,050,000. For strategic reasons Brobeck decided to try the Fresno case first. As it progressed the pleadings and tactical maneuvers in the northern cases went on.

Murray and Connors entered into an agreement that Congressman Steed's deposition could be used in all cases to avoid needless repetition and expense. Murray now moved to be relieved of this agreement but Connors successfully resisted the motion. Brobeck was ordered to amend the complaint because it "is uncertain, ambiguous and unintelligible." DiGiorgio served notice of demand for retractions. The Central Labor Council of Santa Clara County refused. Sackett rejected the notice by publishing the Boehm article a second time with additional comments, saying, "We published what we believed to be true and we will not retract the truth." Putting his resources behind his convictions, Sackett entered into "hold harmless" agreements with the Councils, assuming their liability if they should lose.

With Sackett the Corporation made no progress in shoring up

its case. When it demanded from the publisher an admission that
the original of the report "was holographically signed by Richard
Nixon, Thruston B. Morton and Tom Steed," Sackett replied: "If
you will show me an original of the report referred to . . . and
examples of the signatures of the persons mentioned therein, I shall
compare those examples with the signatures on the original of the
report and shall be glad to give you my opinion." Connors continued to argue that the authenticity of the report was established
beyond doubt by the fact that it was printed in the Appendix, that
this print was perpetuated in a permanently bound volume of the
Congressional Record, its official character being further proved
by the fact that this volume was to be found in hundreds of libraries
throughout the country. Sackett was not impressed.

Now clearly on the defensive Brobeck relied on testimony and
evidence already in hand, leaving further discovery up to Murray,
with which he proceeded.

The best aid to the discovery of the truth is not what an attorney
knows the adversary has in the way of evidence; it is what he does
not know the opponent does not have that makes the risk of impeachment and possible perjury too high to take. It was not what
Brobeck was certain that Murray knew, but what Brobeck was not
sure that Murray did not know that tipped the balance in favor of
the defendants.

Murray first obtained a series of helpful admissions. The Corporation returned sworn statements that there was no letter of
transmittal with the Nixon-Morton-Steed report; that no one in
the firm of Brobeck, Phleger and Harrison had received by telephone from Washington the text of document 612–53, and that
the only document in existence purporting to be the report of
Special Subcommittee Number 1 was the one that had appeared
in the Appendix.

Murray again called Dungan to give a deposition, his third in the
various lawsuits.

He confirmed that Brobeck had in fact had correspondence with
the subcommittee after the Bakersfield hearings. This was a covering letter referring to a brief about which Murray had no previous
knowledge:

> MURRAY: You mentioned 'brief.' Would you describe, gen-
> erally what the document was that you have said
> was sent . . . ?

DUNGAN: . . . when the hearing was held in Bakersfield . . .
the subcommittee gave us leave to file a brief in
response to that [Union] brief . . . we did prepare
such a brief and sent it to the committee in Washington, D.C. Now precisely to whom it was addressed I do not recall.

Connors, sensing trouble, interjected: "Mr. Gregory Harrison tells
me he has no recollection that we did file a brief."

DUNGAN: Well, I am under oath here, and I am telling you
we did.

By this it was obvious to Murray that the three Brobeck law
partners, Harrison, Dungan and Connors, were in disagreement on
a new and important development in the case.

Murray now brought Dungan around to the more than seventy
discrepancies between his document 612–53 and the printed text
of the report in the Appendix. Dungan had previously testified
that the former was teletyped or telephoned from Washington,
appearing in San Francisco as a transcription in mimeographed
duplicates. Now he explained in full:

DUNGAN: I believe that the report of the Subcommittee . . .
shortly after it was filed with the Committee or
shortly after it was filed by a majority of the subcommittee with the Chairman of the subcommittee,
was teletyped to the office of what was then known
as the DiGiorgio Fruit Corporation in San Francisco
and that from that teletype, after making the emendations that are necessary by reason of errors that
are inherent in the transmission of teletype messages, [the report] was retyped in the office of
DiGiorgio and by them transmitted to us. That
involves a whole series . . . of imperfect recollections
and all the rest of it. But that's the conclusion I
have come to.

Dungan fixed the receipt of his copy of this text as March 10,
the day on which both Harrison and he first saw it. He did not
know "and never did" who sent it. Informed by Murray that the
records of the Bell Telephone Company did not show a teletype
installation in Baltimore, where Connors suggested it had origi-

nated, Dungan, taking a tip from Connors, said that "it could have
come over the AP (Associated Press) wire." In any event Dungan
again testified that what he had in his file on March 10 marked
"612–53" was "a Photorapid copy of certain mimeographed sheets
that came over to our office from DiGiorgio." Dungan concluded
by answering a question on the origin of the document saying that
its transmission by telephone from Washington was "an equally
eligible guess as the guess that they came by teletype."

Murray next took a deposition from Robert DiGiorgio. It was
perfunctory. The intricate explanations were being left to Dungan;
Steed remained the anchor man on the authorship of the Werdel
document, its official status, the sources from which it was prepared
and as to whether it had been signed and properly filed. For the
rest, DiGiorgio covered himself with the familiar denials—as of
February 1968, he did not know the source of document 612–53,
or of any agent of the Corporation who had ever searched for the
original of the report. He had nothing to do with the preparation
of *A Community Aroused.*

There was in fact no witness for the Corporation who could
satisfactorily explain another peculiarity of Werdel's Extension
which now became evident. There were in the report statements
which could not be attributed to the published printed volume of
the hearings, the only acknowledged and official record of the evidence taken in Bakersfield. There were 55 lines of such new matter.
Some of those lines had a striking similarity to words which
appeared in DiGiorgio's 1949 complaint for libel against Flannery
and others. This complaint was not submitted to the subcommittee,
so it could not have been a source from which the congressmen
could have copied the lines. Some of the new matter came from the
brief which the Union filed with the Subcommittee at the hearings.
This brief was not read orally in Bakersfield but was accepted as
an extension of the record. It was reproduced in the printed volume
of the hearings. It will be recalled that the volume appeared a
month after Werdel's Extension, and therefore the brief could not
have been before the congressmen early in March.

Evidently the text had been "beefed up," as Steed put it, with
some 450 words which could not be accounted for in the available
public record. One thing was certain: they had been written by a
person or persons well informed on DiGiorgio's troubles with the

Union and the course of controversy between October 1947 and March 1950.

The union brief from which some of the new material came now served another use. Six copies had been handed to Mr. Bussey, the majority clerk, in Bakersfield. This was on 12 November 1949. No copies were given to the Corporation. Murray assumed that Brobeck would have needed a copy of the Union document to prepare its own responding brief. He subpoenaed it. Connors handed over one of the six copies, on the cover of which there was an acknowledgement of receipt by Gregory Harrison dated 21 November 1949.

A case now turned up that proved unusually pertinent to the admissibility of subcommittee reports as evidence in a court of law. This was *Marks v. Orth*, decided by the Indiana Supreme Court in 1889, in which the Court said:

> The question is presented as to the admissibility of this document, pamphlet or book in evidence. It purports to be a printed copy of a report of a subcommittee of the House of Representatives, but it is in no way authenticated. It is not certified by any officer. It is not identified by any testimony. It is not even identified by the *Journal* of the House, nor does it purport to be incorporated in or a part of the authenticated *Journal*. . . . It is not even a publication required to be made or a record required to be kept by the House of Representatives. It is not such a document as is entitled to admission and under no rule of law is it admissible. . . .[190]

In the next round in court Brobeck would have to deal with *Marks v. Orth*.

Serendipity, the arranger of happy and unexpected discoveries, now gave Murray a helping hand. As a Stanford University library attendant took down from the shelf a dusty copy of the hearings print requested by Galarza for a recheck of the testimony, a thin pamphlet slipped out stuck to the heavy volume of the hearings. A mischance in shelving years before had joined what Brobeck was still trying to put asunder. The pamphlet was a report by Special Subcommittees 1 and 2 based on hearings dealing with school problems in areas of heavy concentration of war production workers and their families.

The report was an unnumbered "committee print." The letter

of transmittal to Chairman Lesinski carried the names of Cleveland M. Bailey and Thomas H. Burke, chairmen respectively of
Special Subcommittees Number 1 and Number 2. In their letter the
two chairmen wrote that they, "having concluded their [sic]
work in accordance with House Resolution 75 of the Eighty-first
Congress, hand you herewith its [sic] report and recommendations regarding the educational phases of its [sic] study."

The committee print, 149 pages long, was distributed sometime
after March 1950. It said nothing about the DiGiorgio matter; and
since Bailey and Burke were concluding their assignment, it was
clear that there would be no report on the "labor disturbance" in
Arvin. What Bailey and Burke handed Lesinski, in the proper order
of House business, was a majority report. On it appeared the names
of Richard M. Nixon, Thruston B. Morton, and Tom Steed. There
were no holographic signatures, and no dissenting views.

The case that was now moving forward was that of DiGiorgio
v. Monterey Labor News, set for trial on 14 February 1968. On
motion of Connors this was postponed to June 10, but the Corporation was slowing down in its pursuit. June passed and there was no
trial. Then, on July 11, Brobeck entered a motion for dismissal of
the three lawsuits. There was no settlement, no payment of money,
no compromise. The Fresno case remained pending until 7 April
1969, when Brobeck filed a motion for dismissal, a choice that
seemed in accord with the

New Perspectives. / Between 1950 and 1964 the momentum
in the long series of lawsuits came from the Corporation. Brobeck's
arguments had not varied: the film *Poverty* was a libelous defamation; it was condemned by a responsible committee of Congress;
a congressional report had vindicated DiGiorgio's opposition to
unionism in agriculture; the congressional report was an unbiased
and authoritative verdict on the nature of the film and the character of the Union and its leaders; the report had been written and
signed by three honorable Members of the House; the Corporation
had absolutely nothing to do with the report; the report was issued
in the course of the regular and official proceedings of the House;
its publication had no relation to the strike in 1950, or to the
resistance of the Corporation to the AOWC in 1960.

With these propositions Brobeck had won several victories and contrived the stalemate of San Francisco. In combination they made a weighty package, the most of which was the Werdel text. On the face of it the case they made was sufficient. No additional information was necessary and Brobeck did not turn any up. Side issues, such as the possibility that the original report had been stolen by Union sympathizers, were raised by DiGiorgio but never pursued. There was no need to. Like an icebreaker Brobeck's package continued to crush the defendants before incurious judges and trusting juries.

Between 1964 and 1968 the drift of the controversy changed course. The facts which came to view in this period forced the burden of proof on the Corporation, a burden which by all the precedents and rules rested squarely on its adversaries. The evidence was not direct, but circumstantial. For all that Connors insisted they were "not worth a darn," the pattern they were falling into was one the Corporation could not ignore.

The copy of the Union brief produced by Connors showed that his partner, Harrison, had received it on 21 November 1949. It could have come only from some member of the subcommittee or its staff. Clearly, then, Brobeck was in communication with the subcommittee after the hearings, which Robert DiGiorgio had denied. In addition to this, it was now possible to trace certain wording in both the Werdel text and document 612-53 to the Union brief. These words could not have been taken from the printed Hearings or from the carbon copy of the reporter's transcript in DiGiorgio's possession. The printed volume reproduced the text of the Union brief, but it was not delivered to the subcommittee until April.

Murray now had been led to believe that Brobeck had filed a responding brief to counteract that of the Union. The filing probably took place after 12 November 1949 and before 9 March 1950. This corroborated the fact that Brobeck had been in communication with the subcommittee in the period between the hearings and the publication of the Werdel Extension. Necessarily the responding brief was prepared after November 21. It was transmitted to the subcommittee in Washington whereupon it dropped from sight. It was not included in the printed Hearings. Harrison told Connors that such a responding brief was never prepared and Dungan told Murray that their file copy—the copy of a document

that never existed—had been lost. The covering letter sent with
the responding brief could not be located by Brobeck. A thorough
search in the files of the House Committee on Education and
Labor and in the National Archives failed to produce any trace of
the responding brief.

The new matter in the Werdel Extension text raised additional
questions about its sources. Aside from the wording taken from
the Union brief, there were passages which could be accounted for
in neither the reporter's typescript nor the printed Hearings, theoretically identical. Facts which had not been presented at Bakersfield now appeared in both document 612-53 and the Extension
of Remarks. The language in the report relating to the shacks
shown in *Poverty* had been credited to the congressmen. It was,
however, language which had a familiar ring. It was used in Dungan's 1949 complaint, which the congressmen did not read.

Not only had they not read the language, but they did not see
that which they so vividly described in their report. Dungan told
Murray: "We had investigated the motion picture in great detail,
which the subcommittee had not done. . . . I had actually gone out
and . . . determined where those shacks were . . . which the committee had no time or interest in doing, going into that detail."
There were other details on the Corporation's controversy with the
Union which did not appear in any other documentary source
available to the subcommittee in the preparation of its report. Werdel's Extension had been "beefed up" from as yet invisible sources
and by as yet unknown persons.

The crux of strategy for Murray now was to establish that these
persons and sources were the Corporation and its agents; for Connors, to prevent at all costs such a connection. Document 612-53
threatened to become the missing link. The document was in Brobeck's file on March 10. It had no marks of identification as to
date or place or origin or sender. The original explanation that it
was teletyped from Baltimore to San Francisco to Brobeck via
DiGiorgio had collapsed. So had the story of a telephoned transmission from Nixon's office to Brobeck or DiGiorgio. The last
defense—that it had been copied from an Associated Press dispatch
—was too feeble to stand up. No wire service editor interested in
keeping his job would have sent over a nationwide network some
4400 words taken from the Appendix of the *Congressional Rec-*

ord. Dungan's various versions of a wire transmission of 612-53 to Brobeck assumed that the long message was taken down by a stenographer, typed, stencilled, mimeographed and distributed within a matter of four or five hours on 10 March 1950.

There was something else. In his last deposition Dungan was obliged to explain the more than seventy errors and deviations in document 612-53 from the Werdel text. The explanation was astonishing: Such errors are normal in teletype transmission. The teletyped text that DiGiorgio received had been edited and emendations made to conform it to a correct text.

But where had the correct text come from? Was it in San Francisco on March 10? If not, to what model was the garbled 612-53 made to conform? And most intriguing of all, why had the botched transmission been mimeographed, distributed, and carefully filed, and the corrected text discarded?

DiGiorgio and his counsel fell back to an unusual defense—they began to lose important documents. Both the Corporation and Brobeck kept records on the Werdel matter; combined they comprised "a multitude of documents," as Dungan phrased it. Murray was now making demands for production of some of them and Brobeck was pleading that they were lost. The first to disappear was the carbon copy of the reporter's typescript, which Connors could not produce for the Fresno trial. Nor could Brobeck tell Murray what had happened to the original or any file copy of the responding brief. The correspondence relating to the brief was gone. So was the correspondence that the Corporation had with Werdel during 1949 before the Bakersfield hearings. Apparently Brobeck was prepared to lose any document that Murray demanded by subpoena, for Dungan told Murray that the file copy of the responding brief was lost, and that it "has that characteristic in common with a great many things that went into our files . . ."

Two other respects in which DiGiorgio lost ground were the discovery of the *Marks v. Orth* case and the final appearance of Bailey's official report. *Marks* posed the problem for Brobeck of producing a rule, a precedent or a case which would overcome that decision, by which the Werdel Extension was now disqualified as an official report creditable as evidence. Bailey's report established that Subcommittee Number 1 did complete its assignment under House Resolution 75 and that its authentic, genuine and official report, duly filed with Chairman Lesinski, made no reference whatever to the DiGiorgio investigation. It further established that three of the congressmen who had "signed" Bailey's official report—Nixon, Morton and Steed—had also "signed" Werdel's "majority report."

In the next chapter these and other defects which were now showing up like checks on the glazed finish of Brobeck's propositions will be examined more closely. The matter had to be viewed from the perspective of

The New DiGiorgio. / Between 1948 and 1968 agriculture in California was transformed from a way of life to a business, agribusiness. Family farming as a significant characteristic of the industry was finished. This change was no longer spoken of in regretful tones or diffident whispers. It was proclaimed by the First Annual Agricultural Forum of the Los Angeles Chamber of Commerce, held in January 1969. Henry Schacht reported some of the conclusions of the Forum: "Agriculture will continue its trend toward larger farms and ranches, greater capital investment, widespread mechanization and professional management, accelerated integration of various functions all the way from the producer to the retailer. . . ."

As the past had belonged to farming, so the future now belonged to agribusiness, with "great pressure in favor of the corporate type of organization" generated by "integration, powerful and irreversible."[191] California was already fulfilling the vision of S. M. Miller, Martin Rein and Pamela Roby: "In the year 2000 the U. S. farmer, like the automobile manufacturer, will be a sophisticated urban executive with a computer for a foreman."[192] A new breed of money makers was methodizing an ancient husbandry, remolding it to the formula given by Monsieur Homais, the pragmatist of *Madame Bovary,* "one must keep up with science." To his question: "Do you think that to be an agriculturist it is necessary to have tilled the earth, or fattened fowls oneself?" agribusinessmen were giving a snorting answer: "Of course not."

In favor of agribusiness there was developing another radical shift in the social structure of the state, the spread of the metropolis. By the 1960s California's largest cities could no longer hold their growing suburbs under compression. These invaded the countryside in snaking overflows of tracts and subdivisions. The green country between Los Angeles and San Diego, Fresno and Sacramento, San Francisco and Gilroy began to fill with commuter communities. In this process the smaller marginal farms were squeezed still more. The holdings of corporation farmers gained in value from the resulting land boom.

The DiGiorgio Fruit Corporation was in the mainstream of all this, and in a position to collect its capital increments. It began to plan the liquidation of its farm properties. In Borrego Valley, east of San Diego, a combined farming operation and resort project had an estimated growth profit potential of $10,000,000. Sierra Vista's nearly 5,000 acres near Delano were valued on the books at $1,000,000 and in the market at $7,000,000. With more than 16,000 acres still under intense cultivation, DiGiorgio was figuring closely how to trim and sell the fat, keeping the lean and compact remainder that would still be profitable in agricultural production. The sale of parcels at Sierra Vista was under way in 1968.

Farming was no longer the principal part of the Corporation's business. Its nonagricultural revenues as percentage of all income increased from 15 percent in 1955 to 87 percent in 1964. It dropped the word "Fruit" from its business title and became simply the DiGiorgio Corporation. "We are," said its annual report of 1964, "a dramatically different enterprise," changed from a family-dominated business in fruits and vegetables to a "publicly held, profit oriented processor, distributor and marketer of foods." By 1965 the Corporation controlled fifteen nonfarming subsidiaries including the Bay Counties Finance Company, Klamath Lumber, S and W Foods, the New York Fruit Auction and the Los Angeles Drug Company. Investments and directorships tied it into the network of large enterprise with the Bank of America, Pacific Gas and Electric, Southern California Edison, Firemen's Fund Insurance Company, Foremost Dairies and Pacific Telephone.

The new Corporation did exceedingly well. Its consolidated balance sheet for 1965 showed $81,869,000 in assets compared to $2,205,000 in 1933. The sales volume, $1,333,000 in 1958, surpassed the $100,000,000 mark by 1965, making it ninth in rank as to rate of sales growth among the nation's top five hundred corporations.

The hand at the helm of so much enterprise was no longer

Joseph DiGiorgio's but Robert's. It was under Robert that another
dramatic transformation took place. This was in relation to labor
policy. Joseph DiGiorgio, in his report to the stockholders of 1950,
said: "I take this opportunity to reiterate the position which I have
steadfastly maintained, that there is no place for a union on a
farm." In 1964 Robert was still declaring in a deposition, "This is
still the company policy."[193]

It was the last such declaration. DiGiorgio negotiated a contract
with the United Agricultural Workers Union of Delano. The Corporation reported to the stockholders that in 1966 "labor relations
were satisfactory" and that the Corporation had "provided leadership which resulted in free, secret elections." The new era in agrin-
dustrial democracy had been initiated "by our insistence on each
worker's right to decide whether or not he wished to be represented by a union." Robert testified in the Fresno trial: "If the
employees wish an election, they should have one and if they want
a union they certainly should have one."

In the changed perspective that time had wrought it was also
necessary to consider

The New Nixon, Morton and Steed. / For more than twenty
years DiGiorgio had made the most of the endorsement of the
Werdel text by its three putative signers—Richard M. Nixon,
Thruston B. Morton and Tom Steed. To the name of the first, time
and the fortunes of politics had added a prestige and a luster that
judges considered with respect and juries with reverence. "And this
report, ladies and gentlemen of the jury," Connors might be imagined intoning, "was signed, personally signed, by a then honorable
Member of the House and now the President of the United
States." The Honorable Thruston B. Morton had earned in those
two decades a promotion to the senate and into the inner circles of
Republican strategy. The Honorable Tom Steed remained a wheel-
horse of the House but had become a Member of considerable
seniority, a paragon in his own way of the durabilities of a Democrat, some of whose best friends were Republicans.

There was an ambivalance in the old Nixon which in the long
run cost the farm worker's Union its life. In the late 1940s there
was the Nixon of critical mental faculties, the alert lawyer, the legal
craftsman who paid minute attention to the least of details. Two

years before Bakersfield, Nixon the perspicacious and unrelenting prosecutor had "examined and re-examined transcripts" of Whitaker Chambers's testimony to prepare the cross-examination that was the undoing of Alger Hiss. As chairman of a subcommittee of the House Un-American Activities Committee Nixon acted from the sense of "a grave responsibility to be sure of our facts before any more charges are aired in public." To protect the innocent and punish perjurers, Nixon's subcommittee "diligently pursued the truth." He was distressed at the possibility that "the truth would never be determined." He knew and he feared that "if the Committee failed to follow through on the Hiss case, the effectiveness of all congressional investigations might be impaired for years."[194]

These were the same intellectual qualities that Nixon brought to bear in his campaign for senator against Mrs. Helen Gahagan Douglas. His most damaging charges against her as a fellow-traveller and pink lady "went before the voters as a carefully researched leaflet."[195] His assistants microscoped the *Congressional Record* for hard facts upon which the innuendo was solidly banked. "You have to state it," he advised Senator Joseph McCarthy, "in the context of what is probable."

What is remarkable is that the Bakersfield hearings occurred midway between Hiss and Douglas. In that short but for the Union fatal interlude Nixon's agile mine became merely a filter for an anonymous writing and his name the co-signature on a blank check for DiGiorgio's publicity. It was, moreover, a writing tipped with libel and betrayed by inconsistencies of fact and logic.

It was hard to explain; for in the same Appendix, on another date, Nixon had inserted a speech by David Beck, president of the Teamsters Union, in which Beck said: "Neither labor nor industry has a right to enter into collusive action or conspiracy, for that will not stand the test of time. . . ."

The test of time, which Beck was applying to high level labor-management relations, was now catching up with the Werdel document bearing the name of Nixon. Time had not yet shown whether it was the product of a collusive or conspiratorial action, but it was falling apart in logic and fact, and the supporting documents were getting lost.

Until time and discovery finished their work, it was not likely that the Corporation would try again to cash its blank check

against Nixon's credit. It was not only that a new DiGiorgio had a
lesser need for a questioned document; there was also a new Nixon
in whose career the Werdel affair was trivial beyond recollection.

The politician who in 1968 could say "There is never enough of
me" was in a position to determine what portions of his prestige
could be used by others to serve their interests. In 1950 it served
the interests of both DiGiorgio and Nixon that his name appear on
the Werdel Extension. In 1968 it could serve DiGiorgio, but not
Nixon. Few had risen so swiftly to the heights from which Nixon
was pondering "the lessons of public office." He surveyed the
world from the White House as Vice-President.[196]

High-level insight had come to Nixon which would make it
unlikely that he would ever permit DiGiorgio again to use him. In
Bakersfield he was advised that there was at the moment a case
before the Superior Court of Los Angeles relating to the matters
brought before the subcommittee by DiGiorgio, and Nixon the
congressman received the testimony that Nixon the attorney would
have shunned on professional principles. Years later, in another
context, he stressed publicly the impropriety of public declarations
that might interfere with the processes of justice. His political
biographers discovered other qualities that were perhaps not new,
certainly not evident in the Werdel matter, but in any case now
uppermost in the character of the man. Unlike Judge Popovich,
he was not one to favor ghost-writing. He was for re-establishing
the principle that men should be accountable for what they do.
"Truth," his long-time friend and assistant, Herbert Klein, said,
"would become the hallmark" of Nixon's public life. Campaigning
for the presidency he demanded that both Republicans and Democrats "stop talking what is smart politically and start talking what
is right morally." He was now listening "to the voices of quiet
anguish," not just to those of agribusinessmen. The new keynote
was compassion. Power was not to be served but dispersed.

Of the other two signers, Morton had not gone through such a
transformation, but his philosophy now set him apart from things
as strange and inexplicable as the Werdel report. The mature Morton was suspicious of brainwashing since President Johnson had
been victimized by it at the hands of the military-industrial complex. About DiGiorgio's lawsuits he had been discreet through the
years, his silence alone serving to disembrangle him from the con-

fusion that the report had become. His comment about senators, "Most of us are under suspicion," might or might not have included the recollection of matters to which he testified but had never seen or heard. In any event, as a pragmatist he said in 1957, as he measured his prospects with Rockefeller or with Nixon, "I'm a professional. I'm looking for a winner." The Werdel Extension of Remarks was looking less and less like a winner.

Tom Steed, the last of the three in the order of seniority on the Werdel print, remained the most loyal witness for DiGiorgio. But his devotion, too, had run low. In his last deposition he was contrite. He was the only one of the three who at last expressed regret at the damage that had been done by the derelictions that surrounded the Werdel affair. Perhaps he was also beginning to realize that the testimony was becoming more conflicting, the facts more compromising.

Murray's repeated attempts to glean the full story from Nixon, Morton and Steed between 1960 and 1968 might have at rare intervals put them in mind of these things. Some tacit accord, some unspoken consensus, could be supposed. It was said somewhere in the official guide to the House that "Here, too, the past has a way of cropping up," in disquieting contrast with Nixon's own philosophical view that "You must never look back." Or, as it is taught in law schools, *"non quieta movere."*

For all three the political credits of the Werdel incident were exhausted. It was one of those "old, unhappy far-off things and battles long ago." Contradictions were running rife through the record of nine lawsuits, not a few suggesting impeachment, some trailing implications of perjury. Like Pooh-Bah, the onetime responsible committeemen of Congress had a right to ask: "Am I to understand that all of us high Officers of State are required to perjure ourselves to ensure your safety?"

Not, indeed, for such a diminished cause. The residue of twenty years of litigation was little more than the debris of Brobeck's ten propositions.

NOTES

188. Reporter's transcript. Case number 122891, Vol. III, p. 689.
189. "(The trial court) excluded the Bridges speech because it would be unfair to allow appellants to avail themselves of a publication which their agent had prepared and submitted for delivery on the Senate floor." *Utah State Farm Bureau v. National Farmers Union Service Corporation.* 198 Fed 2d., 20. For the speech by Senator Bridges and documents introduced by him in the Senate proceedings see the *Congressional Record,* 7 September 1950, pp. 14276–14296.
190. *Marks v. Orth.* 121 Indiana Rep. 10–14.
191. *San Francisco Chronicle.* 22 January 1969.
192. Roby, Miller and Rein. "Social problems of the future." 1968, p. 19. Mimeographed.
193. Robert DiGiorgio. Deposition. 16 December 1964, p. 6.
194. Richard M. Nixon. *Six Crises,* pp. 11, 13, 15.
195. Mazo and Hess. *Nixon—A Political Portrait,* p. 73.
196. Ibid., p. 307.

PART FOUR

PART FOUR

13

THE BROKEN WEB

Of the nine suits for libel instituted between 1948 and 1966 the first was dismissed. The second was not settled on the legal merits. As if doubting that it could win solely on those merits, the Corporation applied the drastic political pressure of the Werdel Extension of Remarks. To that pressure the California Federation of Labor yielded, forcing the surrender of the National Farm Labor Union, which could not contest the court action alone.

In the working code of agribusiness the test of this strategy was that it worked. The obnoxious film was suppressed, a strike was broken, a labor organizing campaign in the Central Valley was repulsed, DiGiorgio freshened his laurels as the champion of farmers big and little, and a scorching indictment of agricultural unionism passed unchallenged. Contrary to legal canons the case against the Union was tried in the news media during judicial proceedings. DiGiorgio's complaint was before the Superior Court of Los Angeles County when the *Los Angeles Times* carried the story that a congressional committee had found the film untrue and libelous. One attorney, Robert DiGiorgio, asked a congressional committee to take official notice and pass judgment on the complaint. Two other attorneys—Richard M. Nixon and Thomas H. Werdel —approved.

The third suit was dismissed. Not until the fourth lawsuit did it become clear that *Poverty* and Werdel's Extension were interchangeable parts in DiGiorgio's strategy. In Stockton the Nixon-Morton-Steed text was given full faith and credit as the report of a responsible committee of the House and admissible in evidence for the truth of what it said about the film. Before Judge Buck and the Third District Court of Appeals the record showed that the three congressmen had testified as to the shocking untruthfulness of *Poverty*.

DiGiorgio's abortive third complaint and the press release led to the fifth suit in the series. Brobeck had moved the report to the center of the stage and Murray played it from there. In the proceedings between September 1960 and July 1968 Brobeck's task was no longer to prove that *Poverty* was arrant libel, but that the report was official, genuine and authentic; collaterally but vitally, that DiGiorgio had absolutely nothing to do with its preparation. Both contentions rested on ten propositions, all which came apart in the course of the litigation.

1. That the Nixon-Morton-Steed text was official.

Steed, in one of his depositions, said plaintively "You would almost have to have a book to tell you all the rules" that prescribe the procedure in the House that makes a report official. There was indeed such a book and the Supreme Court had decided in *Christoffel v. United States,* already cited, that the controlling factors were "what rules the House had established and whether they have been followed." And in *Chance v. Cochran* it was settled that "All acts of officials are not official, but only such as are done under some authority derived from law, or in the pursuance of prescribed duties."[197] On these tests the Werdel Extension did not qualify.

House procedure required that only the chairman of a subcommittee may submit a report to the full committee. Werdel, who was not even a member of the subcommittee, presented his document to an unnamed clerk.[198] Reports could be printed only by order of the chairman of the full committee and the Joint Committee on Printing. Werdel, in his prefatory remarks, stated that the report had not been printed. Steed testified that "subcommittees always make reports and present them to the whole committee." This did not happen in the DiGiorgio investigation. Nixon acknowledged that there was no date on his report.

Connors's determined effort to give the Extension an official appearance did not go far. His contention was that the stamp of officialness was given by the fact that the text in question appeared in print in a bound, permanent volume of the Appendix. This volume, he argued, "forms a permanent record of the doings of Congress." But Werdel's prefatory remarks were also in the bound volume and Connors stipulated in Fresno "that they were not part of the report as such." He went further. In his exchange with Sisk, Connors agreed as to the report that "this is not a committee action."[199] In short the only weight of the bound volume was in the paper and covers, not in its supposed official character.

The direct testimony on this point was no less disconcerting:

> JOSEPH DI GIORGIO: The subcommittee held a hearing at Bakersfield. . . . Their official report contains the following statement about the film. . . .[200]
>
> ROBERT DI GIORGIO: All I know is it is an official report of the subcommittee of Congress and was filed.[201] It seems to me that's official enough.[202]
>
> SANBORN: To the best of my knowledge it was an official report.[203]
>
> CONNORS: Whether it is official, unofficial, semi-official, quasi-official, nobody in DiGiorgio has taken a position on it . . . we have never said it was an official House document . . . There is no evidence that DiGiorgio held out the subcommittee report as official.[204]
>
> GUBSER: It is a piece of paper signed by a majority of a committee.[205]
>
> CLERK OF THE HOUSE ROBERTS: It is not a report. It is not an official report.[206]

2. That the Nixon-Morton-Steed text was a majority report.

When Connors asked Ballis if it was not true that three makes a majority of five, Ballis, a college graduate, readily agreed. This was as far as Connors could go in proving mathematically what the House rules would not allow procedurally; no report not submitted by the chairman of a subcommittee could be a report, regardless of the division of votes.

There were other difficulties. In the tradition of the House there are no "majority" reports. There are only reports and minority or dissenting views. There can be no dissenting views unless there is a report to which they can be attached. Steed made it clear that his draft had started out as a statement of dissenting views. When he wrote it, however, there was no report to which it could be appended. "On the assumption," Steed declared, "that the report

. . . would be prepared . . . I was just making comments at variance with the report." This was an unusual form of exegesis—comments upon a text that did not yet exist.

In another sense the word "majority" was a misnomer when applied to the Nixon-Morton-Steed text. The Committee on Education and Labor was, like the House in the 81st Congress, controlled by the Democrats. Steed was of the majority, Nixon and Morton of the minority party. In Brobeck's "majority" report two of the three endorsers were of the minority party. Derrickson called it "other views signed by a majority of the subcommittee." Connors agreed in Fresno that it could be considered as an expression "of views of the majority."

3. That the report originated in the course of the proceedings of the House.

Members of the Senate and the House are reminded at regular intervals of the rule adopted by the Joint Committee on Printing, that there are three categories of material in the *Congressional Record*. These are (1) the proceedings of the Senate, (2) the proceedings of the House and (3) material not germane to the proceedings, which is published in the Appendix. It is further laid down in the House rules themselves that the proceedings are those words and acts which are recorded on the floor of the House by the official reporters. Werdel's Extension was material not germane to the business before the House on 9 March 1950. Contrary to what he testified to in his deposition, he did not deliver either his prefatory remarks or the text of the alleged report in the chamber. What he described as a report was the result of amiable discussions as casual as a western barbecue. The House had long ago taken care that its dignity not be compromised by any confusion between the rigidly controlled agenda in the chamber and privy happenings in the cloak rooms; or between a recipe for bean soup and a floor debate on a national issue.

There was no room for doubt. "The *Journal*," said the Rules, "and not the *Congressional Record* is the official record of the proceedings of the House." Nixon, it will be recalled, thought that any Member who read the *Record* should not be re-elected. Steed regarded the contents of the Appendix as "junk."

4. That the report was signed by the three congressmen.

The Corporation and its attorneys became firmly attached to the contention that Nixon, Morton and Steed had personally affixed their signatures to the report. Persuaded as they were that this made the document official they convinced others including five judges and two juries. The evidence was to the contrary.

Of the six copies that Steed said were signed none was ever produced in court. No one in the Corporation's employ ever saw a copy with the holographic signatures. Nixon, Morton and Werdel were familiar with the fact that only dissenting statements are signed, their signatures having appeared under dissenting views to Report Number 317 of Lesinski's committee during the 81st Congress. The more Connors and Steed insisted that the Werdel piece had been signed the more they established that it was a minority dissent.

Brobeck's argument was categorical enough, but it was trailed by uncertainties and contradictions.

> CONNORS: It was signed by pen and ink as it shows by the names shown here, Richard Nixon, Thruston B. Morton and Tom Steed. . . . They prepared it. They signed it.[207]
>
> SANBORN: I don't know of my own knowledge of its being signed.[208]
>
> NIXON: (I have) no independent recollection of physically affixing my name to the report. . . .[209]
>
> WERDEL: I wasn't present when Mr. Nixon, Mr. Morton and Mr. Steed actually signed the report that would have been filed with the Chairman of the Committee, but there is no doubt in my mind that before I went into the well of the House they told me that they had signed it.[210]
>
> DERRICKSON: An official subcommittee report is not signed by members ever in our committee.[211]

5. That the report was filed in the ordinary course of committee procedure.

As important to DiGiorgio's case as the signatures was the proper filing of the report. This required that it be formally received by Bailey as chairman of the subcommittee, and from Bailey by Lesinski as chairman of the full committee. Neither of these presentations took place. Bailey, in a letter dated 24 August

1960, wrote: "There is no indication that an official report was submitted by the subcommittee to the full committee." In 1966 Brobeck produced a newspaper clipping from the *Los Angeles Times,* 11 March 1950, in which it was reported that the report was "still not formally presented." No proof to the contrary appeared in the sixteen years intervening. The testimony did not indicate that there was such proof.

> WERDEL: There is no doubt about it. . . . It was an official report of the subcommittee and it was filed with the main committee.[212]
>
> NIXON: The subcommittee comes back, gets a report printed, and it is filed with the full committee and through that method becomes public.[213]
>
> STEED: I am not in a position to say that I personally handed it [the report] to him [Bailey].[214] . . . For this one not to have been filed is a very unusual situation.[215]
>
> CONNORS: Bailey said . . . I am not going to bring it up and send it to the chairman of the full committee.[216]
>
> GUBSER: The report . . . was not officially filed by the Democratic majority as an official House report.[217]

6. That the authors of the report were Nixon, Morton and Steed.

Attribution of authorship to the three congressmen went hand in hand with the persistent denial that the Corporation had in any way cooperated in the preparation of the report.

> CONNORS: Did you yourself, Mr. DiGiorgio . . . have any hand in preparing the report?
>
> DI GIORGIO: No, sir.
>
> CONNORS: To your knowledge, did anybody in the employ of DiGiorgio Fruit Corporation have any hand in preparing that report?
>
> DI GIORGIO: No, sir.
>
> CONNORS: To the best of your knowledge, who did prepare the report?
>
> DI GIORGIO: Three congressmen that signed it.[218]

Other witnesses, however, had other answers.

DUNGAN: That document was prepared by the Hon. Tom
Steed.[219]

STEED: I don't know of any report any staff member prepared.[220] Mr. Werdel probably did most of that.[221]
I have in mind that he did most of the work on
it.[222] It was so long ago that I don't recall who did
the actual writing. I would just be guessing to say.
I know it was done by the members.[223]

NIXON: I had nobody on my staff that was an expert in
labor relations.[224]

MURRAY: . . . Mr. Werdel's staff furnished the people to do
the actual typing.

CONNORS: That's not the same as prepared.[225] The only part
that Werdel played in it was to furnish somebody
in his office to type it up.[226]

WERDEL: Now, when the report was drafted and I was
advised that it was signed I obtained a copy of
the report from the minority administrative officer
whose name I believe was Graham.[227] . . . on the
same day or in the same afternoon . . . I extended
my remarks and put it into the Record.[228]

Graham declined to be tagged. He denied that he had written or
edited the report and told Murray that he was under the impression that the text had come to Washington "from somewhere in the
west." By that time Graham must have been well aware that the
search was not for a recipient of a literary award but for a writing
under suspicion.

Morton did not claim the credit. He was not in Bakersfield,
probably had not seen the film and took no discernible interest in
farm labor matters anywhere. He neither testified nor did he give
depositions in any of the DiGiorgio actions. Steed as an author was
not a much better candidate. He was bored with the assignment,
confessed his meager knowledge of California migrant labor problems, and showed only a desultory interest at the Bakersfield hearings. Nixon, the only remaining aspirant for the honor, was not
more likely to have earned it. After November 1949 he was busy
with his senatorial campaign. The Werdel release was of no use to
him as a campaign document. As a perfectionist in literary matters

and a lifetime debater he could not personally and of his own hand have committed the blunders contained in Werdel's text. It was a case of four congressmen in search of an author.

7. That the documentary sources of the report were the printed proceedings of the Bakersfield investigation and the reporter's typescript of those proceedings.

The nine columns of close print of the Werdel Extension were packed with the details of names, places, events, dates and verbal testimony given by witnesses in Bakersfield. The text heavily emphasized that it was based on the evidence taken during the hearings—"the evidence shows that," "not supported by the evidence," "the evidence before the subcommittee establishes that. . . ." The evidence referred to consisted of the 208 pages that appeared in the printed *Hearings* as a committee document.

On this point Werdel and Steed came to a remarkable disagreement:

WERDEL: After the hearings were printed and after they were available, at least, to the members of the subcommittee the majority report was drafted.[229]

STEED: No printed hearings, no, had to work with stenographic copies.[230]

Steed testified in accordance with the facts, Werdel did not. The printed *Hearings* were not released by the Government Printing Office until early April. Nearly a month had passed after the appearance of the Extension before the only official document from which the evidence could have been drawn to prepare it was available to the members of the subcommittee.

Such clairvoyance was even more remarkable in other respects. The subcommittee on its visit to DiGiorgio Farms took testimony from employees which was not recorded in the evidence. Some of this testimony was quoted in the printed report. The film was not again screened for the subcommittee after they saw it, once, in Bakersfield. The report made ten references to the content of *Poverty*. The Corporation had taken the precaution of sending a copy of the Flannery narrative to Governor Warren when he was asked to verify its accuracy; the narrative was not put into the Bakersfield record. In the Werdel text there were over five hundred words constructed in a manner identical, or nearly so, with matter contained in the *Hearings*. These passages referred to dates, acreages, wage costs, income, stock distribution, revenues, number of employees, rentals, philanthropic donations, filing dates and tax payments. Other passages totalling several hundred words did not appear in the evidence at all and represented new matter with which the report had been "beefed up."

These strange feats could still be explained, in the absence of the printed *Hearings,* if the supposed authors had in fact used the original reporter's typescript. When Steed referred to stenographic notes he meant the original or carbon sets typed and bound by the reporter.

This presented even greater difficulties than the printed *Hearings* as the documentary source. Bailey, as chairman of the subcommittee, was the custodian on behalf of the Democratic majority of the reporter's typescripts. Werdel did not say he had obtained them. Instead he up-dated the *Hearings* and testified that they were available before March 9. Moreover, it was never the practice of House committees to distribute among their members carbon typescripts as the source for the preparation of reports. Since Lesinski's committe had twenty-five members, the twenty-fifth carbon would have hardly been legible. Finally, even as the Werdel text was in preparation, the typescripts were already at the Government Printing Office there to be shredded after the completion of the printing.

The only carbon copy that survived this fate was the one that the Corporation had ordered. When last heard of in March 1966 this set was in the possession of either DiGiorgio or Brobeck. It had been obtained for Brobeck's use in preparing a brief to rebut the one the Union had submitted in 1950. Something of this came through in the testimony.

> CONNORS: . . . when House committees hold hearings, a transcript of the testimony is taken down and sent to the committee for their study . . . Yes, otherwise they would have to rely on recollection.[231] Werdel . . . was a member of the committee, but as such, he didn't have the right to deal with the subcommittee.[232]
>
> STEED: The subcommittee didn't have any files in the physical sense of the word. The files are maintained by the House Committee.[233] . . . A great deal of the original report we agreed . . . on

was in longhand on the yellow tab commonly
used by lawyers.[234] . . . I have not reread the
hearings since the day we took the testimony.[235]

DERRICKSON: No, the original transcript we don't keep. That
is sent to GPO. It's cut up in the process of preparing the printing.[236]

8. That between 12 November 1949 and 9 March 1950 there
was no communication between the Corporation and any members
of the subcommittee.

CONNORS: There is absolutely no evidence whatsoever, and
I mean literally now, of any contact between Di-
Giorgio and these three congressmen who wrote
the report.[237]

MURRAY: Before the Bakersfield hearings had you received
any communication from anybody or copies of
letters or reports in relation to the strike?

WERDEL: I think the literal answer to that question—either
as a congressman or an attorney or otherwise—
is no.[238]

CONNORS: . . . did anybody employed by DiGiorgio Fruit
Corporation have any correspondence or communication with those congressmen?

ROBERT DIGIORGIO: No, sir.[239]

MURRAY: Before November 12 and 13, 1949 . . . you knew
that Congressman Werdel was sympathetic with
the position of your corporation in relation to the
picket line?

DIGIORGIO: No, I did not know that at that time.[240]

WERDEL: . . . there were certain things that I wanted the subcommittee to have which I supplied to them. . . .[241]

Werdel did not notice that at the Bakersfield hearings Robert
DiGiorgio had filed for the record certain correspondence between
Joseph DiGiorgio and Governor Warren showing that in May 1949
Werdel was receiving such correspondence from the Corporation.[242]
He was at home in Bakersfield during the Christmas holidays of
1949 but made it a point to explain that he kept in touch with the
strike exclusively through the workers and newspaper reports.
Communication between him and DiGiorgio previous to November
13 was cut off. There followed four months of hermetic silence on

both sides during which, however, Werdel was in touch with the Special Citizens of Kern County and knew of their intense interest in the publication of the report to combat the film.

Eventually facts to the contrary came forward. On November 29 Attorney Dungan, acting for Brobeck, filed with the subcommittee a number of affidavits. He wrote letters accompanying the affidavits, which were printed in the *Hearings*. A week before, on 21 November 1949, Gregory Harrison, a ranking Brobeck partner, received a copy of the union brief. More importantly, sometime between November 13 and March 9 Brobeck filed a responding brief with a member or members of the subcommittee or with the committee staff.

9. That the Corporation had no advance knowledge of the report.

Constituents are free to lobby their congressmen, and do. DiGiorgio chose, in a matter vital to its interests and prestige, to pretend complete and thoroughgoing ignorance of what Werdel, Nixon, Morton and Steed were doing in Washington:

> ROBERT DI GIORGIO: ... the first time I knew about it was when I read it in the morning papers in 1950, or whenever it came out, it was published in the *Examiner* and *Chronicle*.[243]

The witness was referring to the morning editions of March 11 of the San Francisco dailies.

> ROBERT: That was the first time he [Joseph DiGiorgio] knew about it, first any of us knew about it.
>
> CONNORS: Any of us knew about it.[244]

Against this testimony there were certain facts. Twelve prominent citizens of the community, growers and business men, including the publisher of the *Bakersfield Californian,* were acquainted with the text or tenor of the report before March 9. These citizens were close friends of Mr. Joseph. The wire services carried the news from Washington on March 10 and the stories included comments by officials of the Corporation on a report of which Robert DiGiorgio was to learn for the first time on the following morning. There was the text of a "report" in Brobeck's hands on the tenth which Dungan claimed had been received in the DiGiorgio office, mimeographed and relayed to Brobeck in the form of thirteen pages of mimeographed process.

CONNORS: They knew . . . the report was going to come out
and they were waiting for it.[245]

DUNGAN: . . . I knew of it before Mr. Werdel put it in the
Record. I knew of it when it was first signed by the
three members of the subcommittee.[246]

10. That neither the Corporation nor any of its agents had any
part whatever in the preparation of the report.

In 1950 and thereafter the public relations value and the political
effect of the Nixon-Morton-Steed report depended upon its appearance as a spontaneous and completely independent statement by
the subcommittee. To be acceptable at all in the press and in the
courts it had to be official, signed in pen and ink, based on first
hand documentary sources and insulated from any bias in favor
of the company.

There were two difficulties in the way of this proposition. One
was the responding brief. The other was document 612–53.

First, as to the brief.

DUNGAN: . . . when the hearing was held in Bakersfield . . .
the subcommittee gave us leave to file a brief in
response [to the Union brief] . . . we did prepare
such a brief and sent it to the subcommittee in
Washington . . .[247] And I worked on it.

CONNORS: Mr. Gregory Harrison tells me he has no recollection that we did file a brief. . . .

DUNGAN: Well, I am under oath here, and I am telling you
we did.

A covering letter went with the document. Precisely to whom it
was addressed Dungan could not recall, although in Bakersfield
when Bailey granted leave to extend the record he clearly indicated
that additional material was to be mailed to Mr. Frank Boyer, the
majority clerk. There was testimony that a carbon set of the
reporter's typescript was acquired for use in preparing the answering brief. Brobeck's brief did not appear in the printed *Hearings*;
the Union brief did. No copy of it was ever found in Washington.
Neither Werdel nor any of his three associates made any mention
of it. Brobeck was asked to produce a file copy and failed to do so,
explaining that it was lost.

Document 612–53 did not stand up to analysis any better. With the exception of the omitted prefatory remarks and over seventy stylistic errors, its text was identical with that of the Werdel Extension. A subject matter outline of the three related documents showed their striking similarity as to content and arrangement of topics:

UNION BRIEF	WERDEL EXTENSION AND 612–53
Purpose of hearing	Purpose of hearing
DiGiorgio Fruit Corporation	DiGiorgio Fruit Corporation
Properties and holdings	Financial structure
Financial structure	Properties
Subsidiaries	Subsidiaries
Directors	Directors
Working and living conditions	The DiGiorgio Farms
Workers' organization	Union organization
Grievances	The strike
Wages	Non-recognition
Hours	Wages and hours
Housing conditions	Grievances
	Housing conditions
Evictions	Working conditions
Ethnic segregation of the labor force	Rents
Conditions for occupancy	Ethnic segregation
Communist infiltration	Recreational facilities
Poverty in the Valley of Plenty	Welfare provisions
Mexican *braceros*	Workmen's compensation
The *braceros* and the strike	Unemployment insurance
Mexican Wetbacks	Mexican *braceros*
Taft-Hartley Act	Mexican Wetbacks
NLRB proceedings	The *braceros* and the strike
Terms for settlement of the strike	Taft-Hartley Act
Recommendations	NLRB proceedings
State legislation	Fair Labor Standards Act
Federal legislation	Recommendations
Chronology	Federal legislation

The two columns of content and arrangement of text were related to a number of significant facts. The Union brief was submitted on 12 November 1949. Werdel's text appeared in print in Washington on 10 March 1950. On the same date the text was in Brobeck's possession in San Francisco, mimeographed. Between the two dates Brobeck filed a responding brief with the subcommittee. The identical texts of document 612–53 and Werdel's Extension were both, as the columns show, faithfully responsive to the Union brief. So was Brobeck's responding brief.

As to the unproved teletyped transmission from Washington—or Baltimore—Dungan and Connors in the end were not sure whether it had been by way of a private TWX or by Associated Press wires.

> CONNORS: If they have an office in Baltimore and that office teletypes them the text of the report, they will type it up on a typewriter and it's just as simple as that, and there is nothing more to it than that.[248]
>
> DUNGAN: I may have seen it first in teletype form on long yellow sheets.[249] . . . [It] could have come over the AP wire.[250]

The TWX directory proved that there was no private circuit between the DiGiorgio offices in Baltimore and San Francisco. DiGiorgio did not subscribe to the Associated Press or any other wire service by which he could have received the complete text on March 10. No press wire service was known to be sending verbatim nine column items from the Appendix. Besides, he learned of the report for the first time on March 11.

Brobeck made a faint effort to hedge the teletype story by suggesting that the message might have been transmitted over long distance telephone from Washington. Dungan had testified to a call from Nixon's office on March 10.

> MURRAY: At one time you had the impression, Mr. Dungan, that the words that appear on this thirteen-page document came by telephone.
>
> DUNGAN: That could be.
>
> MURRAY: That could be a guess, though?
>
> DUNGAN: Yes, an equally eligible guess as the guess that they came by teletype.

MURRAY: Both are guesses by you?

DUNGAN: That is right.

But it was as to the way in which the mimeographed document 612–53 came into existence as well as the source of its text that the testimony ran in

Circles of Confusion. /

CONNORS: Robert DiGiorgio will testify that . . . he got . . . a copy of the *Congressional Record* containing this report from our law offices, and that it was typed up in his office and mimeographed.[251]

DUNGAN: I have a definite impression that whenever this document became a public document in Washington, that same day, by some means of long distance communication, I saw, in San Francisco, and there was made available at least to Mr. Gregory Harrison and to me . . . the full text of the report of the majority of the subcommittee.[252] . . . a photorapid copy made in our office of a mimeographed paper that came to our office from the office of DiGiorgio Fruit Corporation.[253]

MURRAY: And then it is your testimony that from something that was printed you had this [612–53] typed up?

ROBERT DI GIORGIO: I don't believe that I testified that I had it done, but that it was done.[254]

CONNORS: And do you recall where you got the copy from which it was mimeographed?

DI GIORGIO: I don't recall, but I assume that your office furnished it to us.

SEDGWICK: Do you recall whether or not you had some copies made or mimeographed of that report, wherever you got it?

DI GIORGIO: Well, I believe we did. We had a very fine mimeograph. . . .[255]

SEDGWICK: And it is your recollection that these copies were made on your mimeographing machine in your office here in San Francisco?

DI GIORGIO: Yes.[256]

MURRAY: That was typed up in the DiGiorgio Fruit Corpora-
               tion office?
DI GIORGIO: I don't know that, no.[257]
MURRAY: So you don't know who typed up this exhibit?
DI GIORGIO: No.
MURRAY: Or when it was typed up?
DI GIORGIO: No, I do not.
MURRAY: Or from what?
DI GIORGIO: No, I do not.[258]

Murray, in an interrogatory he sent the Corporation in December 1962, asked: "From what sources did you obtain a copy of a subcommittee report referred to [612–53]?" The answer, given under oath, was: "The source of this copy is unknown."

MURRAY: Now, is the source known to you now?
DI GIORGIO: No, it's not. . . .[259]

The printed copy of the *Congressional Record* which at one point was proposed as the source of 612–53 very likely arrived in San Francisco before Robert DiGiorgio returned from Borrego Springs. The testimony was that several of these copies were in Brobeck's office a few days after Werdel's Extension appeared. "This was a very important thing," Dungan declared, "and that is why it was important to have copies of it right now and for counsel to know and for the company to know what was in it." Werdel instructed his staff to send prints of the Appendix to all "interested persons" immediately. That would have been by air mail which would have delivered them to Brobeck within two or three days. The mimeographed copies of 612–53 were never distributed to the press or associates of DiGiorgio. As Dungan said, "It became unimportant as soon as we had the official printed documents."

Neither explanation for the presence of 612–53 in Brobeck's files on March 10 by way of teletype or by telephone was tenable. Nor were the other two offered by Corporation witnesses: that the document had been reproduced from an Appendix print, and that it had been prepared from a typed manuscript.

If the source was a print mailed to Brobeck by Werdel, it could not have been stencilled and mimeographed in time for Brobeck to have it on March 10, since the print did not arrive in San Fran-

cisco until March 13 or thereafter. Moreover, DiGiorgio testified
that he had seen 612–53 before he saw the printed Appendix version, which could not have been true if 612–53 was developed
from the printing. Brobeck delivered a copy of the printed Appendix to DiGiorgio, in whose office there was produced by mimeograph process a thirteen-page undated and otherwise unidentified
garbled version, a copy of which was then delivered to Brobeck by
DiGiorgio. This copy was identical with the one deposited in Brobeck's file on March 10. But if Robert saw the printed Appendix
first on his return to San Francisco it made no sense that he
ordered mimeographed duplicates which had already become
unimportant.

> CONNORS: Do you recall whether that was the first copy you
> ever saw?
> DI GIORGIO: I believe it was. I believe that was prepared before
> we could get copies of the actual printed . . . *Con-*
> *gressional Record.*
> CONNORS: Do you recall where you got the copy from which
> it was mimeographed?
> DI GIORGIO: I don't recall, but I assume that your office fur-
> nished it to us . . .
> CONNORS: Do you recall where that was mimeographed?
> DI GIORGIO: I believe in our office.[260]

What did Connors mean by "copy"? Not a print, for DiGiorgio
had just so stated. And not a mimeographed process of 612–53,
for this did not yet exist. What Connors meant was a typescript
from which the mimeograph process came forth from DiGiorgio's
office. Brobeck had no mimeograph equipment. Bradford had
already placed the typewriter in the offices of the Corporation.

The sequence would now have been that DiGiorgio received a
text of some sort from Brobeck on March 10, on which day
612–53 was mimeographed and a copy delivered by DiGiorgio to
Brobeck. DiGiorgio read the text for the first time in the newspapers of March 11, some unidentified officials of the Corporation
having already given a statement to the press on March 10. He
returned to San Francisco on or about March 13, asked Brobeck
for a print of the Appendix, had mimeographed copies run from
that, and sent one to Brobeck.

On this roil of inconsistencies, contradictions and guesses, 612–53 kept boggling, like a piece of telltale flotsam. It had surfaced out of Dungan's file as proof that the three congressmen had affixed their signatures to Werdel's insertions. The proof was missing; the evidence remained. It was now the crux of the case: Did the Corporation cooperate or in any way take part in the preparation of the Nixon-Morton-Steed report? The inference was inescapable: it did.

The circumstantial evidence, disdained by Connors, could not be ignored. No one in Washington had been identified as the sender by teletype. DiGiorgio did not have such equipment in Baltimore. The supposed telephone transmission had proved to be a second guess. No one on DiGiorgio's staff received and transcribed the long message on the morning of March 10. Both Werdel's Extension and 612–53 contained new matter which was neither in the printed *Hearings* nor in the reporter's typescript. Passages were quoted closely in both Werdel's Extension and the documents which the congressmen in Washington did not have before them. Werdel's prefatory remarks were written after the text of the report had been prepared and they did not appear in 612–53. Of the life span of 612–53 only a few days were known—March 10 to March 14. During this brief interval the mimeographed copies produced by DiGiorgio's office were not distributed to the press. They carried no dateline. They had not been prepared for Joseph DiGiorgio's immediate use, since he, too, did not know that the report had been released until March 11 or after. He could not have ordered Robert to make them on or after March 11 because they were already in existence on March 10, and one copy was already in Brobeck's possession. On or about March 14, 612–53 became unimportant. It had served its purpose. Only one possible theory remained as to what that was—that it had served as the draft for Werdel's Extension of Remarks. This theory could be proved or disproved by other documents in the file which bore the number 612–53.

The Corporation began to lose those documents.

Murray demanded the Brobeck file copy of the responding brief. Dungan said it was lost. Murray wanted to examine the carbon-copy volumes of the reporter's typescript; Connors declared they were lost. Murray asked for the correspondence relating to the submission of the responding brief. It was reported lost. Murray requested copies of the correspondence between the Corporation and Werdel during 1949. They were gone. Murray subpoenaed the original mimeograph process of 612-53 of which Dungan had given him a photorapid copy. It was lost. Brobeck's copy of the printed Hearings, which both Sedgwick and Plant used in court, was lost.

The words of Supreme Court Chief Justice Burger, spoken in another context, seemed appropriate: the case had lasted "long enough" for the Corporation to "finally reap the natural rewards of lost evidence and fading memories."

NOTES

197. 67 Atl. 320.
198. *Jefferson's Manual and Rules of the House of Representatives.* 81st Congress, section 943.
199. Reporter's transcript. Case number 122891. Vol. III, p. 748.
200. *Report to the Stockholders.* DiGiorgio Fruit Corporation. 1 June 1950.
201. Reporter's transcript. Case number 122891, Vol. I, p. 59.
202. Robert DiGiorgio. Deposition. 16 December 1964, p. 28.
203. Bruce W. Sanborn. Deposition. 2 December 1960, p. 20.
204. Robert DiGiorgio. Deposition. 9 February 1968, p. 20; Reporter's transcript. Case number 122891, Vol. I, p. 26.
205. Charles S. Gubser. Deposition. 28 December 1964, p. 35.
206. Ralph R. Roberts. Deposition. 29 April 1963, p. 32.
207. Reporter's transcript. Case number 122891, Vol. I, p. 17.
208. Bruce W. Sanborn, Deposition, 2 December 1960, p. 20.
209. Richard M. Nixon. Deposition. 7 January 1963, p. 11.
210. Thomas H. Werdel. Deposition. 31 July 1962, p. 30.
211. Russell C. Derrickson. Deposition. 29 April 1963, p. 27.
212. Werdel, deposition cited above, p. 75.
213. Nixon, deposition cited above, p. 22.
214. Tom Steed, Deposition. 13 September 1965, p. 53.
215. Reporter's partial transcript. Testimony of Tom Steed. Complaint number 503735. San Francisco, Calif. 10 March 1964, p. 30.

216. Reporter's transcript. Case number 122891. Vol. IV, p. 840.
217. *Congressional Record.* 24 October 1963, p. 19253.
218. Reporter's transcript. Case number 122891. Vol. I, p. 49.
219. Malcolm T. Dungan. Deposition. 23 January 1968, p. 12.
220. Tom Steed. Deposition. 13 September 1965, p. 8.
221. Steed, testimony cited above. Complaint number 503735.
222. Tom Steed. Deposition. 30 April 1963, p. 22.
223. Ibid., p. 6.
224. Richard M. Nixon, Deposition. 7 January 1963, p. 27.
225. Reporter's transcript. Case number 122891, Vol. III, p. 713.
226. Ibid., p. 928.
227. Thomas H. Werdel. Deposition. 31 July 1962, p. 28.
228. Ibid., p. 29.
229. Ibid., p. 27.
230. Reporter's partial transcript. Testimony of Tom Steed. Complaint number 503735. San Francisco, Calif. 10 March 1964, p. 31.
231. Reporter's transcript. Case number 122891. Vol. II, p. 525.
232. Ibid., Vol. IV, p. 940.
233. Tom Steed. Deposition. 13 September 1965, p. 65.
234. Ibid., p. 10.
235. Reporter's partial transcript. Case number 503735. Testimony of Tom Steed, cited above, p. 21.
236. Russell C. Derrickson. Deposition. 29 April 1963, p. 23.
237. Reporter's transcript. Case number 122891. Vol. IV, p. 842.
238. Thomas H. Werdel Deposition. 31 July 1962, p. 15.
239. Reporter's transcript. Case number 122891. Vol. I, p. 43.
240. Ibid., Vol. I, p. 61.
241. Werdel, deposition cited above p. 16.
242. *Hearings.* Bakersfield 12–13 November 1949, pp. 647, 664.
243. Robert DiGiorgio. Deposition. 9 December 1960, p. 29.
244. Reporter's transcript. Case number 122891. Vol. I, p. 66.
245. Ibid., Vol. I, p. 19.
246. Malcolm T. Dungan. Deposition. 23 January 1968, p. 3.
247. Malcolm T. Dungan. Deposition. 7 February 1966, p. 22.
248. Reporter's transcript. Case number 122891. Vol. IV, p. 830.
249. Dungan. deposition cited above, p. 12.
250. Malcolm T. Dungan, Deposition, 23 January 1968, p. 9.
251. Reporter's transcript. Case number 122891. Vol. I, p. 20.
252. Malcolm T. Dungan. Deposition. 23 January 1968, p. 17.
253. Ibid., p. 23.

254. Reporter's partial transcript. Case number 503735. Testimony of Robert DiGiorgio. 27 February 1964, p. 65.

255. Reporter's transcript. Case number 122891. Vol. I, p. 46.

256. Reporter's partial transcript. Case number 503735, cited above, p. 62.

257. Robert DiGiorgio. Deposition. 16 December 1964, p. 19.

258. Reporter's transcript. Case number 122891. Vol. I, p. 114.

259. Robert DiGiorgio. Deposition. 9 February 1968, p. 28.

260. Reporter's transcript. Case number 122891. Vol. I, p. 46.

14

CONCLUSION
WITHOUT AN END

There is a folk saying that time heals all wounds but folklore has not said that it wounds all heels. Among these are the ingenious mythmakers who succeed, the true deceivers. They are few in number and the pleasure they aspire to is a secret one. Undetected, from a private place they watch mankind wander in peril and distress, grasping not even at straws but at the shadows of straws. They are lone craftsmen without ties of guild or guilt between them. Each in his hole-in-corner, they serve only what Hegel called "the cunning of reason that sets the passions to work for itself, while that which develops its existence through such impulsion pays the penalty, and suffers the loss."

But reason has a dialectic of its own that is at work before it grapples with the world. As music is the food of love, so thesis and antithesis are the food of mind. Strain and tension set the technology of the human brain in motion. As long as there is life that motion continues.

This is vital, but so is that other role of reason. It is the instrument for relating man to man. Beneath and deeper than technical virtuosity in solving puzzles and compromising conflicts is the drive, nearly a hunger, for human kinship, enlarging from the pair of friends or lovers to embrace mankind.

Then man makes a remarkable discovery. The symbols he has invented allow him not only to unravel enigmas or uncover secrets but also to fabricate them, not only to detect traps but to lay them. His own incommunicable experience tells him that being fooled, bamboozled, misled, confused or trapped is evil. What is evil for him organically must be evil for mankind. Reason becomes a miracle of nervous drive tinged with values.

So men must make the choice how they will use the compelling exercise of mind they cannot avoid while they live. The true deceivers are faced with competition from truth searchers, who are even fewer in number. These are people like Professor and Mrs. Sirkin, who rescued James Mill's *History of British India* from H. H. Wilson's pirating; the scholars who removed the poison from the Protocols of Zion; the journalists who told the ingenious fakery of the Zinoviev letter forty years after it toppled Ramsay Mc-Donald's government; and Joseph V. Nobel, museum curator, who noticed "a very thin line running from the tip of the nose" of a bronze horse made after World War II that had supposedly been cast in Italy around 300 B.C.

Fakery in writing, as in painting or sculpture or industrial pro-duction, if the issue is a vital one, encounters minds bent on serving the need of human society for security in man-to-man relationships. Lord Shaw has explained why this is so: "Causation is not a chain but a net. At each point, influences, forces, precedent and simulta-neous, meet, and the radiation from each point extends infinitely." This is a nonbiological description of the human mind. Given time and opportunity it can find its way through the mists of possible truth and possible fiction that spread in all directions from a given fixed point of fact. For no verbal contrivance of men can be com-pletely and purely true, as it cannot be completely and purely false, because it cannot ever be completely complete.

There can be touches of comedy in the process. The Werdel affair was not without them: William Callan, the investigator, call-ing aloud for help in the middle of a deposition; Steed's imagina-tive picture of the three congressmen trudging dutifully through the cloak rooms of the House with bulky volumes of a reporter's tran-script as they drafted their report; Werdel himself receiving and hastily dispatching the typed draft all in the same afternoon as if it were a bit of atomic waste; a crate of fresh asparagus on the reception desk of a congressman eager to give away a succulent conflict of interest; DiGiorgio's private showings of a dead film whose bones had more than once rattled in a courtroom; the Associated Press transmitting nine columns of the Appendix of the

Congressional Record for the private convenience of Joseph
DiGiorgio; documents cherished for twenty years in Brobeck's files
dropping from sight like petals from a withered chrysanthemum,
on command; Murray musing whether document 612-53 had been
transmitted by pony express.

The humor was subdued. The dominant mood was one of prudence, confidentiality, discretion, secrecy, to keep from public view
certain facts. Congress had never extended its demands for open
records in the executive departments to itself. The "proceedings"
described by Steed fitted the legislative permissiveness.

Among the farm workers of Kern County the shattering conse-
quences of the Nixon-Morton-Steed report were never chronicled
and the men and women who remembered them soon scattered.
Local 218 faded away as the National Agricultural Workers Union
spent itself in the resistance of ten years. Farm workers left the
countryside and migrated to the cities. Among them, once more
sorely tried and bitterly frustrated, were hundreds of thousands of
Mexican rural laborers and their families, whose hopes had rested
on a union of their own. Mechanization continued its inroads on
agricultural jobs. The national leaders of organized labor devised
strategies in which there was no place for the NAWU. The Agricultural Workers Organizing Committee displaced it. The center of
controversy shifted from Arvin to Delano. DiGiorgio signed a labor
contract and began to sell its farms. The battle over civil rights
spilled into the Central Valley, and Nixon nibbled in public on a
bunch of grapes. Those who had failed molded in oblivion; those
who had succeeded, mellowed and forgave their victims.

The balance of twenty years showed net gains for the Corporation. *Poverty in the Valley of Plenty* was outlawed. The courts had
legitimated the report that condemned the film. Brobeck still had
over one hundred copies of the Werdel reprint in reserve for whatever the future might bring. The Corporation was $60,000 ahead
in damages collected.

The legal attacks sustained by DiGiorgio for two decades fal-
tered. It was losing money and interest in the matter. It was also
losing vital documents. As these disappeared the chances that the
real author of Werdel's Extension of Remarks would ever be
known diminished. There was both assurance and prophecy in
Connors's observation: "No record will ever show."

No unusual legal principle was settled by the prolonged and expensive lawsuits. Issues of fact took years to clear up, and the central one remained unresolved. As the evidence became more voluminous and complicated juries became more confused. Judges did not detect the flaws in evidence laid before them.

The House of Representatives itself was as it had always been. Gentlemen continued to order reprints of balderdash and constituents continued to distribute them with the Great Seal of the United States and the imprimatur "Proceedings and Debates" of the Congress. There was nothing for the House to correct in the Nixon-Morton-Steed-Werdel matter because there was nothing wrongful that the House itself had done. Four of its children had indulged in a prank. The naughty act helped to destroy a union. This, Senator Morton observed philosophcially, was "water under the bridge."

But had something more than a farm worker's union been washed downstream?

The report this tale is about proved to be a decadent document. It was prepared and published by men who were confident that the myth itself would not decay. Such an idea—that myths can be everlasting—is possible only in a society in which belief in them is cultivated by ignorance and enforced by tyranny. It was a classic example of manipulation, a demonstration "that myths can be manufactured in the same sense and according to the same methods as any other weapons—as machine guns and airplanes," to borrow words from Professor Ernest Cassirer.

The manipulation in this instance was not accomplished by corner grocers conniving with precinct politicians for the petty spoils of a ward. The report was given the stamp of legitimacy by four Members of the House and placed as a dangerous weapon in the hands of a powerful corporation.

Considering its literary quality, its birth in the wastebasket of the *Congressional Record* and its surreptitious uses the document was only a pebble. But it was a pebble used by the Corporation to put an end to Local 218 with the well-aimed publication of the Nixon-Morton-Steed report.

By then DiGiorgio was well on the way to the full stature of industrial corporatism. Its peers, the Big 500, were already claiming to be the axial institutions of American life. Technological com-

pulsions, their vital needs of price stabilization and consumer pre-
dictability, their haunting dependence on aggregate demand, their
will to integrate vertically and horizontally everything in sight,
forced their interest and nerved their intervention into the subtlest
areas of the American spirit. Scholarship, human motivation,
public relations, the political agencies and finally social values were
becoming so many computables of the gross national product.

The aim, eventually, was represented as a spiritual one. It was
a new unity, the master plan of an élite which had already proved
it could produce all Things in abundance. Now there was to be an
abundance of togetherness.

It was a plausible proposition. The American people were to be
togetherized as skillfully and brilliantly as they are fast being com-
puterized. The method was to be the transfer of the skills of the
corporation from technology to sociology. The tooling up of human
beings is feasible. It requires only the services of political artists
and psychological engineers. A corporation can command both.
The Werdel-Nixon-Morton-Steed report was just another demonstration that it can be done.

More than feasible it was crucial. There was an illusion to be
concealed—the illusion of togetherness in a society that gives the
few ownership and control of the most of the productive goods on
which all men depend.

It has been said that "by 1975 only 200 firms will control almost
75 percent of the industrial output" of America, so that "what
happens to large corporations is of utmost social significance."[261]

And so it is, but not only to them.

Towering above the capitol, Freedom in bronze symbolizes a
thoughtful watch over the land. It may also be a vigil over what
happens at its feet in the corridors and cloak rooms of the Congress. This, too, may be of utmost social significance.

NOTES

261. *Kaiser Aluminum News.* Vol. 25, No. 2, p. 31.

BIBLIOGRAPHY

PRINCIPAL SOURCES

GOVERNMENT DOCUMENTS

Business and Professional Code, State of California. 1961. sections 7502, 7521, 7538, 7522.

Biographical directory of the American Congress 1794–1961. U.S. Government Printing Office. Washington, D.C. 1961. House Document 442 85th Congress, second session.

Cannon's Procedures in the House of Representatives. House Document 741. 81st Congress, second session. Government Printing Office, Washington, D.C., 1951.

Congressional Record—House.
  25 May 1876, p. 3339.
  22 March 1948, pp. 3259–3261.
  24 June 1949, p. 8396.
  9 March 1950. Proceedings, pp. 3112, 3127.
                    Daily Digest, p. D-159.
                    Daily edition. Appendix pp. A-1817–A-1820.
  26 April 1960, p. 5818.
  26 September 1951, p. 12175.
  16 October 1963, pp. 18637–18646.
  21 October 1963, pp. 18980-18981.
  24 October 1963, pp. 19252-19254.

Congressional Record—Senate.
  18 February 1955, p. 1703.

Congressional Record. Appendix Volume 96 Part 14, pp. A-1449–A-2862.

Congressional Index. Volume 96, Part 19, p. 630.

Farm Placement Bulletin, Number 75. State of California, Department of Employment. 5 September 1956.

Hearings before a Subcommittee of the Committee on Education and Labor. U.S. Senate pursuant to Senate Resolution 266 (74th Congress). *Violations of Free Speech and Rights of Labor.* U.S. Senate. 76th Congress, second session, Part 48. Washington, D.C. 1940.

Hearings before a Special Subcommittee of the Committee on Education and Labor. House Resolution 2032, U.S. House of Representatives. National Labor Relations Act of 1949. 81st Congress, second session. Washington, D.C. 1949.

Hearings before a Special Investigating Subcommittee of the Committee on Education and Labor. House Resolution 75 . . . Bakersfield, 12–13 November 1949 . . . U.S. House of Representatives, 81st Congress, first session. Washington, D.C., 1950.

Hearings before a Special Investigating Subcommittee of the Committee on Education and Labor. Federal aid to schools in impacted areas. House Resolution 4115, Part 1. U.S. House of Representatives, 81st Congress, first session. Washington, D.C. 1950.

Hearings before a Subcommittee of the Committee on Education and Labor. Fair Labor Standards Act. 85th Congress, first session. Part 2. Washington, D.C. 1957.

Hinds, Asher C. and Clarence Cannon. *Precedents of the House.* Government Printing Office, Washington, D.C. 1907 8 volumes.

House Resolution 75. 81st Congress, first session. *Congressional Record* 2 February 1949.

House Resolution 4115. 81st Congress, first session. *Congressional Record* 8 April 1949.

Joint determination *re* D'Arrigo Brothers. Bureau of Employment Security, 27 October 1959.

Journal. U.S. House of Representatives. 81st Congress second session.

Minutes. Regional Foreign Labor Operations Advisory Committee. Bureau of Employments Security, U.S. Department of Labor. Meeting number 13, 1 February 1957; meeting number 16, 31 October 1957.

Monthly Catalog of United States Government Publications

Number 664. May 1950, p. 30. Superintendent of Documents. Washington, D.C.

Report of Special Investigating Subcommittees numbers 1 and 2. Committee print. Unnumbered. House Resolution 4115. Federal assistance for educating children in localities affected by Federal activities. Committee on Education and Labor. U.S. House of Representatives. 81st Congress, second session. Washington, D.C. 1950.

Report on the Farm Labor Transportation Accident at Chualar, California on September 17, 1963. Committee print. Unnumbered. Committee on Education and Labor. U.S. House of Representatives. 88th Congress, second session. Washington, D.C. April 1964.

Report on *Strangers in Our Fields.* Bureau of Employment security U.S. Department of Labor, Region X. San Francisco, California. No date.

Serial Index and numerical lists of Congressional Documents.
80th Congress, 1947–1948
81st Congress, 1949–1950
82nd Congress, 1951–1952
83rd Congress, 1953–1954
Government Printing Office, Washington, D.C.

Statements given before the Hon. Hugh M. Burns, State Senator, Vice-chairman of the Senate Committee on Un-American Activities at DiGiorgio, Kern County, California, and Bakersfield, California. 16 January 1948.

Statements and reports: DiGiorgio Fruit Corporation. Securities and Exchange Commission. 1945–1965. Washington, D.C.

LEGAL DOCUMENTS

Agreement between DiGiorgio Fruit Corporation and Harry W. Flannery, National Farm Labor Union, Hollywood Film Council. Los Angeles, California, 23 May 1950.

Answers to Interrogatories propounded to Defendants. *Galarza v. DiGiorgio Fruit Corporation.* Complaint Number 503735, in the Superior Court in and for the County of San Francisco, 12 December 1962.

Appellant's opening brief. 5 Civil no. 740 in the Court of Appeal of the State of California. Fifth Appellate District. *DiGiorgio Fruit Corporation v. Valley Labor Citizen,* 26 March 1967.

Brief for plaintiff and respondent. 5 Civil no. 740 in the Court of Appeal of the State of California. Fifth Appellate District. *DiGiorgio Fruit Corporation v. Valley Labor Citizen,* 27 July 1967.

Brief as *amicus curiae* in support of appellants. San Francisco-Oakland Newspaper Guild. 5 Civil 740 in the Court of Appeal of the State of California. Fifth Appellate District, 9 October 1967.

Brief for plaintiff and respondent in reply to Brief as *amicus curiae.* 5 Civil no. 740 in the Court of Appeal of the State of California. Fifth Appellate District. 30 October 1967.

Clerk's transcript. Complaint number 122891. *DiGiorgio Fruit Corporation v. Valley Labor Citizen.* In the Superior Court in and for the County of Fresno, filed 2 August 1966.

Consent Judgment. Complaint number 566888. *DiGiorgio v. Harry W. Flannery, et al.* In the Superior Court in and for the County of Los Angeles, filed 24 May 1950.

Brief for plaintiff and respondent. 3 Civil no. 10522. *DiGiorgio Fruit Corporation v. American Federation of Labor, et al.* In the Court of Appeal of the State of California, Third Appellate District.

Reporter's transcript on appeal. Case number 122891. *DiGiorgio Fruit Corporation v. Valley Labor Citizen.* In the Court of Appeal of the State of California, Fifth District Court. Volumes I–IV.

Trial transcript. 3 Civil no. 10522. *DiGiorgio Fruit Corporation v. American Federation of Labor et al.* In the Court of Appeal of the State of California. Third Appellate District. Volume I.

LAW REPORTS

Advance California Appellate Reports. 215 A.C.A. No. 2. 14 May 1963. Civil No. 10522. *DiGiorgio Fruit Corporation v. American Federation of Labor, et al.* pp. 632–653.

West's California Reporter. Civil no. 740. *DiGiorgio Fruit Corporation v. Valley Labor Citizen, et al.,* 22 April 1968. 67 California Reporter, pp. 82–92.

DEPOSITIONS

H. L. Mitchell	9 January 1950
M. Albert O'Dea	30 November 1960
Bruce W. Sanborn, Jr.	2 December 1960
Robert DiGiorgio	9 December 1960
Glenn E. Brockway	20 December 1960
Alfred J. Norton	27 February 1961
Louis Krainnock	8 May 1961
Malcolm T. Dungan	7 November 1961
Thomas H. Werdel	31 July 1962
Ernesto Galarza	27 December 1962
Richard M. Nixon	7 January 1963
Edward F. Hayes	22 January 1963
Louis Krainnock	19 April 1963
Ralph R. Roberts	29 April 1963
Russell C. Derrickson	29 April 1963
Tom Steed	30 April 1963
William R. Callan	18 September 1963
Robert M. Perkins	14 July 1964
Lloyd Myers	14 July 1964
George Ballis	25 July 1964
Jeff Boehm	28 October 1964
Robert DiGiorgio	16 December 1964
Charles S. Gubser	28 December 1964
Sheldon F. Sackett	15 March 1965
Wallace E. Sedgwick	7 July 1965
Tom Steed	13 September 1965
Malcolm T. Dungan	7 February 1966
Malcolm T. Dungan	23 January 1968
Robert DiGiorgio	9 February 1968

CASES

Babcock v. McClatchy Newspapers. 82 CA 2d., 528. (1947)
Blake v. Hearst Publication, Inc. 75 CA 2d, 6. (1946)
Brayton v. Crowell-Collier Publishing Company. 205 Fed 2d, 644 (1953).
Brown v. Paramount Publix Corporation. 270 New York Sup., 544. (1934)

Campbell v. New York Evening Post. 157 NE 155. (1927)

Christoffel v. U.S. 338 U.S. 85–88. (1949)

Corbett v. American Newspapers. 5 Atl. 2d, 245. (1939)

Cowley v. Pulsifer. Mass. Rpts. Vol. 137, 394. (1886)

Davis v. RKO Pictures. 191 Fed. 2d, 901. (1951)

DiGiorgio Fruit Corporation v. American Federation of Labor, et al. 215 A.C.A. No. 2, 632–653. (1963)

DiGiorgio Fruit Corporation v. Valley Labor Citizen. 67 Cal. Rep. 82–92. (1968)

Emde v. San Joaquin County Central Labor Council. 23 CA 2d, 146. (1943)

Felix Youssoupoff v. Columbia Broadcasting System, Inc., 265 N.Y. Sup. 2d, 757. (1965)

Grigorieff v. Winchell. 45 N.Y. Sup. 2d, 31. (1943)

General Talking Pictures Corp. v. Hyatt. 199 Pac. 2d, 147. (1948)

Houston v. Interstate Circuits. 132 SW 2d, 906. (1939)

Hartman v. Winchell. 171 ALR 764. (1947)

Hughes v. Washington Daily News Co. 193 Fed. 2d, 293. (1951)

Kelly v. Loew's. Inc. 76 Fed. Supp. 473. (1948)

Kuhn v. Warner Brothers Pictures. 29 Fed. Supp. 800. (1939)

Kurata v. Los Angeles News Publishing Co. 40 Pac. 2d, 520. (1935)

Lyon v. Fairweather. 636 A 194. (1923)

Marks v. Orth. 121 Indiana Rep. 10. (1889)

Merle v. Sociological Research Film Corp. 99 ALR 878. (1915)

Near v. Minnesota. 283 U.S. 714. (1930)

Newby v. Times-Mirror Co. 46 CA 110. (1920)

Pennsylvania Iron Works v. Henry Voght Machinery Co. 96 SW 551. (1906)

Princess Irina Alexandrovna Youssoupoff v. Metro-Goldwyn-Mayer Pictures, Ltd. 99 ALR 864. (1934)

Sullivan v. Warner Brothers Theaters. 42 CA 2d, 660. (1941)

South Hetton Coal Co. v. N.E. News Association. 1 QB 133. (1894)

U.S. v. California Fruit Exchange, DiGiorgio Fruit Corporation, et al. complaint and consent decree. District Court of the U.S. Southern District of California. (1942)

Utah State Farm Bureau Federation v. National Farmers Union Service Corporation. 198 Fed. 2d, 20. (1952)
Warner Brothers v. Stanly. 192 SE 311. (1937)

MISCELLANEOUS DOCUMENTS

Agricultural Labor at DiGiorgio Farms, California (612–53), no date, no author, no publisher, no imprint. Photocopy of mimeograph process.

Letter by Malcolm T. Dungan for Brobeck, Phleger and Harrison to Mssrs. Gilbert, Nissen and Irvin, San Francisco, California, 18 May 1960.

Memorandum-brief on the DiGiorgio strike and conditions among the agricultural workers of California. National Farm Labor Union. Bakersfield, California, 12 November 1949.

Notes for Director Goodwin, Bureau of Employment Security, U.S. Department of Labor *re* Ernesto Galarza. State of California Department of Employment, 4 September 1956.

Notice to Grower-Members. Northern California Growers Association. Yuba City, California, 11 November 1957.

Press release. DiGiorgio Fruit Corporation. San Francisco, California, 18 May 1960.

Report of examination of Summons and Complaint, 7 November 1949, and purported draft of a manuscript (612–53). Lowell W. Bradford, 21 October 1963.

Reporter's transcript of Hearings of Subcommittee Number 1, Bakersfield, California, 12–13 November 1949, pp. 67–98. Photocopy of carbon copy. DiGiorgio Fruit Corporation. San Francisco, California, no date.

BOOKS

American Bar Association. *Canons of Professional Ethics.* 1967 edition.

Acheson, Dean. *A Citizen Looks at Congress.* Harper and Brothers. 1957.

Ashley, Paul P. *Say it Safely.* University of Washington Press. 1966.

Bailey, Stephen K. and Howard D. Samuel. *Congress at Work.* Anchor Books. 1965.

Beck, Carl. *Contempt of Congress*. Hauser Press. 1959.

Berman, David O. *In Congress Assembled*. MacMillan. 1964.

Boyd, Anne Morris. *United States Government Publications*. H. W. Wilson. 1941.

Cardozo, Benjamin N. *The Growth of the Law*. Yale University Press. 1924.

————— *The Paradoxes of Legal Science*. Columbia University Press. 1927.

Chambers, Clarke E. *California Farm Organizations*. University of California Press. 1952.

Crompton, John. *The Life of the Spider*. New American Library. 1954.

Dean, Joseph. *Hatred, Ridicule or Contempt*. MacMillan, 1954.

Drinker, Henry S. *Legal Ethics*. Columbia University Press. 1961.

Downey, Sheridan. *They Would Rule the Valley*. Published by the author. No imprint, San Francisco. 1947.

Galarza, Ernesto. *Merchants of Labor*. McNally & Loftin. 1964.

Gavin, Clark. *Foul, False and Infamous*. Abelard Press. 1950.

Goldschmidt, Walter. *As You Sow*. Harcourt, Brace. 1947.

Hand, Learned. *The Spirit of Liberty*. Irving Dillard, editor. Knopf. 1952.

Hartman, Dennis. *Motion Picture Law Digest*. No imprint. Los Angeles, California. 1947.

Holmes, Oliver Wendell. *The Common Law*. Harvard University Press. 1963.

Keating, Kenneth B. *Government of the People*. World Book Co. 1964.

Lindley, Alexander. *Entertainment, Publishing and the Arts*. Clark, Boardman Co. Ltd. 1963.

MacNeil, Neil. *Forge of Democracy*. David McKay Co. 1963.

Marchetti, Roger. *Law of Stage, Screen and Radio*. Suttonhouse Ltd. 1936.

Martindale-Hubbell. *Law Directory*. 1967 edition. Vol. I.

Mazo, Earl and Stephen Hess. *Nixon—a Political Portrait*. Popular Library. 1967.

Miller, Clem. *Member of the House*. John W. Baker, editor. Scribner's. No date.

Nelson, Harold L. *Libel in News of Congressional Investigating Committees.* University of Minnesota Press. 1961.

Nixon, Richard M. *Six Crises.* Doubleday and Co. 1962.

Pound, Roscoe. *Law Finding Through Experience and Reason.* University of Georgia Press. 1960.

Prosser, William A. *Handbook of the Law of Torts.* West Publishing Co. 1941.

Spring, Samuel. *Risks and Rights in Publishing, Radio, Motion Pictures, Advertising and the Theater.* W. W. Morton. 1956.

Taylor, Telford. *Grand Inquest.* Ballantine Books. 1961.

Thomas, Ella Cooper. *The Law of Libel and Slander.* Legal Almanac Series. Oceana Publications. 1963.

PAMPHLETS

A Community Aroused. Kern County Special Citizens Committee. Walter Kane, chairman. 1947.

Report to the Stockholders. DiGiorgio Fruit Corporation. 1 June 1950.

We, the People. United States Capitol Historical Society. 1966.

Joseph DiGiorgio, a Tribute. Kern County Board of Supervisors. February 1937.

DIRECTORIES AND MANUALS

City of Baltimore Telephone *Directory.* June 1950.

Martin-Hubbell Law Directory. Martin-Hubbell. 1968.

Moody's Manual of Investments. 1950.

Polk's Bakersfield City Directory. 1949.

Standard and Poor's Corporation Reports. 1949.

Teletypewriter Directory. American Telephone and Telegraph Co. 1949–1950 issue.

MAGAZINE AND HOUSE ORGANS

AWOC Organizer. October 1959–March 1960.

Fortune Magazine. "Joseph DiGiorgio." August 1946, p. 97 ff.

Gilbert, Robert W. "Privileged Publications in Labor Disputes Under California Libel Laws." *Southern California Law Review,* December 1956, p. 35.

Hall, John M. "Pleadings in Libel Actions in California." *Southern California Law Review*, March 1939. p. 225.
_____, "Proof in Libel Actions in California." *Southern California Law Review*. July 1951, p. 339.
Hollywood Film Council. *Important Notice to Your Organization*. 12 June 1950.
News Letter. Council of California Growers. 17 November 1961, 8 July 1963.
Northern California Growers Association. *Bulletin*. 16 August 1957. Yuba City, Calif.
The Associated Farmer. 15 November 1947
                            21 April 1948
                            22 November 1948
                            March–April 1950
                            August 1950
                            June–July 1951
                            June–July 1954
                            August 1955
                            August 1959

NEWSPAPERS

Appeal-Democrat. Marysville, Calif. 6 July 1960; 14 July 1960; 16 July 1960; 18 July 1960; 23 July 1960; 29 July 1960; 30 July 1960; 14 September 1960.
Bakersfield Californian. 10 November 1947; 4 February 1948; 1 November 1949; 13 November 1949; 10 December 1949; 11 March 1950.
Bakersfield Press. 9 November 1949; 13 November 1949; 14 March 1950.
Daily Commercial News. San Francisco. 20 May 1960; 16 March 1964.
Fresno Bee. 23 March 1948; 6 April 1948; 12 December 1948; 11 September 1949; 14 March 1950; 23 November 1951; 13 September 1962.
Inland Empire Labor Review. Marysville, California. September 1957.
Los Angeles Examiner. 9–12 February 1948.

Los Angeles Times. 17 May 1949; 8 November 1949; 11 March 1950; 26 February 1951; 9 March 1952; 15 January 1961; 13 September 1962.

New York Times. 18 August 1957.

Oakland Tribune. 26 February 1948.

Palo Alto Times. 27 September 1967.

People's World. 6 June 1959.

Sacramento Union. 14 September 1960.

San Francisco Chronicle. 26 June 1949; 11 March 1950; 15 March 1950; 8 June 1957; 13 August 1957; 19 March 1959; 19 May 1960; 31 July 1960; 19 August 1960; 14 February 1963; 21 November 1964.

San Francisco Examiner. 30 June 1960; 3 October 1966.

San Francisco News-Call Bulletin. 20 November 1964.

San Jose Mercury. 28 September 1967; 30 January 1968.

San Jose News. 13 September 1962.

Stockton Record. 10 March 1960; 19 May 1960; 18 November 1961.

Union Gazette. Olympic Press. 13 March 1964; 17 April 1964; 10 July 1964.

Valley Labor Citizen. 6 May 1960; 24 April 1964.

APPENDIX

EXTENSION OF REMARKS*
OF
HON. THOMAS H. WERDEL
OF CALIFORNIA
IN THE HOUSE OF REPRESENTATIVES
Thursday, March 9, 1950

Mr. WERDEL. Mr. Speaker, a matter of great importance to many Members of the House has just occurred.

After the adjournment of the first session of the Eighty-first Congress, a subcommittee of the House Committee on Education and Labor, entitled Subcommittee No. 1, investigated alleged agricultural labor disturbances at the Di Giorgio Ranch, in Kern County, Calif. The ranch belongs to the Di Giorgio Fruit Corp.

The committee's interest and the interest of this House was aroused by the release of a movie film and narrations which depicted deplorable conditions and physical disabilities of men purporting to result from the unconscionable actions of the employer, Di Giorgio Fruit Corp. The film was shown to the Committee on Education and Labor during hearings on pertinent labor legislation.

I recommend as the majority report of the subcommittee, signed by three members thereof, to all Members of this House who have any doubt about the libelous nature of the film as narrated by Mr. Harry W. Flannery. This majority report is conclusive proof that for 30 pieces of silver, more or less, Mr. Harry W. Flannery and his associates deliberately fabricated falsehoods. The officers of the National Farm Labor Union then admittedly used the fabrication to collect hundreds of thousands of dollars from workingmen throughout the country to finance a purported strike that did not exist. The majority report is another disclosure of corrupt men deliberately bearing false witness to do untold damage to employers and employees, as well as disservice to the legitimate American Labor movement, for a pittance by way of gain for themselves.

I am, therefore, including herein a copy of the majority report which has been signed by three members of the five-man Subcommittee No. 1.

* As printed in the *Congressional Record*.

My purpose in offering it today is that the Di Giorgio Ranch, referred to in the report, lies entirely within the Tenth District of California, which I represent. Public opinion in the area of the Di Giorgio Ranch is incensed over the falsehoods embraced in the said moving picture and narration and the fraud that has been perpetrated to the advantage of a handful of men. That area is desirous of immediately correcting the unfavorable publicity resulting from the libelous action. I am including the report in the RECORD today inasmuch as it may be several weeks before it is distributed in printed form by the subcommittee. It follows:

AGRICULTURAL LABOR AT DI GIORGIO FARMS, CALIFORNIA

Special Subcommittee No. 1, Committee on Education and Labor, House of Representatives, was constituted by the following authority:

The Honorable CLEVELAND M. BAILEY,
   House of Representatives, Washington, D. C.

DEAR COLLEAGUE: By virtue of the authority vested in me as chairman of the Committee on Education and Labor, and pursuant to House Resolution 75 of the Eighty-first Congress, first session, I hereby appoint you as chairman of Special Investigating Subcommittee No. 1 of the Committee on Education and Labor. Other members of the subcommittee will be the Honorable LEONARD IRVING of Missouri, the Honorable TOM STEED of Oklahoma, the Honorable RICHARD M. NIXON of California, and the Honorable THRUSTON BALLARD MORTON of Kentucky.

You are hereby authorized and directed to investigate conditions to provide for the education of children residing on certain nonsupporting federally owned property and children residing in localities overburdened with increased school enrollments resulting from Federal activities in the area and for other purposes as outlined in H. R. 4115.

You are further authorized and directed to conduct a thorough study and investigation of labor-management relations at the Di Giorgio fruit corporation known as the Di Giorgio Farms, in Di Giorgio, Calif.

You are further directed to hold such public or executive sessions as you may deem advisable, and you are hereby authorized and designated by me to issue and have served such subpenas as may be necessary in this investigation.

Upon completion of your study and investigation you are directed to prepare a report to the Congress with such recommendations for legislation or otherwise as in the judgment of your subcommittee the facts warrant.

Very sincerely yours,

JOHN LESINSKI
Chairman, Committee on Education and Labor.

Pursuant to the authorization and direction of the whole Committee, the subcommittee met on November 12–13, 1949, at Bakersfield, Calif. It heard sworn testimony from witnesses called by the National Farm Labor Union, the subcommittee, and the Di Giorgio Fruit Corp. It also viewed two motion pictures, one submitted by the union and one by the fruit corporation; and it visited the Di Giorgio farms, Di Giorgio, Calif., and the surrounding area.

The hearing at Bakersfield and the visit to Di Giorgio farms were for the purpose of inquiring into the background of a labor disturbance which occurred on October 1, 1947 at Di Giorgio farms and thereafter. At least theoretically, it continues to the present day. There was a large volume of testimony on the part of the union concerning conditions of living and working on farms owned by corporations in general; and in a brief filed with the subcommittee the union took the position that such testimony was germane to the Di Giorgio farms disturbance. There was also some testimony concerning conditions prevailing at Di Giorgio farms in the past, going as far back as 1934. The subcommittee has been compelled, in order to report upon the issues involved in its investigation, to separate all such extraneous matter from that relevant to the question involved.

The subcommittee's view is that its authority and instructions were to investigate: (1) The hours, wages, working conditions and living conditions of the employees of Di Giorgio Farms Corp. at Di Giorgio farms during the period relevant to the labor disturbance there, i.e. roughly the period from June 1, 1947 to date; (2) the nature and history of the dispute; (3) consideration of proposed legislative changes suggested in connection with the foregoing.

I. THE DI GIORGIO FRUIT CORPORATION AND ITS DI GIORGIO FARMS

Di Giorgio Fruit Corp. is a Delaware corporation, with its principal office in San Francisco, Calif. Its business is the production and marketing of fruits and vegetables, and the activities incidental to that business. In 1946 its total assets were somewhat over $19,500,000, its total revenue over $18,000,000. Its founder and principal stockholder is Joseph Di Giorgio, who owns 43.9 percent of the class A common stock, 39.8 percent of the class B common stock, and 31.4 percent of the cumulative preferred stock. The remainder of the stock is owned by some 5,000 stockholders.

The corporation owns 11 orchards and one farm in Florida, and 8 orchards and vineyards in California. It also owns some interests in 3 fruit auction markets on the eastern seaboard, a box company and a wine company.

Joseph Di Giorgio is chairman of the board of directors of the corporation; his address is Di Giorgio, Calif. The president of the corporation is Philip Di Giorgio of New York City. One of the vice presidents, J. A. Di Giorgio, resides on Di Giorgio farms. The other officers of the corporation reside either at New York or San Francisco; the directors in New York, San Francisco, Southern California, or Florida, and one in Cuba.

Di Giorgio Farms is a tract of almost 11,000 acres, or 18 square miles, in the San Joaquin Valley, about 15 miles southeast of Bakersfield, in Kern County, Calif. The development of the land to its present condition began with the purchase in 1919 of 2,000 acres of Kern County land by the fruit corporation's predecessor. At that time there was no significant agricultural production in Kern County; the land was dry and barren. Joseph Di Giorgio was active in the management of the company and the development of Di

Giorgio Farms. By drilling deep wells for irrigation and experimenting with suitable crops, the land was brought to production and presently bears grapes, plums, potatoes, and asparagus, in order of importance.

Selection of crops by the fruit corporation has depended on two factors: (1) Individual crops which were suitable for the soil and weather of the area; (2) a combination of crops which would enable it to employ a relatively stable permanent labor force throughout the year. Employment ranges from approximately 1,200 permanent employees to 2,500 at harvest season; other growers in the area may have a temporary-permanent employment ratio of as much as 15 to 1.

II. THE DISPUTE OF THE FRUIT CORPORATION WITH THE NATIONAL FARM LABOR UNION

Early in 1947 the National Farm Labor Union sent Hank Hasiwar to Kern County as its western representative, to organize the farm workers there. He established Kern County Farm Union Local 218 and proceeded to organize some Di Giorgio Farm employees. In September of 1947 he requested the fruit corporation to recognize the local as the exclusive bargaining agent of its employees, claiming to represent a majority of them. The fruit corporation declined recognition, contending that Local 218 did not represent its employees or any substantial number of them. Thereupon, on October 1, 1947, Local 218 established a picket line at Di Giorgio Farms.

The evidence before the subcommittee, including the testimony of the secretary of the California State Federation of Labor, establishes that the sole issue in this dispute is recognition. Members of the union testified to various grievances concerning wages, hours, working conditions, and living conditions, but all of these were obviously after-thoughts and makeweights. This strike was solely one for the purpose of organization.

The National Farm Labor Union does not hold any collective bargaining contracts in the State of California. Yet it has maintained a picket line against a single employer for over 2 years, and its representatives and others have testified that the wages, hours, working conditions, and living conditions on that employer's farm are not inferior to those elsewhere; the subcommittee finds that they are, for the most part, superior. Wages, hours, working conditions, and living conditions have never been a real issue in the Di Giorgio strike.

III. WAGES AND WORKING CONDITIONS AT DI GIORGIO FARMS

Although these issues are not actually present in the dispute between the fruit corporation and the union, there is much testimony in the record concerning them, and the subcommittee deems it desirable to report on wages, working conditions, and living conditions at Di Giorgio Farms. The union presented its film, Poverty in the Valley of Plenty, which is designed to represent living and working conditions at Di Giorgio Farms. The fruit corporation presented its film, The Di Giorgio Story, relating to the same matters.

The union film was also shown to the committee during its hearings on H. R. 2032 in Washington on March 16, 1949. The committee has been seriously imposed upon by the union by the presentation of the film Poverty in the Valley of Plenty at that time. The film itself, and the president of the union in presenting it, represented to the committee that the conditions depicted in the film existed on Di Giorgio Farms and led up to a strike there. The committee's belief in the truth of these statements induced it to authorize and instruct this subcommittee to investigate the facts. The union's president now takes the position that the film relates, not to Di Giorgio Farms but to corporate farms in general. The educational director and the western representative of the union insist that the film is a true picture of the Di Giorgio Farms. The subcommittee finds that, insofar as it purports to represent conditions existing on Di Giorgio Farms, the film Poverty in the Valley of Plenty was made in disregard of the truth.

The film purports to relate the facts surrounding the wages, working conditions, and living conditions of employees of the fruit corporation at Di Giorgio Farms. The subcommittee finds the facts to be as follows:

Wages: The lowest wage paid at Di Giorgio Farms is 80 cents per hour for field work. The highest is $1.10 per hour for loaders. These wage levels are, if not the highest, at least as high as any in the area. Neighboring farmers testified that the fruit corporation had always been the leader in the matter of raising wage scales, which the other farmers followed in order to keep their employees. There is testimony in the record by a union witness to show that wages at Di Giorgio Farms rose from a depression-born low during the midthirties by steady progression to their present levels.

Wages are not a grievance or a strike issue.

Working conditions: Individual members of the union testified to various grievances over a 15-year period. One of these was that persons often came to Di Giorgio Farms seeking employment, and if not hired were not paid. There was no evidence that the fruit corporation ever called in a worker and failed to hire or pay him. Another grievance was that foremen were given the power to discharge field workers; another that foremen and supervisors were extended privileges not extended to field workers; that drinking water in the fields was not iced; that workers in refrigerating rooms were not given extra pay; that foremen had to supervise too large groups of employees.

Insofar as the afore-mentioned grievances are concerned, the subcommittee found that in some instances they were not supported by the evidence, in others they were inconsequential and that in no event did they constitute an issue in the strike.

In its motion-picture film, Poverty in the Valley of Plenty, the union said that the fruit corporation required its irrigators to work 12 hours, but paid them for only 11. This statement was wholly false, as witnesses both for the fruit corporation and the union agreed.

Living conditions: The union film also represents that living conditions on Di Giorgio farms consist of disreputable, filthy shacks, and that the living habits of the occupants are substandard and squalid.

The film contains unmistakable innuendoes that the houses pictured in it are on Di Giorgio farms. None of the houses shown is fit for human beings to live in. They are in varying states of disrepair, unpainted and sordid. They are surrounded with junk and with undernourished children and dogs. Near one is a shower, said to be used by 25 or 30 families, lacking in hot water, and situated next to a cow pen. The film charges that the fruit corporation rents washing machines to employees for 50 cents per hour, and that women are compelled to heat water over open fires. No one could doubt that these charges are leveled straight at the corporation.

All of these representations are false. The shacks portrayed, said to exist on Di Giorgio farms, are not on the farm. It is inferred that the fruit corporation charges its employees $26 per month for such housing; all the witnesses agreed that $3 per month is the maximum ever charged; and that at present all company housing is rent-free.

In fact, the National Farm Labor Union film, Poverty in the Valley of Plenty, insofar as it purports to represent conditions existing on Di Giorgio farms, is a shocking collection of falsehoods, almost wholly unrelieved by any regard whatever for the truth and the facts. The subcommittee believes that responsible labor leadership will join with it in decrying the attempt of the National Farm Labor Union's organizers to win their case by dishonest presentation. The cause of organized labor is not aided when one group of union organizers are willing to besmirch the public reputation of labor as a whole, in order to advance their own interests.

The evidence and the subcommittee's visit to the premises demonstrated that the housing conditions at Di Giorgio farms are at least as good as any to be found on similar properties in agriculture. The fruit corporation maintains several types of housing: cottages for supervisory personnel; smaller houses (2–4 rooms) for field and shed workers; apartments; and dormitories for single men. The houses are respectable, though not pretentious, enjoy modern facilities, including electricity, and in addition have garbage disposal service and fire protection at company expense. Separate facilities are maintained for workers whose backgrounds give them different dietary tastes, and they are provided with food which is acceptable to them. All the union witnesses agreed that the food furnished by the company is better than average.

Recreational, educational, and religious facilities: The union represented to the committee that Di Giorgio workers were deprived of all recreational, educational and religious opportunities. The evidence shows that the fruit corporation provides swimming pools and tennis courts for all employees. It does not maintain any schools or churches. However, there are ample, modern well-equipped schools in the vicinity, including a new high school in Arvin. A new grammar school building near the farm was made possible by a gift of 40 acres of land and $150,000 cash by the fruit corporation. The fruit corporation supports these schools by payment of 64 percent of the taxes of Di Giorgio school district; and it has contributed land or cash or both to the churches in the area.

Welfare provisions: The union in its film represented that Di Giorgio workers were without any protection in case of accidental injury, and depicted a maimed worker in the fields who, it said, would receive no compensation for his injuries from the Di Giorgio farms. The evidence shows that this individual was not injured on the DiGiorgio farms and that in fact the fruit corporation has always maintained full workmen's compensation insurance protection for all of its employees, though not required to by law. Such statements have convinced the subcommittee that the union did not make a fair and truthful presentation.

An official of the fruit corporation testified that the company did not provide unemployment insurance for its workers; had no pension plan; provided no old-age insurance. However, the fruit corporation offers employees of 1 year's standing a group life insurance policy, on which the company pays 60 percent of the premiums.

Mexican labor: The union in its film "Poverty in the Valley of Plenty" insinuated that the fruit corporation engaged in a program of smuggling Mexican aliens, wetbacks, across the border to work in its fields. At the hearing it did not charge smuggling but did complain at length of the hiring of Mexican nationals by the fruit corporation.

The fruit corporation had participated in the program instituted by the Federal Government during the war of hiring Mexican nationals to supplement the Nation's farm labor force. One hundred thirty of these nationals remained at Di Giorgio farms when the union set up its picket line on October 1, 1947. After the situation was explained to them by a representative of the Department of Agriculture, they unanimously signified their desire to continue to work, and did so. The fruit corporation contends that the farm labor union brought pressure to bear on the State Department and, in violation of the Government's contract, these nationals were removed from Di Giorgio farms.

Illegal aliens have from time to time been found on Di Giorgio farms, just as they have been found on almost every farm in Texas, New Mexico, Arizona, and southern California. There is no evidence that the fruit corporation ever smuggled any alien into the United States, or hired an illegal alien knowing his status. The union's charges in this respect appear to be completely unfounded. In any event they throw no light whatever on the issues involved in the labor disturbances, and have no real place here.

IV. THE LABOR DISPUTE AT DI GIORGIO AND THE
LABOR-MANAGEMENT RELATIONS ACT

After the picket line was set up at Di Giorgio farms the work of growing, harvesting, and shipping the produce of the farm continued. A majority of the employees of the fruit corporation continued to work, or returned to work within a few weeks. There were allegations of a few isolated cases of violence by both sides in the early months of the strike; but the picket line may be regarded as a relatively peaceful one, and the subcommittee finds that the union made it its policy to discourage violence.

Since the picket line failed to affect the operations of the fruit corporation or to accomplish the organization of its employees, the union embarked upon a series of secondary activities. In this it had the aid of a few of the members of a winery local at Di Giorgio Winery, and of some other trade unions. The Farm Labor Union picketed the winery; it picketed another distant winery, owned by a wholly separate company; it placed a mass picket line across the tracks of the railroads which serve Di Giorgio farms, and it boycotted the produce of Di Giorgio farms in southern California cities by picketing distributors in that area.

After an investigation of complaint, the general counsel of the National Labor Relations Board sued out an injunction against this conduct, which was granted by the United States District Court for the Southern District of California against the unions involved, including the Farm Labor Union and other unions acting in concert with it, under section 10 (j) of the Labor-Management Relations Act of 1947.

The fruit corporation thereafter filed unfair labor practice charges with the Board against the same unions under section 8 (b) (1) (A) and 8 (b) (4) (A) of the act. The trial examiner found that all the factual charges in the complaint were true. He exonerated all the respondents under section 8 (b) (1) (A). He recommended that the Board's order issue under section 8 (b) (1) (A) against all the unions except the Farm Union and a teamster's local, both of which purported to represent for the purpose of the proceedings, agricultural workers only. The theory of the trial examiner was that the Board could not impose sanctions upon the Farm Union, since, he said, the act does not extend its benefits to the Farm Union. The fruit corporation and the general counsel of the Board filed exceptions to the trial examiner's report, and the matter has been submitted to the Board.

The Farm Union takes the position in its brief before the subcommittee that it is inconceivable that any group could be subjected to the sanctions provided by the act, unless it were extended privileges and benefits under the act. Counsel for the fruit corporation, in a statement to the subcommittee, said that the position of the fruit corporation is that Congress "need not purchase compliance with the laws of the United States at the price of benefits and privileges."

V. RECOMMENDATIONS FOR LEGISLATION GROWING OUT OF THE DI GIORGIO LABOR DISTURBANCE

The law, the strike issues, and the investigation: The hearing and investigation at Bakersfield and Di Giorgio farms were held at the request of the National Farm Labor Union. The reason stated for this request was that a situation existed on Di Giorgio farms which called for immediate action in order to prevent further unfair and ill treatment of agricultural workers at Di Giorgio farms. The committee was told that legislation was required in order to correct the abuses of corporation farmers and their lobbies.

Relying on this request and these representations, the subcommittee came to Bakersfield and visited Di Giorgio farms. Witnesses were called by both sides, and the subpena power of the subcommittee was made available to the union and the fruit corporation. The union called no pickets to testify; and there was no picket line at the farm when the subcommittee went there. No employee of Di Giorgio Fruit Corp. was called by the union to testify to his wish to become a member of the Farm Labor Union, and the fruit corporation's thwarting of his wish. The subcommittee interviewed Di Giorgio employees and no one of them signified a desire to become a member of the union or his acquaintance with any other employee who held such a desire. No witness called by the union testified to anything which represented a substantial strike issue, or even approximated the charges depicted in the union's film, Poverty in the Valley of Plenty.

The contrast between that film, with the testimony accompanying it in Washington last March, and the case made by the union at the Bakersfield hearing and investigation, is most striking. The way in which the union presented its evidence shows that this committee has been induced to spend its time and the taxpayers' money to publicize the leadership of a labor organization which has no contracts, no grievances, no strike, no pickets, and only a handful of members; its only apparent reason for existence is its voluble leaders.

The processes of the Congress of the United States have been perverted and misused by the National Farm Labor Union in order to furnish a soundingboard for its claims. The committee should certainly not be without power to prevent the recurrence of this kind of abuse of its functions and impositions upon its energies.

Workmen's compensation: The question of workmen's compensation is not relevant here since, contrary to the charges of the union, the fruit corporation has always provided full compensation-insurance protection for all its employees, including agricultural workers of every description.

Fair-labor standards: This matter likewise has no bearing on the present issues. The undisputed evidence shows that the fruit corporation had a minimum-wage level of 80 cents per hour long before the Fair Labor Standards Act was amended to provide even 75 cents.

Old-age and unemployment insurance: The fruit corporation has not provided benefits of this character. However, the question whether its employees should be covered has been repeatedly considered by the Congress, and the Congress has repeatedly found that they should not be. Lack of coverage is the result of exemptions in the law, and not the action of the fruit corporation. The fruit corporation does provide low-cost life-insurance as a measure of welfare protection.

The National Farm Labor Union recommends removal of the exemptions of agricultural labor from labor legislation. Agricultural labor has been exempted from all labor relations legislation ever written. The evidence before the subcommittee shows that it would be harmful to the public interest and to all responsible labor unions to legislate otherwise. The evidence shows that a strike of any serious proportions in agriculture would choke off interstate commerce in necessary foodstuffs, would cause incalculable harm to the public, and would antagonize public opinion to the cause of trade-unionism. It would not only result in temporary distress of a character more serious than has ever been experienced, it would result in permanent loss of farm employment and permanent loss to the public of farm production, and, of course, permanent ruin to the farmers of the Nation.

The union has suggested that the fruit corporation is of such a size and character that it should be differentiated from other farm producers. The union did not, however, suggest any valid basis for differentiation of small farmers from large ones, or of corporate farms from farms owned by individuals or other forms of business organization. In fact, the union disclaims taking the position that the mere bigness of the fruit corporation is a vice. This must be apparent to anyone who has seen Di Giorgio farms. It is perfectly obvious that, were this acreage distributed to its permanent workers, none of the 1,200 could make a living on his 9 acres. If Di Giorgio farms had not been developed and operated by a corporation, or some individual or organization possessing comparable capital, it could never have been developed or operated at all.

Mere size is not a sound basis for differentiating between farmers. It is evident that any condition imposed by law upon a large farmer, automatically becomes a condition under which every farmer, however small, must operate. It is idle to contend that 1 or 2 or 10 farms in Kern County may be subjected to congressionally imposed standards, without subjecting their neighbors to the same standards.

The subcommittee finds that the exemption of agricultural labor from the Labor Management Relations Act is sound, being based upon facts which clearly differentiate agriculture from industry in this regard.

Other legislative recommendations: The fruit corporation contended that the exemption of labor organizations from the anti-trust laws resulted in serious abuses which required repeal of the exemption. The evidence before the subcommittee showed that the farm union possesses no collective bargaining contracts, at least in California, and has created no labor disturbance except at Di Giorgio farms. The only conduct of the union which violates the antitrust laws is its secondary boycott activity, and in this regard the exemption is created by Supreme Court decisions construing the Norris-LaGuardia Act. Since the secondary boycott is already made unlawful by the Labor Management Relations Act, as discussed above, no recommendation is here made with respect to this contention of the fruit corporation.

The union made certain recommendations for State legislation which the subcommittee does not deem it appropriate to discuss.

It also recommended certain Federal legislation, most of which is discussed above. The evidence shows that all of the union recommendations not previously discussed have no application to the facts at Di Giorgio farms, and the subcommittee therefore considers them irrelevant.

RICHARD NIXON
THRUSTON B. MORTON
TOM STEED

INDEX

Admission of evidence, 112

Admissions, 234

Advance knowledge of "report," 188, 198, 261

Adversary proceedings, 121

A.F.L., 55

A.F.L.-C.I.O., 88, 92, 106, 111, 196

Agreement of May 23, 1950, 64, 90, 99, 104, 116, 123, 148, 149, 150, 190

Agribusiness, 4, 60, 63, 76, 77, 82, 83, 84, 117, 124, 139, 140, 163, 189, 242, 246, 251

Agricultural corporations, 158

Agricultural integration, 242

Alternative to lawsuit, 190

Amalgamated Meat Cutters and Butcher Workmen of America, 88

Ancient document, 90, 110, 124

Appellate Bench, Fresno, 223

Appellate decision, Fresno, 224

Appellate procedure, 222

Appendix of the *Congressional Record*, 29, 50, 51, 54, 59, 67, 68, 111, 112, 115, 118, 120, 121, 151, 158, 159, 162, 168, 169, 170, 176, 186, 187, 191, 192, 200, 204, 212, 215, 216, 217, 223, 232, 234, 245, 252, 264, 267

Arvin, 18, 31, 33, 74, 113, 238

Asparagus, gift of, to Congressman Steed, 61

Associated Farmers, 27, 42, 59, 81, 84, 85, 98, 155, 176

Authenticity of "Subcommittee report," 175, 185, 214, 219

Authorship of "Subcommittee report," 112, 175, 182, 213, 218, 225, 256

Agricultural Workers Organizing Committee, 4, 5, 88, 92, 93, 94, 95, 101, 102, 105, 106, 115, 122, 123, 124, 136, 148, 175, 176, 195

campaign, 121, 189

publications, 155, 190

Bailey, Cleveland M., 36, 37, 41, 43, 44, 46, 48, 55, 67, 68, 69, 157, 158, 161, 170, 175, 184, 188, 191, 192, 202, 203, 215, 216, 218, 239, 241, 256

Ballis, George, 196, 198, 199, 200, 201, 202, 213, 214, 253,

Beck, David, 245

Bennett, Ralph K., 168

Bierce, Ambrose, 27

Boehm, Jeff, 195, 196, 197, 199, 201, 211, 214, 215, 219, 221, 223, 224, 229, 231

Boycott, 77

Boyd, Anne Morris, 58

Boyer, Frank, 42, 45, 48, 67, 184, 262

Braceros, 23, 24, 67, 68, 75, 77, 78, 79, 80, 82, 89, 95, 97, 163, 189

Bradford, Lowell W., 180, 215, 218, 267

Brobeck, Phleger and Harrison, 31, 37, 38, 39, 40, 60, 61, 62, 63, 64, 66, 90, 95, 97, 99, 101, 102, 105, 106, 108, 109, 110, 116, 122, 123, 136, 151, 152, 153, 157, 159, 173, 177,

"Junk" in the Congressional Rec-
ord, 176, 186, 254
Jury, Fresno trial, 209, 210
Jury, San Francisco trial, 174

Kane, Walter, 68
Kelly, Hon. Augustus, 35
Kennedy, Hon. John F., 35
Klein, Herbert, 166, 246
Krainnock, Louis, 95, 96, 106,
108, 123

Labor contractors, 78
Labor question, 123, 151, 177,
189
Leadership training, N.F.L.U., 74
Legal firm, 225
Legal mind, 143, 225
Legal reasoning, 131
Legal tactics, 173
Legislative proceedings, 223
Lesinski, Hon. John, 35, 36, 37,
41, 48, 55, 66, 67, 157, 158,
175, 192, 242, 255
Letter of authorization, 54, 66,
162
Letter of submittal, 54, 162, 188
Libel, 38, 39, 109, 128, 129, 130,
131, 134
insurance, 152
lawsuits for, 251
litigation, 147
per quod, per se, 109, 129, 134,
137
Libelous publication, 117
Library of Congress, 111
Lobbying of committees, 231
Local 218, N.F.L.U., 1, 4, 22, 45,
52, 63, 65, 66, 73, 74, 78,
107
strike, 1-2, 22, 23, 24, 37, 41,
44, 52, 62, 64, 65, 66, 69, 73,
188
Los Angeles Central Labor Council, 32, 37, 62, 64

Lost documents, 109, 206, 207,
208, 226, 239, 245, 262, 268
Loustalot, Sheriff John, 2, 23, 67
Lucey, Emmet E., 111, 206

McCarthy, Hon. Joseph P., 41,
128, 245
Madison, James, 227
Majority report, 59, 160, 162,
172, 188, 191, 203, 218, 253
Malice, 114
Malicious prosecution, 150, 156
Mason, Walter, 55, 204
Mechanization of agriculture, 86
Migrants, 18, 19, 31
Miller, S.M., 243
Milton, John, 150
Mimeograph copies, 177, 179,
180, 183, 205, 207, 211, 235,
261, 265, 266, 267
Minority report, 59, 111, 172,
184, 191, 218
Minority statement, 202
Minority views, 255
Minutes, Committee, 103, 173,
192
Misrepresentations, 198
Mitchell, H.L., 26, 32, 34, 36, 42,
44, 46, 48, 55, 58, 60–64, 73,
81, 86, 99, 102, 106, 117,
123, 139, 148, 170, 211
Monthly Catalogue of Government Publications, May
1950, 170, 184
Morton, Hon. Thruston B., 3, 35,
43, 48, 53, 112, 113, 115,
121, 124, 141, 142, 154, 158,
161, 175, 179, 182, 186, 187,
191, 192, 197, 203, 204, 206,
213, 238, 241, 244, 246, 247,
255, 257
Motion pictures, sound, 119, 130,
131, 132, 134, 137, 140–142
Murray, James, 90, 104, 150–159,
161, 162, 165-169, 171, 173-
181, 184, 185, 189, 195, 199,